Scattered Context Grammars and their Applications

Scattered Context Grammars and their Applications

A. Meduna & J. Techet

Brno University of Technology, Czech Republic

WIT*PRESS* Southampton, Boston

A. Meduna & J. Techet
Brno University of Technology, Czech Republic

Published by

WIT Press
Ashurst Lodge, Ashurst, Southampton, SO40 7AA, UK
Tel: 44 (0) 238 029 3223; Fax: 44 (0) 238 029 2853
E-Mail: witpress@witpress.com
http://www.witpress.com

For USA, Canada and Mexico

WIT Press
25 Bridge Street, Billerica, MA 01821, USA
Tel: 978 667 5841; Fax: 978 667 7582
E-Mail: infousa@witpress.com
http://www.witpress.com

British Library Cataloguing-in-Publication Data

A Catalogue record for this book is available
from the British Library

ISBN: 978-1-84564-426-0

Library of Congress Catalog Card Number: 2009931446

The texts of the papers in this volume were set individually by the authors or under their supervision.

Printed in Great Britain by MPG Books Group, Bodmin and King's Lynn.

In Memory of Roman

Contents

Preface

Objective

Many modern information technologies cope with processing broadly scattered pieces of mutually related information throughout various computer systems. As a result, a mathematical exploration of scattered information processing based upon adequate formal models represents an important investigation area of today's informatics. In formal language theory, which often provides informatics with formal models, information processing of this kind is formalized by *scattered context grammars*. As these grammars formalize scattered information processing in a very natural and rigorous way, it comes as no surprise that formal language theory has devoted to their investigation a great number of studies since their introduction four decades ago. Although these studies have achieved many remarkable results, published in many international computer science journals and conferences, formal language theory lacks any monograph that systematically and compactly summarizes them. To fill this gap, the principal goal of the present book is to provide informatics with a monograph like this. This book gives an in-depth exploration of scattered context grammars and their languages from a theoretical point of view. In addition, from a practical point of view, it sketches how to process scattered information by these grammars in linguistics.

Approach

This book is primarily a theoretically oriented treatment of scattered context grammars. As a result, it introduces all formalisms with enough rigor to make all results clear and valid. Every complex concept defined in the text is immediately illustrated by some examples and every complicated mathematical passage is followed by its intuitive explanation, so the reader should easily follow every proof in the book. By describing their applications in linguistics and sketching several other application areas, the text also demonstrates their use in practice.

Organization

The text consists of the following three parts.

Part I consists of two chapters. Chapter 1 gives a rudimentary introduction to scattered context processing and its formalization by scattered context grammars. It explains why this formalization and its investigation is important in today's informatics. Chapter 2 reviews basic mathematical concepts, including fundamental notions of formal language theory. Most importantly, it rigorously defines scattered context grammars and their languages.

Part II, consisting of Chapters 3 through 7, presents the theory of scattered context grammars and their languages, and as such, it represents the core of this monograph. Chapters 3 and 4 establish crucial properties concerning the languages generated by scattered context grammars. Chapter 5 discusses several restricted and extended versions of scattered context grammars. Compared to the first three chapters of Part II, which are mostly mathematically oriented, Chapters 6 and 7 represent theoretical treatments with significant consequences regarding the use of scattered context grammars in practice. Chapter 6 explains how to describe these grammars in an economical way. In particular, it studies their reduction with respect to some of their components, such as the number of symbols or productions. As obvious, compared to their general versions, the resulting grammars described in this succinct way are easier to use in practice. Chapter 7 studies parsing based upon scattered context grammars. Apart from its interesting theoretical properties, parsing plays an important role in several pragmatically oriented areas of computer science and informatics, such as computational linguistics and compiler writing. As a result, this final chapter of Part II brings its theoretical discussion to the application-oriented discussion of the third part.

Part III consists of Chapters 8 and 9. To demonstrate the use of scattered context grammars, Chapter 8 describes their applications in linguistics. Finally, Chapter 9 closes the monograph by making several remarks, suggesting further theoretically oriented investigation areas concerning scattered context grammars, and bringing the reader's attention to some attractive application fields of these grammars, such as compiler writing and biology.

Prerequisites

No previous knowledge concerning the subject of this book is assumed on the part of the reader. Indeed, this book is self-contained in the sense that no other sources are needed for understanding all the presented material. Nonetheless, some background in today's formal language theory is definitely helpful to grasp the material of this monograph easily, and for this purpose, we recommend *Handbook of Formal Languages* (see [1]), which gives both an introduction to this theory and an overview of its recent trends.

Use

Principally, this monograph is meant as a general source of information about scattered context grammars, and therefore, it is useful to everybody interested in theoretical fundamentals of scattered information processing. Secondarily, it can be used as a textbook for a graduate-level course in formal language theory. Although it contains enough material for a full semester, we recommend to use it as a complementary text for a part of such a course, covering some selected essential topics of scattered context grammars. The text allows the flexibility needed to make a selection of this kind. Further backup materials related to this book, such as suggestions for further reading, are available at

`http://www.fit.vutbr.cz/~meduna/books/scg/`

Acknowledgments

We are indebted to many people for their assistance in various aspects of creating this book. We have greatly benefited from conversations with many of our colleagues at Brno University of Technology. Our special thanks go to Zbyněk Křivka and Tomáš Masopust, whose help was enormous. We are grateful to Elizabeth Cherry and Brian Privett at WIT Press, who were always helpful and encouraging during the preparation of this book. We gladly acknowledge the support of the GACR 102/05/H050, GACR 201/07/0005, and MSM 0021630528 grants. Most importantly, we thank our families for their constant support during our work on this book.

Alexander Meduna & Jiří Techet

PART I

Introduction

CHAPTER 1

Motivation

Making use of highly effective computation performed in parallel, modern computer science technologies are designed to work with information of enormous size. During a single computational step, however, a computational process usually needs only some selected elements of the information. Typically, it selects only a finite number of scattered, but often mutually related elements of the information, intuitively referred to as *scattered information* in this book, and simultaneously derives new pieces of information from these elements. By substituting the new pieces of information for the selected elements, it produces new information and, thereby, completes such a computational step. The newly obtained information is subsequently processed in the same selective way during the next computational step. This computational process successfully ends when some terminating conditions concerning the information are fulfilled; as a rule, these conditions simply require that the information consists solely of elements from a prescribed terminating set. Although this way of scattered computation processing frequently underlies modern information technologies, computer science has not monographically formalized this processing so far, so it lacks any systematic body of knowledge regarding this important kind of information processing. The present book fills this gap.

In general, to discuss some kind of information processing in a rigorous way in computer science, we often formalize the corresponding information processors by formal language models, such as suitable grammars. Then, by studying these grammars and the way they yield their languages in strictly mathematical terms of formal language theory, we actually rigorously investigate the processors that work with the information under discussion. Following this mathematical approach, we formalize the scattered information processors by scattered context grammars, introduced by formal language theory several decades ago (see [2]). We have chosen the theory of formal languages because it straightforwardly and naturally allows us to formalize the scattered information within information i by *scattered context* of symbols, A_1 through A_n, occurring in i as $i = x_0A_1x_1A_2x_2 \ldots A_nx_n$, where the x's represent parts of i irrelevant to the current computational step. A computational rule according to which the computational step, referred to as *derivation step* in formal language theory, is made, has the form $(A_1, A_2, \ldots, A_n) \rightarrow (y_1, y_2, \ldots, y_n)$, where y_1 through y_n represent the new piece of information derived from A_1 through A_n.

In this way, we formalize all the computational rules according to which the computational process performs its steps. As these *scattered context rules* actually define how the words are changed, the set containing these rules forms a *scattered context grammar* as a whole. These rules operate over two sets of symbols. The grammar contains a finite set of *terminal symbols*. Apart from the terminal symbols, it also contains finitely many *nonterminal symbols*, one of which is defined as the *start symbol*. Beginning from the start symbol, the formalized computational process consisting of a sequence of derivation steps successfully ends when the derived words consist solely of terminal symbols. A terminal word derived in this way is included into the language of this grammar, which contains all words derived in this way. As proved later in this book, scattered context grammars are equivalent to Turing machines in the sense that both define the family of recursively enumerable languages. As a result, these grammars represent not only an elegant formalization of scattered information processing, but also a powerful generator of languages.

To illustrate the formalization of scattered information processing, consider a file f in its binary form. Double f by attaching f to its duplicate as ff, which is a common file operation in practice. Suppose we want to specify the generative process that produces the set of all files doubled in this way. More formally speaking, we want to generate the language $L = \{ff : f \in \{0, 1\}^*\}$. Generating this set requires to guarantee that every member of this set is formed by a binary word followed by an equally long binary word that coincides with the preceding word. In greater detail, we need to make sure that both words consist of the same number of binary digits and, in addition, the ith binary digit in the first word coincides with the ith binary digit in the second word. In this case, scattered information processing consists in verifying the identity of the ith binary digit in the first f and the ith binary digit in the second f. The start rule derives FF from the start symbol S by a rule of the form $(S) \to (FF)$. Then, to guarantee that the ith binary digit in the left word coincides with the ith binary digit in the right word, we simultaneously derive two identical binary digits from the left and from the right F by the scattered context rules $(F, F) \to (0F, 0F)$ and $(F, F) \to (1F, 1F)$. To complete this process, we simultaneously erase both F's by $(F, F) \to (\varepsilon, \varepsilon)$, where ε is the empty word, which consists of no symbols at all. For instance, 0101 is derived by a sequence of derivation steps S, FF, $0F0F$, $01F01F$, 0101.

To enhance the reason why we have chosen scattered context grammars as a proper grammatical formalization of scattered information processing, we now consider how some other fundamental formal grammars describe context dependencies and perform their derivation steps in order to see why these grammars are less appropriate for this formalization than scattered context grammars. Regarding the context description, we can divide grammatical rules into context-dependent and context-independent rules in the theory of formal languages. Accordingly, we distinguish between context-dependent grammars, such as phrase-structure grammars or interactive Lindenmayer systems, and context-independent grammars, such as context-free grammars. Context-independent rules are applied quite independently of other symbols, so they are obviously incapable of formalizing the mutually related elements of scattered information. Besides, they are significantly less powerful than scattered context grammars; in fact, they cannot even generate the trivial language L above. Context-dependent grammars are more powerful; however, their context-dependent rules depend on the context surrounding the rewritten symbol, so they fail to appropriately formalize widely scattered elements of information. Concerning the description of scattered context, all these grammars are thus less suitable than scattered context grammars. The performance of derivation steps in grammars should obviously reflect the way scattered information is processed in reality. Therefore, sequential grammars, such as context-free grammars, can hardly serve as a proper formalization of scattered information processing because they rewrite only a single symbol during a derivation step. Although totally parallel grammars, such as L systems, reflect scattered information processing more appropriately, this reflection is still inadequate from a realistic point of view. Indeed, these grammars work in a completely parallel way because they rewrite all symbols of a word during a single derivation step. However, due to hardware-related limitations, only a finite number of symbols can be processed during one computational step in practice. As scattered context grammars simultaneously rewrite finitely many selected symbols during a single derivation step while leaving the other symbols unchanged, they formalize scattered information processing most appropriately.

CHAPTER 2

Definitions

This chapter, divided into three sections, gives an overview of theoretical concepts and notions used later in the book. Sections 2.1 and 2.2 review the fundamental mathematical notions needed to follow all the text clearly and accurately. Section 2.3 introduces scattered context grammars and notions related to these grammars, which are specific for this book. For readers having a solid background in the mathematical theory of formal languages, this chapter can be skimmed and treated as a reference for notions and definitions.

2.1 Mathematical background

This section recalls the basic notions concerning sets, sequences, and relations, whose understanding is necessary to follow the rest of the book.

Sets

A *set* A is a collection of elements taken from some prespecified universe. If A contains an element a, then we symbolically write $a \in A$ and refer to a as a member of A. On the other hand, if a is not in A, we write $a \notin A$. If A has a finite number of members, then A is a *finite set*; otherwise, A is an *infinite set*. An infinite set A is *countably infinite* if there is a bijection from A to the set of all integers (the notion of a bijection is defined later in this section). The *cardinality* of a finite set A, $|A|$, is the number of members of A. The set that has no member is the *empty set*, denoted $\emptyset$; note that $|\emptyset| = 0$. A finite set A is customarily specified by listing its members; that is, $A = \{a_1, \ldots, a_n\}$, where a_1 through a_n are all members of A. An infinite set B is usually specified by a property π, so that B contains all elements satisfying π; in symbols, this specification has the general format $B = \{a : \pi(a)\}$. Sets whose members are other sets are usually called *families of sets* rather than sets of sets.

Let A and B be two sets. A is a *subset* of B, symbolically written as $A \subseteq B$, if every member of A also belongs to B. A is a *proper subset* of B, written as $A \subset B$, if $A \subseteq B$ and B contains an element that is not in A. If $A \subseteq B$ and $B \subseteq A$, A equals B, denoted by $A = B$. The *power set* of A, denoted by 2^A, is the set of all subsets of A. For two sets A and B, their *union*, *intersection*, and *difference* are denoted by $A \cup B$, $A \cap B$, and $A - B$, respectively, and defined as

$$A \cup B = \{a : a \in A \text{ or } a \in B\},$$
$$A \cap B = \{a : a \in A \text{ and } a \in B\},$$
$$A - B = \{a : a \in A \text{ and } a \notin B\}.$$

For a property π, the union of elements of A satisfying this property is defined as

$$\bigcup_{\pi} A = \big\{a : a \in A, \text{ and } \pi(a)\big\}.$$

For a set A over a universe U, the *complement* of A is the set $U - A$.

A *sequence* is a list of elements from some universe U. A sequence is *finite* if it represents a finite list of elements; otherwise, it is *infinite*. The *length* of a finite sequence x, denoted by $|x|$, is the number of elements in x. The *empty sequence*, denoted by ε, is the sequence consisting of no element—that is, $|\varepsilon| = 0$. A finite sequence is usually specified by listing its elements. For $V \subseteq U$, $|x|_V$ denotes the number of occurrences of elements from V in a sequence x. For instance, consider a finite sequence x specified as $x = 0, 1, 0, 0$, and observe that $|x| = 4$ and $|x|_{\{0\}} = 3$.

Relations

For two objects a and b, (a, b) denotes the *ordered pair* consisting of a and b in this order. Analogically, the *ordered n-tuple* is denoted by $(a_1, \ldots, a_n)$, for some objects $a_1, \ldots, a_n$. Let A and B be two sets. The *Cartesian product* of A and B, $A \times B$, is defined as

$$A \times B = \big\{(a, b) : a \in A, b \in B\big\}.$$

A *binary relation* or, briefly, a *relation* ρ from A to B is any subset of $A \times B$; that is, $\rho \subseteq A \times B$. The *domain* of ρ, denoted by domain(ρ), and the *range* of ρ, denoted by range(ρ), are defined as

$$\text{domain}(\rho) = \big\{a : (a, b) \in \rho, \text{ for some } b \in B\big\}, \text{ and}$$
$$\text{range}(\rho) = \big\{b : (a, b) \in \rho, \text{ for some } a \in A\big\}.$$

If $A = B$, then ρ is a *relation on A*. A relation σ is a *subrelation* of ρ if $\sigma \subseteq \rho$. The *inverse* of ρ, denoted by ρ^{-1}, is defined as

$$\rho^{-1} = \big\{(b, a) : (a, b) \in \rho\big\}.$$

Instead of $(a, b) \in \rho$, we often write $b \in \rho(a)$ or $a\rho b$; in other words, $(a, b) \in \rho$, $a\rho b$, and $b \in \rho(a)$ are used interchangeably.

A *function* from A to B is a relation ϕ from A to B such that for each $a \in A$,

$$\Big|\big\{b : b \in B, (a, b) \in \phi\big\}\Big| \leq 1.$$

Let ϕ be a function from A to B. If domain$(\phi) = A$, ϕ is *total*; otherwise, ϕ is *partial*. If for each $b \in B$

$$\left|\{a : a \in A, (a, b) \in \phi\}\right| \leq 1,$$

ϕ is *injective*. If for each $b \in B$

$$\left|\{a : a \in A, (a, b) \in \phi\}\right| \geq 1,$$

ϕ is *surjective*. If ϕ is both surjective and injective, then ϕ is called *bijective*. An injective, surjective, and bijective function is briefly called *injection*, *surjection*, and *bijection*, respectively. If ϕ is a function, we usually write $b = \phi(a)$ instead of $b \in \phi(a)$.

We say that a set A is *closed under a binary operation* $\circ$ if for each $a, b \in A$, $a \circ b \in A$. A set that is closed under an operation is said to satisfy a *closure property*. A closure under an n-ary operation is defined analogically. Let ρ be a relation on a set A. For $k \geq 0$, the *k-fold product* of ρ, ρ^k, is recursively defined as (1) $a\rho^0 b$ if and only if $a = b$, and (2) $a\rho^k b$ if and only if $a\rho c$ and $c\rho^{k-1}b$, for some c and $k \geq 1$. The *transitive closure* of ρ, ρ^+, is defined as $a\rho^+ b$ if and only if $a\rho^k b$, for some $k \geq 1$, and the *reflexive and transitive closure* of ρ, ρ^*, is defined as $a\rho^* b$ if and only if $a\rho^k b$, for some $k \geq 0$.

2.2 Basics of formal language theory

In this section, we define fundamental mathematical notions and concepts underlying formal language theory, such as languages, language operations, language families, and various grammars.

Languages

An *alphabet* T is a finite non-empty set whose members are called *symbols*. A finite sequence of symbols from T is a *string* or, synonymously, a *word* over T; specifically, ε is referred to as the *empty string*. By convention, we omit all separating commas in strings. That is, we write $a_1 \ldots a_n$ instead of $a_1, \ldots, a_n$. By T^*, we denote the set of all strings over T, and $T^+ = T^* - \{\varepsilon\}$. Any subset $L \subseteq T^*$ is a *language* over T. If L represents a finite set of strings, L is a *finite language*; otherwise, L is an *infinite language*. For instance, T^*, called the universal language over T, is an infinite language while $\emptyset$ and $\{\varepsilon\}$ are finite. If $\varepsilon \notin L$, then L is an *ε-free language*.

By alph(x) we denote the set of all symbols occurring in a string x. Set

$$\text{alph}(L) = \bigcup_{x \in L} \text{alph}(x).$$

Let $x, y \in T^*$ be two strings. The *concatenation* of x with y, denoted by xy, is the string obtained by appending y to x. Observe that for every $w \in T^*$, $w\varepsilon = \varepsilon w = w$.

We say that x is a *prefix* of y if there exists $u \in T^*$ such that $xu = y$; in addition, if $x \notin \{\varepsilon, y\}$, x is a *proper prefix* of y. Similarly, x is a *suffix* of y if there exists $u \in T^*$ such that $ux = y$; in addition, if $x \notin \{\varepsilon, y\}$, x is a *proper suffix* of y. Finally, x is a *substring* of y if there exists $u, v \in T^*$ such that $uxv = y$; in addition, if $x \notin \{\varepsilon, y\}$, x is a *proper substring* of y. For all $i \geq 0$, the ith *power of* x, denoted by x^i, is recursively defined as (1) $x^0 = \varepsilon$, and (2) $x^i = xx^{i-1}$, for $i \geq 1$. The *reversal* of x, denoted by $\mathrm{rev}(x)$, is x written in reverse order.

As languages represent sets, all set operations apply to them. Let $L_1, L_2 \subseteq T^*$ be two languages over T. Then, $L_1 \cup L_2$, $L_1 \cap L_2$, and $L_1 - L_2$ denote the union, intersection, and difference of languages L_1 and L_2, respectively. There are, however, some operations specific to languages. The *concatenation* of L_1 and L_2, denoted by L_1L_2, is defined as

$$L_1L_2 = \{xy : x \in L_1, y \in L_2\}.$$

The *right quotient* of L_1 with respect to L_2, denoted by L_1/L_2, is defined as

$$L_1/L_2 = \{y : yx \in L_1, \text{ for some } x \in L_2\};$$

similarly, the *left quotient* of L_1 with respect to L_2, denoted by $L_2\backslash L_1$, is defined as

$$L_2\backslash L_1 = \{y : xy \in L_1, \text{ for some } x \in L_2\}.$$

We also use a special type of the right and the left quotient. The *exhaustive right quotient* of L_1 with respect to L_2, denoted by $L_1 /\!\!/ L_2$, is defined as

$$L_1 /\!\!/ L_2 = \{x : x \in L_1/L_2, \text{ and no string in } L_1/L_2 \text{ is a proper prefix of } x\};$$

similarly, the *exhaustive left quotient* of L_1 with respect to L_2, denoted by $L_2 \backslash\!\!\backslash L_1$, is defined as

$$L_2 \backslash\!\!\backslash L_1 = \{x : x \in L_2\backslash L_1, \text{ and no string in } L_2\backslash L_1 \text{ is a proper suffix of } x\}.$$

Apart from binary operations, we also make some unary operations with languages. Let $L \subseteq T^*$. The ith *power* of L, L^i, is defined as (1) $L^0 = \{\varepsilon\}$ and (2) $L^i = LL^{i-1}$, for $i \geq 1$. The *Kleene star* of L, L^*, is defined as

$$L^* = \bigcup_{i \geq 0} L^i,$$

and the *Kleene plus* of L, L^+, is defined as

$$L^+ = \bigcup_{i \geq 1} L^i.$$

Notice that $L^+ = LL^* = L^*L$ and $L^* = L^+ \cup \{\varepsilon\}$. The *complement* of L is the language $T^* - L$. The *reversal* of L, denoted by $\mathrm{rev}(L)$, is defined as

$$\mathrm{rev}(L) = \big\{\mathrm{rev}(x) : x \in L\big\}.$$

Let T and U be two alphabets. A total function τ from T^* to 2^{U^*} such that $\tau(uv) = \tau(u)\tau(v)$, for every $u, v \in T^*$, is a *substitution* from T^* to U^*. By this definition, $\tau(\varepsilon) = \{\varepsilon\}$ and $\tau(a_1 \dots a_n) = \tau(a_1) \dots \tau(a_n)$, where $n \geq 1$, and $a_i \in T$, for all $1 \leq i \leq n$, so τ is completely specified by defining $\tau(a)$ for each $a \in T$. For $L \subseteq T^*$, we extend the definition of τ to

$$\tau(L) = \bigcup_{w \in L} \tau(w).$$

A substitution is ε-free if it is defined from T^+ to 2^{U^+}. A total function χ from T^* to U^* such that $\chi(uv) = \chi(u)\chi(v)$ for every $u, v \in T^*$ is a *homomorphism* from T^* to U^*. As any homomorphism is obviously a special case of a substitution, we specify χ by analogy with the specification of τ. For $L \subseteq T^*$, we extend the definition of χ to

$$\chi(L) = \{\chi(w) : w \in L\}.$$

Sets whose members are languages are called *families of languages*, denoted by $\mathscr{L}$. A family of languages $\mathscr{L}$ is ε-free if for every $L \in \mathscr{L}$, $\varepsilon \notin L$. The closure of a language family under an operation is defined by analogy with the definition of the closure of a set. Next, we define three closure properties, which we discuss later in the book.

Definition 2.1. A family of languages $\mathscr{L}$ is said to be *closed under linear erasing* if for every $L \in \mathscr{L}$, homomorphism h, and integer k such that $|w| \leq k|h(w)|$, for every $w \in L$, $h(L) \in \mathscr{L}$.

Definition 2.2. A family of languages $\mathscr{L}$ is said to be *closed under c-substitution* if for every $L \in \mathscr{L}$ and a substitution τ from T^* to $(T \cup \{c\})^*$ such that $\tau(a) = \{c\}^*\{a\}\{c\}^*$, for each $a \in T$, where $c \notin T$ is a new symbol, $\tau(L) \in \mathscr{L}$.

Definition 2.3. A family of languages $\mathscr{L}$ is said to be *closed under k-limited erasing*, where k is a positive integer, if whenever $c \notin T$ and $L \in \mathscr{L}$ with

$$L \subseteq \Big(T\big(\{\varepsilon\} \cup \{c\} \cup \dots \cup \{c\}^k\big)\Big)^*,$$

$h(c) = \varepsilon$ and $h(a) = a$, for each $a \in T$, then $h(L) \in \mathscr{L}$.

Theorem 2.4 (see [3]). *Any ε-free family of languages closed under intersection with a regular language, c-substitution, and k-limited erasing is closed under inverse homomorphism.*

The following definition introduces a language family closed under several operations defined above.

Definition 2.5. An *abstract family of languages* (see [4]) is a language family $\mathscr{L}$ satisfying the following properties:

- T is a countably infinite set of symbols;
- for every $L \in \mathscr{L}$, there is a finite set $T_1 \subseteq T$ such that $L \subseteq T_1^*$;
- $L \neq \emptyset$, for some $L \in \mathscr{L}$;
- $\mathscr{L}$ is closed under union, concatenation, Kleene plus, inverse homomorphism, ε-free homomorphism, and intersection with a regular language.

Theorem 2.6 (see [2]). *If an abstract family of languages is closed under intersection, it is closed under ε-free substitution.*

Finally, we introduce some additional definitions used in this book. For a finite set of integers I, $\max(I)$ denotes the maximal element of I.

Definition 2.7. Let $\text{perm}(t)$ be the set of all permutations of $\{1, \ldots, t\}$, where $t \geq 1$. For some $m, n \geq 0$, where $m + n \geq 1$, define

$$\text{perm}(m, n) = \big\{(i_1, \ldots, i_{m+n}) : (i_1, \ldots, i_{m+n}) \in \text{perm}(m + n), \\ i_k < i_l, \text{ for } k < l, i_k < m, i_l \leq m\big\}.$$

Let T be an alphabet. For all $x_1, \ldots, x_m \in T^+$ and $(i_1, \ldots, i_m) \in \text{perm}(m)$, define

$$\text{reorder}\big((x_1, \ldots, x_m), (i_1, \ldots, i_m)\big) = (x_{i_1}, \ldots, x_{i_m}).$$

Example 2.8. Let $m = 4$, $n = 3$, and $T = \{a, b, c, d, e, f, g\}$. Then,

$$(1, 6, 2, 7, 3, 5, 4) \in \text{perm}(m + n).$$

As the order of 1 through 4 is preserved in this permutation,

$$(1, 6, 2, 7, 3, 5, 4) \in \text{perm}(m, n).$$

Then,

$$\text{reorder}\big((a, b, c, d, e, f, g), (1, 6, 2, 7, 3, 5, 4)\big) = (a, f, b, g, c, e, d).$$

Grammars

This section reviews the basics of grammars. Specifically, it defines several types of grammars, including phrase-structure, context-sensitive, context-free, linear, right-linear, and regular grammars. In addition, basic results concerning all these grammars are recalled.

Definition 2.9. A *phrase-structure* grammar is a quadruple

$$G = (V, T, P, S),$$

where

- V is the *total alphabet*;
- $T \subset V$ is the set of *terminal symbols* or, briefly, *terminals*;
- $P \subseteq V^*(V-T)V^* \times V^*$ is a finite relation;
- $S \in V - T$ is the *start symbol* of G.

The symbols in $V - T$ are referred to as *nonterminal symbols* or, briefly, *nonterminals*. In what follows, each $(x, y) \in P$ is called a *production* or a *rule* and written as

$$x \to y \in P;$$

accordingly, P is called the *set of productions* in G. Given a production $p = x \to y \in P$, we set $\text{lhs}(p) = x$ and $\text{rhs}(p) = y$, which represent the *left-hand side* and the *right-hand side* of the production p, respectively. If $y = \varepsilon$, p is called *erasing production*. The relation of a *direct derivation* in G is a binary relation over V^* denoted by $\Rightarrow_G$ and defined in the following way. If $u = z_1xz_2$, $v = z_1yz_2$, and $x \to y \in P$, where $z_1, z_2 \in V^*$, then G makes a *derivation step* from u to v according to $x \to y$, symbolically written as

$$u \Rightarrow_G v\ [x \to y].$$

When no confusion exists, we simplify $u \Rightarrow_G v\ [x \to y]$ to $u \Rightarrow_G v$. By $\Rightarrow_G^k$, we denote the k-fold product of $\Rightarrow_G$. Furthermore, let $\Rightarrow_G^+$ and $\Rightarrow_G^*$ denote the transitive closure of $\Rightarrow_G$ and the reflexive and transitive closure of $\Rightarrow_G$, respectively. If $S \Rightarrow_G^* x$, for some $x \in V^*$, x is called a *sentential form*; in addition, if $x \in T^*$, x is called a *sentence*. If $S \Rightarrow_G^* w$, where $w \in T^*$, $S \Rightarrow_G^* w$ is said to be a *successful derivation* of G. If $S \Rightarrow_G^* v$, where $v \in V^*$, and there is no derivation $v \Rightarrow_G^* w$, where $w \in T^*$, $S \Rightarrow_G^* v$ is said to be an *unsuccessful derivation* of G. Set

$$F(G) = \{x : x \in V^*, S \Rightarrow_G^* x\}.$$

The *language of* G, denoted by $L(G)$, is defined as

$$L(G) = \{w : w \in T^*, S \Rightarrow_G^* w\}.$$

A *recursively enumerable language* is a language generated by a phrase-structure grammar. In the literature, the phrase-structure grammars are also often defined with productions of the form

$$xAy \to xuy,$$

where $u, x, y \in V^*$, and $A \in V - T$ (see [5]). Both definitions are interchangeable in the sense that the grammars defined in these two ways generate the same family of languages—the family of recursively enumerable languages, denoted by $\mathscr{L}(RE)$.

Definition 2.10. A *context-sensitive grammar* is a phrase-structure grammar

$$G = (V, T, P, S)$$

such that every production $x \to y \in P$ satisfies

$$|x| \leq |y|.$$

A *context-sensitive language* is a language generated by a context-sensitive grammar. The family of context-sensitive languages is denoted by $\mathscr{L}(CS)$.

Definition 2.11. A *context-free grammar* is a phrase-structure grammar

$$G = (V, T, P, S)$$

such that every production in P is of the form

$$A \to x,$$

where $A \in V - T$ and $x \in V^*$. A *context-free language* is a language generated by a context-free grammar. The family of context-free languages is denoted by $\mathscr{L}(CF)$.

Definition 2.12. A *linear grammar* is a phrase-structure grammar

$$G = (V, T, P, S)$$

such that every production in P is of the form

- $A \to xBy$, or
- $A \to x$,

where $A, B \in V - T$ and $x, y \in T^*$. A *linear language* is a language generated by a linear grammar. The family of linear languages is denoted by $\mathscr{L}(LIN)$.

Definition 2.13. A *regular grammar* is a phrase-structure grammar

$$G = (V, T, P, S)$$

such that every production in P is of the form

- $A \to aB$, or
- $A \to a$,

where $A, B \in V - T$ and $a \in T$. A *regular language* is a language generated by a regular grammar. The family of regular languages is denoted by $\mathscr{L}(REG)$.

Alternatively, the family of regular languages is characterized by right-linear grammars, defined next.

Definition 2.14. A *right-linear grammar* is a phrase-structure grammar

$$G = (V, T, P, S)$$

such that every production in P is of the form

- $A \to xB$, or
- $A \to x$,

where $A, B \in V - T$ and $x \in T^*$. The family of languages generated by right-linear grammars is denoted by $\mathscr{L}(RLIN)$.

For the families of languages generated by regular, right-linear, linear, context-free, context-sensitive, and phrase-structure grammars, it holds:

Theorem 2.15 (see [5]).

$$\mathscr{L}(REG) = \mathscr{L}(RLIN) \subset \mathscr{L}(LIN) \subset \mathscr{L}(CF) \subset \mathscr{L}(CS) \subset \mathscr{L}(RE).$$

Theorem 2.16 (see [6]). *For every recursively enumerable language L, there exist ε-free context-free languages L_1, L_2 and a homomorphism h such that $L = h(L_1 \cap L_2)$.*

Lemma 2.17 (Kuroda Normal Form of Context-Sensitive Grammars, see [7]). *Let $L \in \mathscr{L}(CS)$. Then, there exists a context-sensitive grammar $G = (V, T, P, S)$ such that $L = L(G)$ and every production in P is of the form*

- $AB \rightarrow CD$,
- $A \rightarrow BC$, *or*
- $A \rightarrow a$,

where A, B, C, $D \in V - T$, and $a \in T$.

Lemma 2.18 (Kuroda Normal Form of Phrase-Structure Grammars, see [7]). *Let $L \in \mathscr{L}(RE)$. Then, there exists a phrase-structure grammar $G = (V, T, P, S)$ such that $L = L(G)$ and every production in P is of the form*

- $AB \rightarrow CD$,
- $A \rightarrow BC$,
- $A \rightarrow a$, *or*
- $A \rightarrow \varepsilon$,

where A, B, C, $D \in V - T$, and $a \in T$.

Lemma 2.19 (Geffert Normal Form of Phrase-Structure Grammars, see [8]). *Let $L \in \mathscr{L}(RE)$. Then, there exists a phrase-structure grammar*

$$G = \big(\{S, A, B, C, D\} \cup T, T, P \cup \{AB \rightarrow \varepsilon, CD \rightarrow \varepsilon\}, S\big)$$

such that $L = L(G)$, and P contains only context-free productions. In addition, the context-free productions are of the form

- $S \rightarrow zSa$, *where* $z \in \{A, C\}^*$, $a \in T$;
- $S \rightarrow uSv$, *where* $u \in \{A, C\}^*$, $v \in \{B, D\}^*$;
- $S \rightarrow uv$, *where* $u \in \{A, C\}^*$, $v \in \{B, D\}^*$.

Apart from phrase-structure grammars, we also use simple matrix grammars, programmed grammars, state grammars, Extended Post Correspondence, and queue grammars to describe languages in this book. We start with the definition of linear simple matrix grammars.

Definition 2.20. A *simple matrix grammar of degree n* (see [9]) is an $(n + 3)$-tuple

$$G = (V_1, \ldots, V_n, T, P, S),$$

where $n \geq 1$, V_1, ..., V_n are alphabets, $T \subset V_i$, for all $1 \leq i \leq n$, $(V_1 - T)$, ..., $(V_n - T)$ are pairwise disjoint, $S \notin V_1 \cup \cdots \cup V_n$, and P is a finite set of productions of the following three forms:

- $(S) \rightarrow (x_{11}A_{11}x_{12}A_{12} \ldots x_{1k}A_{1k} \ldots x_{n1}A_{n1}x_{n2}A_{n2} \ldots x_{nk}A_{nk}y)$, where $y \in T^*$, and $A_{ij} \in V_i - T$, $x_{ij} \in T^*$, for all $1 \leq i \leq n$, $1 \leq j \leq k$, for some $k \geq 1$;
- $(A_1, \ldots, A_n) \rightarrow (x_{11}A_{11} \ldots x_{1k}A_{1k}y_1, \ldots, x_{n1}A_{n1} \ldots x_{nk}A_{nk}y_n)$, where y_i, $x_{ij} \in T^*$, A_i, $A_{ij} \in V_i - T$, for all $1 \leq i \leq n$, $1 \leq j \leq k$, for some $k \geq 1$;
- $(A_1, \ldots, A_n) \rightarrow (x_1, \ldots, x_n)$, where $A_i \in V_i - T$, $x_i \in T^*$, for all $1 \leq i \leq n$.

If

- either $u = S$ and $p = (S) \rightarrow (v) \in P$
- or $u = y_1A_1z_1 \ldots y_nA_nz_n$, $v = y_1w_1z_1 \ldots y_nw_nz_n$, where $y_i \in T^*$, $z_i \in V_i^*$, for all $1 \leq i \leq n$, and $p = (A_1, \ldots, A_n) \rightarrow (w_1, \ldots, w_n) \in P$,

then G makes a derivation step from u to v according to p, symbolically written as $u \Rightarrow_G v\ [p]$. Let $\Rightarrow_G^+$ and $\Rightarrow_G^*$ denote the transitive closure of $\Rightarrow_G$ and the reflexive and transitive closure of $\Rightarrow_G$, respectively. The language of G is denoted by $L(G)$ and defined as

$$L(G) = \{x : x \in T^*, S \Rightarrow_G^* x\}.$$

The family of languages generated by simple matrix grammars of degree n is denoted by $\mathscr{L}(SM, n)$, and

$$\mathscr{L}(SM) = \bigcup_{n=1}^{\infty} \mathscr{L}(SM, n).$$

Definition 2.21. A *linear simple matrix grammar of degree n* (see [10]) is a simple matrix grammar

$$G = (V_1, \ldots, V_n, T, P, S),$$

where P is a finite set of productions of the following three forms:

- $(S) \rightarrow (x_1A_1 \ldots x_nA_nx_{n+1})$, where $A_i \in V_i - T$, $x_j \in T^*$, for all $1 \leq i \leq n$, $1 \leq j \leq n + 1$;
- $(A_1, \ldots, A_n) \rightarrow (x_1B_1y_1, \ldots, x_nB_ny_n)$, where A_i, $B_i \in V_i - T$, x_i, $y_i \in T^*$, for all $1 \leq i \leq n$;

- $(A_1, \ldots, A_n) \to (x_1, \ldots, x_n)$, where $A_i \in V_i - T$, $x_i \in T^*$, for all $1 \le i \le n$.

The family of languages generated by linear simple matrix grammars of degree n is denoted by $\mathscr{L}(SM, LIN, n)$, and

$$\mathscr{L}(SM, LIN) = \bigcup_{n=1}^{\infty} \mathscr{L}(SM, LIN, n).$$

Definition 2.22. A *right-linear simple matrix grammar of degree n* (see [9]) is a linear simple matrix grammar

$$G = (V_1, \ldots, V_n, T, P, S),$$

where P is a finite set of productions of the following three forms:

- $(S) \to (x_1 A_1 \ldots x_n A_n)$, where $A_i \in V_i - T$, $x_i \in T^*$, for all $1 \le i \le n$;
- $(A_1, \ldots, A_n) \to (x_1 B_1, \ldots, x_n B_n)$, where A_i, $B_i \in V_i - T$, $x_i \in T^*$, for all $1 \le i \le n$;
- $(A_1, \ldots, A_n) \to (x_1, \ldots, x_n)$, where $A_i \in V_i - T$, $x_i \in T^*$, for all $1 \le i \le n$.

The family of languages generated by right-linear simple matrix grammars of degree n is denoted by $\mathscr{L}(SM, RLIN, n)$, and

$$\mathscr{L}(SM, RLIN) = \bigcup_{n=1}^{\infty} \mathscr{L}(SM, RLIN, n).$$

Theorem 2.23 (see [9, 10]). *For every $n \ge 1$,*

$$\mathscr{L}(SM, n) \subset \mathscr{L}(SM, n+1),$$
$$\mathscr{L}(SM, LIN, n) \subset \mathscr{L}(SM, LIN, n+1),$$
$$\mathscr{L}(SM, RLIN, n) \subset \mathscr{L}(SM, RLIN, n+1),$$

and

$$\mathscr{L}(SM, RLIN, n) \subset \mathscr{L}(SM, LIN, n) \subset \mathscr{L}(SM, n).$$

Theorem 2.24 (see [9, 10]).

$$\mathscr{L}(CF) - \mathscr{L}(SM, LIN) \neq \emptyset,$$
$$\mathscr{L}(CF) - \mathscr{L}(SM, RLIN) \neq \emptyset,$$

and

$$\mathscr{L}(SM, RLIN) \subset \mathscr{L}(SM, LIN) \subset \mathscr{L}(SM) \subset \mathscr{L}(CS).$$

Lemma 2.25 (see [9]). $\{a^n b^n c^n : n \ge 1\}^+ \notin \mathscr{L}(SM)$.

Next, we define a programmed grammar.

Definition 2.26. A *programmed grammar* (without appearance checking, see [11]) is a quadruple

$$G = (V, T, P, S),$$

where V is an alphabet, $T \subset V$, $S \in V - T$ is the start symbol, and P is a finite set of pairs

$$(A \to x, \phi),$$

where $A \in V - T$, $x \in V^*$, and $\phi \subseteq P$. If $u = (rAs, p)$, $v = (rxs, q)$, and $p = (A \to x, \phi) \in P$, where $q \in \phi$, and $r, s \in V^*$, then G makes a derivation step from u to v according to p, symbolically written as $u \Rightarrow_G v\ [p]$ or, simply, $u \Rightarrow_G v$. Let $\Rightarrow_G^+$ and $\Rightarrow_G^*$ denote the transitive closure of $\Rightarrow_G$ and the reflexive and transitive closure of $\Rightarrow_G$, respectively. The language generated by a programmed grammar G, denoted by $L(G)$, is defined as

$$L(G) = \left\{x : x \in T^*, (S, p) \Rightarrow_G^* (x, q), \text{ for some } p, q \in P\right\}.$$

The family of languages generated by programmed grammars without erasing productions and with erasing productions is denoted by $\mathscr{L}(P)$ and $\mathscr{L}(P, \varepsilon)$, respectively.

Theorem 2.27 (see [11]). $\mathscr{L}(CF) \subset \mathscr{L}(P) \subset \mathscr{L}(CS)$.

Theorem 2.28 (see [12]). *All languages over one-letter alphabets in $\mathscr{L}(P, \varepsilon)$ are regular.*

Corollary 2.29. $\mathscr{L}(P) \subseteq \mathscr{L}(P, \varepsilon) \subset \mathscr{L}(RE)$.

Next, we define state grammars.

Definition 2.30. A *state grammar* (see [13]) is a sextuple

$$G = (V, T, K, P, S, p_0),$$

where V is an alphabet, $T \subset V$, K is a finite set of states, $S \in V - T$, $p_0 \in K$, and P is a finite set of productions of the form

$$(A, p) \to (x, q),$$

where $A \in V - T$, $x \in V^+$, and $p, q \in K$. If $u = (rAs, p)$, $v = (rxs, q)$, and $(A, p) \to (x, q) \in P$, where $r, s \in V^*$, and for each $(B, p) \to (y, t) \in P$ it holds that $B \notin \text{alph}(r)$, then G makes a derivation step from u to v according to $(A, p) \to (x, q)$, symbolically written as $u \Rightarrow_G v\ \left[(A, p) \to (x, q)\right]$ or, simply, $u \Rightarrow_G v$. To emphasize that the jth nonterminal in u is rewritten during a derivation step, we write $u\ {}^j\!\!\Rightarrow_G v$. Let $\Rightarrow_G^+$ and $\Rightarrow_G^*$ denote the transitive closure of $\Rightarrow_G$ and the reflexive and transitive closure of $\Rightarrow_G$, respectively. The language generated by G is defined as

$$L(G) = \{x : x \in T^*, (S, p_0) \Rightarrow_G^* (x, q), \text{ for some } q \in K\}.$$

A *state language* is a language generated by a state grammar. The family of all state languages is denoted by $\mathscr{L}(ST)$. An *n-limited derivation*, denoted by $x \;{}^n\!\!\Rightarrow_G^* y$, is a derivation in which every derivation step $u \;{}^j\!\!\Rightarrow_G v$ satisfies $j \leq n$. Define

$$L(G, n) = \{x : x \in T^*, (S, p_0) \;{}^n\!\!\Rightarrow_G^* (x, q), \text{ for some } q \in K\};$$

clearly,

$$L(G) = \bigcup_{n=1}^{\infty} L(G, n).$$

A state grammar G is *of degree n* if and only if $L(G, n) = L(G)$. A state language is said to be of degree n if there is a state grammar G of degree n with $L = L(G)$. If $L(G, n) \neq L(G)$, for all $n \geq 1$, then G and $L(G)$ are said to be *of infinite degree*. The family of state languages of degree n is denoted by $\mathscr{L}(ST, n)$, and

$$\mathscr{L}(ST, \infty) = \bigcup_{n=1}^{\infty} \mathscr{L}(ST, n).$$

Theorem 2.31 (see [13]). *A state language L is of degree n if and only if $L = L(G, n)$, for some state grammar G.*

Theorem 2.32 (see [13]).

$$\mathscr{L}(CF) = \mathscr{L}(ST, 1) \subset \mathscr{L}(ST, 2) \subset \cdots \subset \mathscr{L}(ST, \infty) \subset \mathscr{L}(ST) = \mathscr{L}(CS).$$

Theorem 2.33 (see [13]). *Every $\mathscr{L}(ST, n)$, where $n \geq 1$, is an abstract family of languages.*

Next, we define an Extended Post Correspondence.

Definition 2.34. For an alphabet $T = \{a_1, \ldots, a_n\}$, an *Extended Post Correspondence* (see [8]) is defined as

$$E = \Big(\big\{(u_1, v_1), \ldots, (u_r, v_r)\big\}, (z_{a_1}, \ldots, z_{a_n})\Big),$$

where $u_i, v_i, z_{a_j} \in \{0, 1\}^*$, for every $1 \leq i \leq r$ and $1 \leq j \leq n$. The language represented by an Extended Post Correspondence E, denoted by $L(E)$, is defined as

$$L(E) = \big\{b_1 \ldots b_k : b_1 \ldots b_k \in T^*, v_{s_1} \ldots v_{s_l} = u_{s_1} \ldots u_{s_l} z_{b_1} \ldots z_{b_k}, \text{ for some } s_1, \ldots, s_l \in \{1, \ldots, r\}, l \geq 1, k \geq 0\big\}.$$

Theorem 2.35 (see [8]). *For every $L \in \mathscr{L}(RE)$, there exists an Extended Post Correspondence E such that $L(E) = L$.*

Finally, we define the notion of a queue grammar and a normal form of its productions, used throughout this book. We prove that for every queue grammar, there exists a queue grammar in this normal form.

Definition 2.36. A *queue grammar* (see [14]) is a sextuple

$$Q = (V, T, W, F, R, g),$$

where V and W are alphabets satisfying $V \cap W = \emptyset$, $T \subset V$, $F \subset W$,

$$g \in (V - T)(W - F),$$

and

$$R \subseteq \big(V \times (W - F)\big) \times (V^* \times W)$$

is a finite relation. If $u = arb$, $v = rxc$, and $(a, b, x, c) \in R$, where $r, x \in V^*$, $a \in V$, and $b, c \in W$, then Q makes a derivation step from u to v according to (a, b, x, c), symbolically written as $u \Rightarrow_Q v\ \big[(a, b, x, c)\big]$, or, simply, $u \Rightarrow_Q v$. The language generated by a queue grammar Q, denoted by $L(Q)$, is defined as

$$L(Q) = \{x : x \in T^*, g \Rightarrow_Q^+ xf, f \in F\}.$$

Theorem 2.37 (see [14]). *For every $L \in \mathscr{L}(RE)$, there exists a queue grammar Q such that $L(Q) = L$.*

Lemma 2.38. *Let Q' be a queue grammar. Then, there exists a queue grammar*

$$Q = \big(V, T, W' \cup \{1, f\}, \{f\}, R, g\big)$$

such that $L(Q') = L(Q)$, where $W' \cap \{1, f\} = \emptyset$, each $(a, b, x, c) \in R$ satisfies $a \in V - T$, and

- *either $b \in W'$, $x \in (V - T)^*$, $c \in W' \cup \{1, f\}$*
- *or $b = 1$, $x \in T$, $c \in \{1, f\}$.*

Proof. Let $Q' = (V', T, W', F', R', g)$ be a queue grammar. Set $\Phi = \{\bar{a} : a \in T\}$. Define the homomorphism α from $(V')^*$ to $\big((V' - T) \cup \Phi\big)^*$ as $\alpha(a) = \bar{a}$, for each $a \in T$, and $\alpha(A) = A$, for each $A \in V' - T$. Set $V = V' \cup \Phi$, $W = W' \cup \{1, f\}$, and $F = \{f\}$. Define the queue grammar

$$Q = (V, T, W, F, R, g)$$

with R constructed in the following way:

1. For each $(a, b, x, c) \in R'$, where $c \in W' - F'$, add $\big(\alpha(a), b, \alpha(x), c\big)$ to R.
2. (a) For each $(a, b, x, c) \in R'$, where $c \in F'$, add $\big(\alpha(a), b, \alpha(x), 1\big)$ to R.
   (b) For each $(a, b, \varepsilon, c) \in R'$, where $c \in F'$, add $\big(\alpha(a), b, \varepsilon, f\big)$ to R.
3. For each $a \in T$, add
   (a) $(\bar{a}, 1, a, 1)$ and
   (b) $(\bar{a}, 1, a, f)$ to R.

Clearly, each $(a, b, x, c) \in R$ satisfies $a \in V - T$ and either $b \in W'$, $x \in (V - T)^*$, $c \in W' \cup \{1, f\}$ or $b = 1$, $x \in T$, $c \in \{1, f\}$.

To see that $L(Q') \subseteq L(Q)$, consider any $v \in L(Q')$. As $v \in L(Q')$, $g \Rightarrow^*_{Q'} vt$, where $v \in T^*$ and $t \in F'$. Express $g \Rightarrow^*_{Q'} vt$ as

$$g \Rightarrow^*_{Q'} axc \Rightarrow_{Q'} vt\ \big[(a, c, y, t)\big],$$

where $a \in V'$, $x, y \in T^*$, $xy = v$, and $c \in W' - F'$. This derivation is simulated by Q as follows. First, Q uses productions from (1) to simulate $g \Rightarrow^*_{Q'} axc$. Then, it uses a production from (2) to simulate $axc \Rightarrow_{Q'} vt$. For $x = \varepsilon$, a production from (2b) can be used to generate $\varepsilon \in L(Q)$ if $\varepsilon \in L(Q')$; otherwise, a production from (2a) is used. This part of the simulation can be expressed as

$$g \Rightarrow^*_Q \alpha(ax)c \Rightarrow_Q \alpha(v)1.$$

At this point, $\alpha(v)$ satisfies $\alpha(v) = \bar{a}_1 \ldots \bar{a}_n$, where $a_i \in T$, for all $1 \le i \le n$, for some $n \ge 1$. The productions from (3a) replace every $\bar{a}_j$ with a_j, where $1 \le j \le n - 1$, and finally, a production from (3b) replaces $\bar{a}_n$ with a_n. As a result, we obtain the sentence vf, so $L(Q') \subseteq L(Q)$.

To establish $L(Q) \subseteq L(Q')$, observe that the use of a production from (2b) in Q before the sentential form has the form $\alpha(ax)c$, where $a \in V'$, $x \in T^*$, $c \in W' - F'$, leads to an unsuccessful derivation. Similarly, the use of the production from (2b) in the case when $x \ne \varepsilon$ leads to an unsuccessful derivation as well. The details are left to the reader. As a result, $L(Q) \subseteq L(Q')$.

As $L(Q') \subseteq L(Q)$ and $L(Q) \subseteq L(Q')$, we obtain $L(Q) = L(Q')$. ■

Consider the queue grammar $Q = (V, T, W, F, R, g)$ from Lemma 2.38. Its properties imply that Q generates every string in $L(Q) - \{\varepsilon\}$ so that it passes through 1. Before it enters 1, it generates only strings over $V - T$; after entering 1, it generates only strings over T. The following corollary expresses this property formally.

Corollary 2.39. *Let Q be a queue grammar that satisfies the properties given in Lemma 2.38. Then, Q generates every $y \in L(Q) - \{\varepsilon\}$ in this way:*

$$
\begin{array}{lll}
a_0 q_0 & \Rightarrow_Q x_0 q_1 & [(a_0, q_0, z_0, q_1)] \\
& \vdots & \\
& \Rightarrow_Q x_{k-1} q_k & [(a_{k-1}, q_{k-1}, z_{k-1}, q_k)] \\
& \Rightarrow_Q x_k 1 & [(a_k, q_k, z_k, 1)] \\
& \Rightarrow_Q x_{k+1} b_1 1 & [(a_{k+1}, 1, b_1, 1)] \\
& \vdots & \\
& \Rightarrow_Q x_{k+m-1} b_1 \dots b_{m-1} 1 & [(a_{k+m-1}, 1, b_{m-1}, 1)] \\
& \Rightarrow_Q b_1 \dots b_m f & [(a_{k+m}, 1, b_m, f)],
\end{array}
$$

where $k, m \geq 1$, $g = a_0 q_0$, $a_1, \dots, a_{k+m} \in V - T$, $b_1, \dots, b_m \in T$, $z_0, \dots, z_k \in (V - T)^*$, $q_0, \dots, q_k$, $1 \in W - F$, $f \in F$, $x_0, \dots, x_{k+m-1} \in (V - T)^+$, and $y = b_1 \dots b_m$. ∎

If some grammars define the same language, they are referred to as *equivalent grammars*. This grammatical equivalence is central to this book because we often discuss how to transform grammars to some other grammars so that both the original grammars and the transformed grammars are equivalent.

2.3 Scattered context grammars

In this section, we define scattered context grammars without erasing productions, introduced in [2], and their generalized version—scattered context grammars with erasing productions, first studied in [15]. In addition, we illustrate these definitions by several examples.

Definition 2.40. A *scattered context grammar* is a quadruple

$$G = (V, T, P, S),$$

where

- V is the total alphabet;
- $T \subset V$ is the set of terminals;
- P is a finite set of productions of the form

  $$(A_1, \dots, A_n) \rightarrow (x_1, \dots, x_n),$$

  where $n \geq 1$, $A_i \in V - T$, and $x_i \in V^*$, for all $1 \leq i \leq n$;
- $S \in V - T$ is the start symbol of G.

If

$$u = u_1 A_1 \dots u_n A_n u_{n+1},$$
$$v = u_1 x_1 \dots u_n x_n u_{n+1},$$

and $p = (A_1, \ldots, A_n) \rightarrow (x_1, \ldots, x_n) \in P$, where $u_i \in V^*$, for all $1 \leq i \leq n+1$, then G makes a derivation step from u to v according to p, symbolically written as

$$u \Rightarrow_G v\ [p],$$

or, simply, $u \Rightarrow_G v$. In addition, if $A_i \notin \text{alph}(u_i)$ for all $1 \leq i \leq n$, then the derivation step is *leftmost*, and we write

$$u\ {}_{lm}{\Rightarrow_G}\ v\ [p];$$

if $A_i \notin \text{alph}(u_{i+1})$ for all $1 \leq i \leq n$, then the derivation step is *rightmost*, and we write

$$u\ {}_{rm}{\Rightarrow_G}\ v\ [p].$$

Set

$$\text{lhs}(p) = A_1 \ldots A_n,$$
$$\text{rhs}(p) = x_1 \ldots x_n,$$

and

$$\text{len}(p) = n.$$

If $\text{len}(p) \geq 2$, p is said to be a *context-sensitive production* while for $\text{len}(p) = 1$, p is said to be *context-free*. The language generated by G is denoted by $L(G)$ and defined as

$$L(G) = \{x : x \in T^*, S \Rightarrow_G^* x\}.$$

A language L is a *scattered context language* if there exists a scattered context grammar G such that $L = L(G)$. The family of languages generated by scattered context grammars is denoted by $\mathscr{L}(SC)$.

Definition 2.41. A *propagating scattered context grammar* is a scattered context grammar

$$G = (V, T, P, S)$$

in which each $(A_1, \ldots, A_n) \rightarrow (x_1, \ldots, x_n) \in P$ satisfies $x_i \in V^+$, for all $1 \leq i \leq n$. A *propagating scattered context language* is a language generated by a propagating scattered context grammar. The family of propagating scattered context languages is denoted by $\mathscr{L}(PSC)$.

Example 2.42. Consider the non-context-free language $L = \{a^n b^n c^n : n \geq 1\}$. This language can be generated by the scattered context grammar

$$G = \big(\{S, A, a, b, c\}, \{a, b, c\}, P, S\big),$$

where

$$P = \big\{(S) \rightarrow (aAbAcA),$$
$$(A, A, A) \rightarrow (aA, bA, cA),$$
$$(A, A, A) \rightarrow (\varepsilon, \varepsilon, \varepsilon)\big\}.$$

For example, the sentence *aabbcc* is generated by G as follows:

$$S \Rightarrow_G aAbAcA \Rightarrow_G aaAbbAccA \Rightarrow_G aabbcc.$$

Notice, however, that the generated language belongs to $\mathscr{L}(PSC)$ because it is also generated by the propagating scattered context grammar

$$G' = \big(\{S, A, a, b, c\}, \{a, b, c\}, P', S\big),$$

where

$$\begin{aligned} P' = \big\{&(S) \to (AAA), \\ &(A, A, A) \to (aA, bA, cA), \\ &(A, A, A) \to (a, b, c)\big\}. \end{aligned}$$

Example 2.43. Consider the non-context-free language

$$L = \big\{(ab^n)^m : m \geq n \geq 2\big\}.$$

This language is generated by the propagating scattered context grammar

$$G = \big(\{S, S_1, S_2, B, M, X, Y, Z, a\}, \{a\}, P, S\big)$$

with P containing the following productions:

$$\begin{aligned} 1 &: (S) \to (MS), \\ 2 &: (S) \to (S_1S_2), \\ 3 &: (S_1, S_2) \to (MS_1, BS_2), \\ 4 &: (S_1, S_2) \to (MX, BY), \\ 5 &: (X, B, Y) \to (BX, Y, b), \\ 6 &: (M, X, Y) \to (X, Y, ab), \\ 7 &: (M, X, Y) \to (Z, Y, ab), \\ 8 &: (Z, B, Y) \to (Z, b, Y), \\ 9 &: (Z, Y) \to (a, b). \end{aligned}$$

Clearly, by applying productions (1) through (4), the grammar generates a string from $\{M\}^+\{X\}\{B\}^+\{Y\}$. In what follows, we demonstrate that the string is of the form $M^{m-1}XB^{n-1}Y$, where $m, n \geq 2$. Production (1) allows G to add M's to the beginning of the sentential form, so $m \geq n$ holds true. Observe that each of the productions (5) through (8) either shifts the last nonterminal Y left or keeps its position unchanged. As a result, always the rightmost nonterminal preceding Y has to be replaced with Y by productions (5) through (7); otherwise, the skipped nonterminals cannot be rewritten during the rest of the derivation. For the same reason, the rightmost nonterminal M preceding X has to be rewritten by the production (6). Productions (5) and (6) are applied in a cycle consisting of $n-1$ applications of (5) and one application of (6):

$$\begin{aligned} M^{m-1}XB^{n-1}Y &\Rightarrow_G^{n-1} M^{m-1}B^{n-1}XYb^{n-1} \; [5^{n-1}] \\ &\Rightarrow_G M^{m-2}XB^{n-1}Yab^n \; [6]. \end{aligned}$$

At this point, the substring preceding Y differs from the original string only in the number of M's decremented by 1, and the cycle can be repeated again. After repeating this cycle $m-2$ times, we obtain $MXB^{n-1}Y(ab^n)^{m-2}$. The derivation is completed as follows:

$$\begin{aligned} MXB^{n-1}Y(ab^n)^{m-2} &\Rightarrow_G^{n-1} MB^{n-1}XYb^{n-1}(ab^n)^{m-2} && [5^{n-1}] \\ &\Rightarrow_G ZB^{n-1}Y(ab^n)^{m-1} && [7] \\ &\Rightarrow_G^{n-1} Zb^{n-1}Y(ab^n)^{m-1} && [8^{n-1}] \\ &\Rightarrow_G (ab^n)^m && [9]. \end{aligned}$$

Example 2.44 (see [16, 17]). Consider the non-context-free language

$$L = \left\{a^{2^n} : n \geq 0\right\}.$$

This language is generated by the propagating scattered context grammar

$$G = \left(\{S, W, X, Y, Z, A, a\}, \{a\}, P, S\right)$$

with P containing the following productions:

$$\begin{aligned} &1 : (S) \to (a), \\ &2 : (S) \to (aa), \\ &3 : (S) \to (WAXY), \\ &4 : (W, A, X, Y) \to (a, W, X, AAY), \\ &5 : (W, X, Y) \to (a, W, AXY), \\ &6 : (W, X, Y) \to (Z, Z, a), \\ &7 : (Z, A, Z) \to (Z, a, Z), \\ &8 : (Z, Z) \to (a, a). \end{aligned}$$

In what follows, we demonstrate that $L(G) = L$. Productions (1) and (2) generate the strings of $\left\{a^{2^n} : n \in \{0, 1\}\right\}$ while (3) starts off the derivation of other strings in L. Consider the following derivation of $a^{16} \in L(G)$:

$$\begin{aligned} S &\Rightarrow_G WAXY && [3] \\ &\Rightarrow_G aWXA^2Y && [4] \\ &\Rightarrow_G a^2WA^3XY && [5] \\ &\Rightarrow_G a^3WA^2XA^2Y && [4] \\ &\Rightarrow_G a^4WAXA^4Y && [4] \\ &\Rightarrow_G a^5WXA^6Y && [4] \\ &\Rightarrow_G a^6WA^7XY && [5] \\ &\Rightarrow_G a^6ZA^7Za && [6] \\ &\Rightarrow_G^7 a^{13}ZZa && [7^7] \\ &\Rightarrow_G a^{16} && [8]. \end{aligned}$$

Observe that in any successful derivation, productions (4) and (5) are applied in a cycle, and after the required number of A's is obtained, the derivation is finished by productions (6), (7), and (8). In greater detail, observe that the production $(W, A, X, Y) \rightarrow (a, W, X, AAY)$ removes one A between W and X, and inserts two A's between X and Y. In a successful derivation, this production has to rewrite the leftmost nonterminal A. After all A's between W and X are removed, the production $(W, X, Y) \rightarrow (a, W, AXY)$ can be used to bring all A's between X and Y back between W and X, and the cycle can be repeated again. Alternatively, production (6) can be used, which initializes the final phase of the derivation in which all A's are replaced with a's by productions (7) and (8).

By adding one more stage, the above grammar can be extended so that it generates the language

$$\left\{a^{2^{2^n}} : n \geq 0\right\}.$$

The first stage, similar to the above grammar, generates 2^n identical symbols that serve as a counter for the second stage. In the second stage, a string consisting of identical symbols, which are different from those generated during the first stage, is doubled 2^n times, thus obtaining 2^{2^n} identical symbols. This doubling starts from a string consisting of a single symbol. See [18] for more details.

Finally, we introduce several measures of the descriptional complexity of scattered context grammars, which we make use of later in the book.

Definition 2.45. Let $G = (V, T, P, S)$ be a scattered context grammar. Then, its *degree of context sensitivity*, symbolically written as $\text{dcs}(G)$, is defined as

$$\text{dcs}(G) = \left|\left\{p : p \in P, \text{lhs}(p) \geq 2\right\}\right|.$$

The *maximum context sensitivity* of G, denoted by $\text{mcs}(G)$, is defined as

$$\text{mcs}(G) = \max\left(\left\{\text{len}(p) - 1 : p \in P\right\}\right).$$

The *overall context sensitivity* of G, denoted by $\text{ocs}(G)$, is defined as

$$\text{ocs}(G) = \text{len}(p_1) + \cdots + \text{len}(p_n) - n,$$

where $P = \{p_1, \ldots, p_n\}$.

PART II

Theory

CHAPTER 3

Basic properties

In this chapter, we state the fundamental properties of scattered context grammars and their languages. Based upon the pioneer study given in [2], in Sections 3.1 and 3.2, we introduce a normal form of propagating scattered context grammars and study their closure properties. Then, in Section 3.3, we investigate the generative power of scattered context grammars with and without erasing productions.

3.1 Normal forms

In this section, we discuss 2-limited propagating scattered context grammars, which represent an important normal form of propagating scattered context grammars. We demonstrate that the family of languages generated by these grammars coincides with the language family generated by ordinary propagating scattered context grammars. First, we rigorously define this normal form.

Definition 3.1. A *2-limited propagating scattered context grammar* is a propagating scattered context grammar $G = (V, T, P, S)$ such that

- $(A_1, \ldots, A_n) \to (w_1, \ldots, w_n) \in P$ implies $n \leq 2$, and for every $1 \leq i \leq n$, $1 \leq |w_i| \leq 2$ and $w_i \in \big(V - \{S\}\big)^*$;
- $(A) \to (w) \in P$ implies $A = S$.

By establishing the next two lemmas, we demonstrate that 2-limited propagating scattered context grammars are as powerful as ordinary propagating scattered context grammars.

Lemma 3.2. *If $L \subseteq T^*$ is a language generated by a propagating scattered context grammar $G = (V, T, P, S)$, and if c is a symbol such that $c \notin T$, then there is a 2-limited propagating scattered context grammar $\bar{G}$ such that $L(\bar{G}) = L\{c\}$.*

Proof. Let $\bar{n}$ be the number of the productions in P. Number the productions of P from 1 to $\bar{n}$. Let $(A_{i1}, \ldots, A_{in_i}) \to (w_{i1}, \ldots, w_{in_i})$ be the ith production. Let C

and $\bar{S}$ be new symbols,

$$W = \{\langle i, j\rangle : 1 \le i \le \bar{n}, 1 \le j \le n_i\},$$
$$\bar{V} = V \cup \{C, \bar{S}\} \cup W \cup \{\langle C, i\rangle : 1 \le i \le \bar{n}\}.$$

Let $G' = (\bar{V}, T \cup \{c\}, P', \bar{S})$ be a propagating scattered context grammar, where P' is defined as follows:

1. For each $1 \le i \le \bar{n}$, add $(\bar{S}) \to (S\langle C, i\rangle)$ to P'.
2. For each i such that $n_i = 1$ and $1 \le k \le \bar{n}$, add $(A_{i1}, \langle C, i\rangle) \to (w_{i1}, \langle C, k\rangle)$ to P'.
3. For each i such that $n_i > 1$, $1 \le j \le n_i - 1$, $1 \le k \le \bar{n}$, add
   (a) $(A_{i1}, \langle C, i\rangle) \to (\langle i, 1\rangle, C)$,
   (b) $(\langle i, j\rangle, A_{i(j+1)}) \to (w_{ij}, \langle i, j+1\rangle)$, and
   (c) $(\langle i, n_i\rangle, C) \to (w_{in_i}, \langle C, k\rangle)$ to P'.
4. (a) For each i such that $n_i = 1$, add $(A_{i1}, \langle C, i\rangle) \to (w_{i1}, c)$ to P'.
   (b) For each i such that $n_i > 1$, add $(\langle i, n_i\rangle, C) \to (w_{in_i}, c)$ to P'.

Clearly, $L(G') = L\{c\}$. Since for some i and j, w_{ij} may satisfy $|w_{ij}| > 2$, G' may not be a 2-limited propagating scattered context grammar. However, by making use of standard techniques, one can obtain a 2-limited propagating scattered context grammar $\bar{G}$ from G' such that $L(\bar{G}) = L(G')$. ■

Lemma 3.3. *If $L \subseteq T^+$, c is a symbol such that $c \notin T$, and $G = (V, T \cup \{c\}, P, S)$ is a 2-limited propagating scattered context grammar satisfying $L(G) = L\{c\}$, then there is a 2-limited propagating scattered context grammar $\bar{G}$ such that $L(\bar{G}) = L$.*

Proof. For each $a \in T \cup \{S\}$, let $\bar{a}$ be a new symbol. Let

$$L_1 = \{A_1A_2A_3 : S \Rightarrow_G^* A_1A_2A_3, A_i \in V, \text{ for all } 1 \le i \le 3\},$$
$$L_2 = \{A_1A_2A_3A_4 : S \Rightarrow_G^* A_1A_2A_3A_4, A_i \in V, \text{ for all } 1 \le i \le 4\}.$$

Let h be the homomorphism from V^* to $(\{\bar{a} : a \in T\} \cup (V - T))^*$ defined as $h(a) = \bar{a}$, for each $a \in T$, and $h(A) = A$, for each $A \in V - T$. Let

$$V' = h(V) \cup T \cup \{S'\} \cup \{\langle a, b\rangle : a, b \in V\}.$$

Let $G' = (V', T, P', S')$, where for all $a, b \in T$, $A_1, \ldots, A_6 \in V$, $A \in h(V)$, P' is defined as follows:

1. (a) For each $a \in T \cap L$, add $(S') \to (a)$ to P'.

(b) For each $A_1A_2A_3 \in L_1$, add
$(S') \rightarrow \big(h(A_1)\langle A_2, A_3\rangle\big)$ to P'.

(c) For each $A_1A_2A_3A_4 \in L_2$, add
$(S') \rightarrow \big(h(A_1A_2)\langle A_3, A_4\rangle\big)$ to P'.

2. (a) For each $(A_1, A_2) \rightarrow (w_1, w_2) \in P$, add
$(A_1, A_2) \rightarrow \big(h(w_1), h(w_2)\big)$ to P'.

(b) For each $(A_1, A_2) \rightarrow (w_1, w_2) \in P$,

(i) where $|w_2| = 1$, add

(A) $\big(A_1, \langle A_2, A_3\rangle\big) \rightarrow \big(h(w_1), \langle w_2, A_3\rangle\big)$, and

(B) $\big(A_1, \langle A_3, A_2\rangle\big) \rightarrow \big(h(w_1), \langle A_3, w_2\rangle\big)$ to P';

(ii) where $w_2 = A_4A_5$, add

(A) $\big(A_1, \langle A_2, A_3\rangle\big) \rightarrow \big(h(w_1), h(A_4)\langle A_5, A_3\rangle\big)$, and

(B) $\big(A_1, \langle A_3, A_2\rangle\big) \rightarrow \big(h(w_1), h(A_3)\langle A_4, A_5\rangle\big)$ to P'.

(c) For each $(A_1, A_2) \rightarrow (w_1, w_2) \in P$,

(i) where $|w_1| = |w_2| = 1$, add
$\big(A, \langle A_1, A_2\rangle\big) \rightarrow \big(A, \langle w_1, w_2\rangle\big)$ to P';

(ii) where $w_1w_2 = A_3A_4A_5$, add
$\big(A, \langle A_1, A_2\rangle\big) \rightarrow \big(A, h(A_3)\langle A_4, A_5\rangle\big)$ to P';

(iii) where $w_1w_2 = A_3A_4A_5A_6$, add
$\big(A, \langle A_1, A_2\rangle\big) \rightarrow \big(A, h(A_3A_4)\langle A_5, A_6\rangle\big)$ to P';

3. For each $a, b \in T$, add

(a) $\big(\bar{a}, \langle b, c\rangle\big) \rightarrow \big(a, \langle b, c\rangle\big)$, and

(b) $\big(\bar{a}, \langle b, c\rangle\big) \rightarrow (a, b)$ to P'.

Note that the construction simply combines the symbol c with the symbol to its left. The reason for introducing a new symbol $\bar{a}$, for each $a \in T$, is to guarantee that there always exists a nonterminal A whenever a production from (2c) is to be applied, and a nonterminal $\bar{a}$ that enables $\langle b, c\rangle$ to be converted to b by a production from (3). Clearly, $L(G') = L$. G' may not be a 2-limited propagating scattered context grammar since in (2c), $\big|h(A_3A_4)\langle A_5, A_6\rangle\big| = 3$. Once again, by standard techniques, we can obtain a 2-limited propagating scattered context grammar $\bar{G}$ from G' such that $L(\bar{G}) = L(G')$. ■

By Lemmas 3.2 and 3.3, any propagating scattered context grammar can be converted to an equivalent 2-limited propagating scattered context grammar as stated in the following theorem.

Theorem 3.4. *If G is a propagating scattered context grammar, then there exists a 2-limited propagating scattered context grammar $\bar{G}$ such that $L(\bar{G}) = L(G)$.* ■

3.2 Closure properties

In this section, the closure properties of the family of propagating scattered context languages under various operations are studied. Most significantly, it is proved that the family of propagating scattered context languages represents an abstract family of languages—that is, it is closed under union, concatenation, Kleene plus, ε-free homomorphism, inverse homomorphism, and intersection with a regular language. As a result, this family is closed under intersection, ε-free substitution, and linear erasing.

First, a preliminary lemma is given.

Lemma 3.5. *The family of propagating scattered context languages is closed under substitution by an ε-free context-free language, intersection with a regular language, and permutations.*

Proof. The theorem is established by Claims 1 through 3 stated below.

Claim 1. The family of propagating scattered context languages is closed under substitution by an ε-free context-free language.

Proof. Let $G = (V, T, P, S)$ be a propagating scattered context grammar. For each $a \in T$, let $\bar{a}$ be a new symbol, and let $T_1 = \{\bar{a} : a \in T\}$. Let h be the homomorphism from V^* to $\big(T_1 \cup (V - T)\big)^*$ defined as $h(a) = \bar{a}$, for each $a \in T$, and $h(A) = A$, for each $A \in V - T$. For each $a \in T$, let L_a be a context-free language, and let $G_a = (V_a, T_a, P_a, S_a)$ be a context-free grammar such that $L(G_a) = L_a$. Without loss of generality, we can assume that for each $a, b \in T$, $a \neq b$,

$$(V_a - T_a) \cap (V - T) = (V_b - T_b) \cap (V_a - T_a) = \emptyset,$$

and P_a contains no production $A \to \varepsilon$. Let

$$\bar{V} = h(V) \cup \bigcup_{a \in T} V_a$$

and

$$\bar{T} = \bigcup_{a \in T} T_a.$$

Let $\bar{G} = (\bar{V}, \bar{T}, \bar{P}, S)$, where $\bar{P}$ is defined as follows:

1. For each $(A_1, \dots, A_n) \to (w_1, \dots, w_n) \in P$, add $(A_1, \dots, A_n) \to \big(h(w_1), \dots, h(w_n)\big)$ to $\bar{P}$.
2. For each $a \in T$, and $A \to w \in P_a$, add
   (a) $(\bar{a}) \to (S_a)$,
   (b) $(A) \to (w)$ to $\bar{P}$.

If τ is the substitution on T^* defined as $\tau(a) = L_a$, then, clearly, $L(\bar{G}) = \tau\big(L(G)\big)$. □

Claim 2. The family of propagating scattered context languages is closed under intersection with a regular language.

Proof. Let L be a propagating scattered context language and R be a regular language. Let $G = (V, T, P, S)$ be a 2-limited propagating scattered context grammar such that $L(G) = L$, and let $G' = (V', T', P', S')$ be a right-linear grammar such that $L(G') = R$. Without loss of generality, assume that productions of G' are of the form $A \to aB$, or $A \to \varepsilon$, where $A, B \in V' - T'$ and $a \in T'$. Define the propagating scattered context grammar $\bar{G} = (\bar{V}, T, \bar{P}, S)$, where

$$\bar{V} = \{\langle A, a, A'\rangle : A, A' \in V' - T', a \in V\} \cup \{\langle A, ab, A'\rangle : A, A' \in V' - T', a, b \in V\} \cup T \cup \{S\},$$

and where $\bar{P}$ is defined as follows:

1. For each $A \to \varepsilon \in P'$, add $(S) \to (\langle S', S, A\rangle)$ to $\bar{P}$.
2. For each $(A, B) \to (w_1, w_2) \in P$ and $C, C', D, D' \in V' - T'$, add $(\langle C, A, C'\rangle, \langle D, B, D'\rangle) \to (\langle C, w_1, C'\rangle, \langle D, w_2, D'\rangle)$ to $\bar{P}$.
3. For each $C, C', C'' \in V' - T'$, and $a, b \in V$, add $(\langle C, ab, C'\rangle) \to (\langle C, a, C''\rangle\langle C'', b, C'\rangle)$ to $\bar{P}$.
4. For each $A \to aB \in P'$, and $a \in T$, add $(\langle A, a, B\rangle) \to (a)$ to $\bar{P}$.

Clearly, $L(\bar{G}) = L(G) \cap R$. □

Claim 3. The family of propagating scattered context languages is closed under permutations.

Proof. Let L be a propagating scattered context language, and let $G = (V, T, P, S)$ be a propagating scattered context grammar such that $L(G) = L$. Set $T_1 = \{\bar{a} : a \in T\}$. Let h be the homomorphism from V^* to $(T_1 \cup (V - T))^*$ defined as $h(a) = \bar{a}$, for each $a \in T$, and $h(A) = A$, for each $A \in V - T$. Let $\bar{V} = V \cup T_1$,

$$\bar{P} = \{(A_1, \ldots, A_n) \to (h(w_1), \ldots, h(w_n)) : (A_1, \ldots, A_n) \to (w_1, \ldots, w_n) \in P\} \cup \{(\bar{a}, \bar{b}) \to (\bar{b}, \bar{a}) : a, b \in T\} \cup \{(\bar{a}) \to (a) : a \in T\},$$

and $\bar{G} = (\bar{V}, T, \bar{P}, S)$. Clearly, $L(\bar{G})$ contains all and only permutations of members of $L(G)$. □

The theorem immediately follows from Claims 1 through 3. ■

From Lemma 3.5, we obtain the following corollary.

Corollary 3.6. *The family of propagating scattered context languages is closed under ε-free homomorphism.* ■

In what follows, it is demonstrated that the family of propagating scattered context languages is an abstract family of languages. Before this demonstration, however, three preliminary lemmas are established. The first of them, established next, says that the family of propagating scattered context languages is closed under reversal.

Lemma 3.7. *If L is a propagating scattered context language, then* $\mathrm{rev}(L)$ *is a propagating scattered context language.*

Proof. Let $G = (V, T, P, S)$ be a 2-limited propagating scattered context grammar such that $L(G) = L$. Let

$$P_r = \Big\{(S) \to (w) : (S) \to \big(\mathrm{rev}(w)\big) \in P\Big\} \\ \cup \Big\{(A, B) \to (w_1, w_2) : (B, A) \to \big(\mathrm{rev}(w_2), \mathrm{rev}(w_1)\big) \in P\Big\}.$$

Let $G_r = (V, T, P_r, S)$. Clearly, $\mathrm{rev}(L) = L(G_r)$. ■

Next, a special type of homomorphism is considered.

Definition 3.8. A homomorphism h from T_1^* to T_2^* is *k-restricted* on $L \subseteq T_1^*$, if $h(w) = \varepsilon$ for $w \in L$ implies $w = \varepsilon$, and for every string in L, each its substring z such that $|z| \geq k$ satisfies $h(z) \neq \varepsilon$. A family of languages $\mathscr{L}$ is said to be *closed under restricted homomorphism* if $h(L) \in \mathscr{L}$ whenever $L \subseteq T_1^*$ is in $\mathscr{L}$ and h is a homomorphism on T_1^* that is $k - 1$ restricted on L, for some k.

As proved next, the family of propagating scattered context languages is closed under restricted homomorphism.

Lemma 3.9. *The family of propagating scattered context languages is closed under restricted homomorphism.*

Proof. Let $G = (V, T, P, S)$ be a 2-limited propagating scattered context grammar, and let h be a homomorphism on T^* that is k-restricted on $L(G)$. Let

$$L_1 = L(G) \cap \big\{x : x \in T^+, |x| < k\big\}, \\ L_2 = \big\{x : S \Rightarrow_G^* x, k \leq |x| \leq 2k + 1\big\}.$$

For every $x \in V^+$ such that $k \leq |x| \leq 2k + 1$, let $\langle x \rangle$ be a new symbol, and

$$S_1 = \big\{\langle x \rangle : x \in V^+, k \leq |x| \leq 2k + 1\big\}, \\ S_2 = \big\{\langle x \rangle : x \in V^+, k \leq |x| \leq 2k - 1\big\}.$$

Let $\bar{S}$ be a new symbol, $\bar{V} = T \cup S_1 \cup \{\bar{S}\}$, and $\bar{G} = (\bar{V}, T, \bar{P}, \bar{S})$, where $\bar{P}$ is defined as follows:

1. (a) For each $x \in L_1$, add
   $(\bar{S}) \to (h(x))$ to $\bar{P}$.
   (b) For each $x \in L_2$, add
   $(\bar{S}) \to (\langle x \rangle)$ to $\bar{P}$.
2. For each $(A, B) \to (w_1, w_2) \in P$, $\langle x_1 A y_1 \rangle, \langle x_2 B y_2 \rangle \in S_2$, and $\langle x_3 A z B y_3 \rangle \in S_2$, add
   (a) $(\langle x_1 A y_1 \rangle, \langle x_2 B y_2 \rangle) \to (\langle x_1 w_1 y_1 \rangle, \langle x_2 w_2 y_2 \rangle)$, and
   (b) $(\langle x_3 A z B y_3 \rangle) \to (\langle x_3 w_1 z w_2 y_3 \rangle)$ to $\bar{P}$.
3. For each $\langle x \rangle, \langle y \rangle, \langle z \rangle \in S_1$ and $x = yz$, add
   $(\langle x \rangle) \to (\langle y \rangle \langle z \rangle)$ to $\bar{P}$.
4. For each $\langle x \rangle \in S_2$, where $x \in T^*$, add
   $(\langle x \rangle) \to (h(x))$ to $\bar{P}$.

Since $h(x) \neq \varepsilon$, for $x \in T^*$, $\bar{G}$ is a propagating scattered context grammar. Clearly, $L(\bar{G}) = h(L(G))$. ■

Corollary 3.10. *The family of propagating scattered context languages is closed under inverse homomorphism.*

Proof. By Theorem 2.4, any ε-free family of languages closed under intersection with a regular language, c-substitution, and k-limited erasing, is closed under inverse homomorphism. Since c-substitution is a special case of context-free substitution, and since k-limited erasing is a special case of a k-restricted homomorphism, the family of propagating scattered context languages is closed under inverse homomorphism. ■

Lemma 3.11. *If $L \subseteq T^+$ is a propagating scattered context language and c is a symbol such that $c \notin T$, then $\{c\}(L\{c\})^+$ is a propagating scattered context language.*

Proof. Let $G = (V, T, P, S)$ be a 2-limited propagating scattered context grammar such that $L(G) = L$. Let c, C_1, C_2, and $\bar{S}$ be new symbols and $\bar{V} = V \cup \{c, C_1, C_2, \bar{S}\}$. Let $\bar{G} = (\bar{V}, T \cup \{c\}, \bar{P}, \bar{S})$, where $\bar{P}$ is defined as follows:

1. (a) Add $(\bar{S}) \to (C_1 S C_2)$ to $\bar{P}$.
   (b) For each $(S) \to (w) \in P$, add
   $(C_1, S, C_2) \to (C_1, w, C_2)$ to $\bar{P}$.
2. For each $(A, B) \to (w_1, w_2) \in P$, add
   $(C_1, A, B, C_2) \to (C_1, w_1, w_2, C_2)$ to $\bar{P}$.
3. Add $(C_1, C_2) \to (c, C_1 S C_2)$ to $\bar{P}$.
4. Add $(C_1, C_2) \to (c, c)$ to $\bar{P}$.

Observe that derivations in $L(\bar{G})$ proceed in phases:

$$\bar{S} \Rightarrow_{\bar{G}}^* C_1 w C_2 \Rightarrow_{\bar{G}} cwC_1 S C_2 \Rightarrow_{\bar{G}} \cdots$$

Between applications of the production $(C_1, C_2) \to (c, C_1SC_2)$, the derivation simulates a derivation in $L(G)$. Thus,

$$C_1SC_2 \Rightarrow^*_{\bar{G}} C_1wC_2$$

if and only if

$$S \Rightarrow^*_G w.$$

If $\bar{G}$ uses a production from (3) before the string of symbols between C_1 and C_2 is over T, then

$$C_1SC_2 \Rightarrow^*_{\bar{G}} C_1xAyC_2 \Rightarrow_{\bar{G}} cxAyC_1SC_2.$$

Now, the nonterminal A can never be rewritten and thus a terminal string cannot be derived. Clearly, $L(\bar{G}) = \{c\}\big(L\{c\}\big)^+$. ■

The crucial closure property concerning the family of propagating scattered context languages follows next.

Theorem 3.12. *The family of propagating scattered context languages is an abstract family of languages.*

Proof. Recall that a family of languages is an abstract family of languages if it is closed under union, Kleene plus, ε-free homomorphism, inverse homomorphism, and intersection with a regular language. It has been demonstrated that the family of propagating scattered context languages is closed under ε-free homomorphism, inverse homomorphism, and intersection with a regular language. Thus, it is only needed to prove that it is closed under union and Kleene plus.

Claim 1. The family of propagating scattered context languages is closed under union.

Proof. For $i \in \{1, 2\}$, let $G_i = (V_i, T_i, P_i, S_i)$ be a propagating scattered context grammar. Without loss of generality, let

$$(V_1 - T_1) \cap (V_2 - T_2) = \emptyset.$$

Let S be a new symbol, $V = V_1 \cup V_2 \cup \{S\}$, $T = T_1 \cup T_2$,

$$P = \big\{(S) \to (S_1), (S) \to (S_2)\big\} \cup P_1 \cup P_2,$$

and $G = (V, T, P, S)$. Clearly, $L(G) = L(G_1) \cup L(G_2)$. □

Claim 2. The family of propagating scattered context languages is closed under Kleene plus.

Proof. Let $L \subseteq T^*$ be a propagating scattered context language and c be a symbol such that $c \notin T$. By Lemma 3.11, $\{c\}\big(L\{c\}\big)^+$ is a propagating scattered context language and, since $\varepsilon \notin L$, by Lemma 3.9, L^+ is a propagating scattered context language. □

Because the family of propagating scattered context languages is closed under union, Kleene plus, ε-free homomorphism, inverse homomorphism, and intersection with a regular language, it is an abstract family of languages. ■

Corollary 3.13. *The family of propagating scattered context languages is closed under concatenation.* ■

Next, we prove that the family of propagating scattered context languages is closed under linear erasing, intersection, and substitution. More specifically, we first demonstrate that this family is closed under a special case of intersection and linear erasing. Making use of these specific results, we then achieve the desired closure properties in general.

Lemma 3.14. *If $L \subseteq T^+\{c\}T^+$, where c is a symbol such that $c \notin T$, is a propagating scattered context language, then $L \cap \{wcw : w \in T^+\}$ is a propagating scattered context language.*

Proof. Let $G = \big(V, T \cup \{c\}, P, S\big)$ be a 2-limited propagating scattered context grammar such that $L(G) = L$. Let $\bar{c}, d, \bar{S}, C_1, C_2$, and C_3 be new symbols, and for each $a \in T$, let $\bar{a}$ and $\hat{a}$ be new symbols. Let h be the homomorphism from V^* to

$$\Big(\big\{\bar{a} : a \in T \cup \{c\}\big\} \cup (V - T)\Big)^*$$

defined as $h(a) = \bar{a}$, for each $a \in T$, $h(c) = \bar{c}$, and $h(A) = A$, for each $A \in V - T$. Let

$$\bar{V} = V \cup \{\bar{c}, d, \bar{S}, C_1, C_2, C_3\} \cup \{\bar{a} : a \in T\} \cup \{\hat{a} : a \in T\}.$$

Let $\bar{G} = \big(\bar{V}, T \cup \{c, d\}, \bar{P}, \bar{S}\big)$, where $\bar{P}$ is defined as follows:

1. Add $(\bar{S}) \to (C_1SC_2)$ to $\bar{P}$.
2. (a) For each $(S) \to (w) \in P$, add $(C_1, S, C_2) \to \big(C_1, h(w), C_2\big)$ to $\bar{P}$.
   (b) For each $(A, B) \to (w_1, w_2) \in P$, add $(C_1, A, B, C_2) \to \big(C_1, h(w_1), h(w_2), C_2\big)$ to $\bar{P}$.
3. For each $a, b \in T$, add
   (a) $(C_1, \bar{a}, \bar{c}, \bar{a}, C_2) \to (d, \hat{a}, C_3, \hat{a}, C_2)$,
   (b) $(\hat{a}, \bar{b}, C_3, \hat{a}, \bar{b}, C_2) \to (a, \hat{b}, C_3, a, \hat{b}, C_2)$, and
   (c) $(\hat{a}, C_3, \hat{a}, C_2) \to (a, c, a, d)$ to $\bar{P}$.

Productions from (1) and (2) generate strings of the form

$$C_1\bar{a}_1 \ldots \bar{a}_n\bar{c}\bar{b}_1 \ldots \bar{b}_mC_2,$$

where $a_1 \ldots a_ncb_1 \ldots b_m \in L$. Productions from (3a) introduce two identical symbols from $\{\hat{a} : a \in T\}$, which are placed right behind C_1 and $\bar{c}$. Note that a production from (3a) can be applied only once. Productions from (3b) cause the tagged symbols to synchronously propagate left to right and compare symbols. As the symbols are compared, they are converted to terminals. If any symbol is skipped, it can never become a terminal. Finally, an application of a production from (3c) removes the tagged symbols from the string. It is easy to demonstrate that

$$L(\bar{G}) = \{d\}\big(L \cap \{wcw : w \in T^+\}\big)\{d\}.$$

The details of the proof are left to the reader. It follows from Lemma 3.9 that $L \cap \{wcw : w \in T^+\}$ is a propagating scattered context language. ■

Consider the construction given in Lemma 3.14. Observe that it is based upon passing two special symbols through a string, and by using them, it checks whether the symbols occurring in the string coincide. It performs this check in a strictly one-direction way. As a result, if a symbol is skipped, the derivation is eventually blocked, so it cannot produce a terminal string. The same technique is applied to show that the family of propagating scattered context languages is closed under a very restricted type of linear erasing.

Lemma 3.15. *Let $c, d \notin T$ be symbols. If*

$$L \subseteq \left\{d^k cw : |w| = k, k \geq 1, w \in T^+\right\}$$

is a propagating scattered context language, then

$$L_1 = \{w : d^k cw \in L, \textit{ for some } k\}$$

is a propagating scattered context language.

Proof. Let $\bar{c}$, $\bar{d}$ be new symbols and for each $a \in T$, let $\bar{a}$ be a new symbol. Let

$$T_1 = T \cup \{\bar{c}, \bar{d}\} \cup \{\bar{a} : a \in T\},$$

and let h be the homomorphism defined from $\big(T \cup \{c, d\}\big)^*$ to $(T_1 - T)^*$ as $h(c) = \bar{c}$, $h(d) = \bar{d}$, and $h(a) = \bar{a}$, for each $a \in T$. Then, $L_2 = h(L)$ is a propagating scattered context language. Let $G = (V, T_1, P, S)$ be a 2-limited propagating scattered context grammar such that $L(G) = L_2$. Let C, $\hat{d}$, S' be new symbols, and let $\hat{a}$ be a new symbol, for each $a \in T$. Let $\bar{G} = \big(\bar{V}, T \cup \{c, d\}, P', S'\big)$ be a propagating scattered context grammar, where

$$\bar{V} = V \cup \{C, c, d, \hat{d}, S'\} \cup \{\hat{a} : a \in T\},$$

and P' is defined as follows:

1. (a) For each $dca \in L$, where $a \in T$, add $(S') \rightarrow (acdc)$ to P'.
   (b) Add $(S') \rightarrow (SC)$ to P'.
2. (a) For each $(S) \rightarrow (w) \in P$, add $(S, C) \rightarrow (w, C)$ to P'.

(b) For each $(A, B) \rightarrow (w_1, w_2) \in P$, add
$(A, B, C) \rightarrow (w_1, w_2, C)$ to P'.

3. For each $a, b \in T$, add

(a) $(\bar{d}, \bar{c}, \bar{a}, C) \rightarrow (\hat{d}, c, \hat{a}, c)$,
(b) $(\hat{d}, \bar{d}, \bar{d}, \hat{a}, \bar{b}) \rightarrow (a, d, \hat{d}, \bar{d}, \hat{b})$, and
(c) $(\hat{d}, \bar{d}, \hat{a}, \bar{b}) \rightarrow (a, d, b, d)$ to P'.

Productions from (1a) generate $acdc$, where $a \in T$, while (1b) starts off the derivation of other strings. Productions from (2) simulate the derivations of G so that $S' \Rightarrow^*_{\bar{G}} wC$ corresponds to $S \Rightarrow^*_G w$. Productions from (3a) tag the first $\bar{d}$ and the first $\bar{a}$ after $\bar{c}$ and guarantee that only productions from (3b) and (3c) can be applied from this point on. If the wrong symbol is tagged, the derivation is blocked. Productions from (3b) swap every second d at the beginning of the string with the first unswapped symbol from $\{\bar{a} : a \in T\}$. In a successful derivation, every production from (3b) is applied as follows:

$$za_l d\hat{d}\bar{d}\bar{d}x\hat{a}_{l+1}\bar{a}_{l+2}y \Rightarrow_{\bar{G}} za_l da_{l+1}d\hat{d}x\bar{d}\hat{a}_{l+2}y.$$

If a symbol is skipped, it can never become terminal, and the derivation is blocked. The derivation has to end by an application of a production from (3c), which removes the tags from the sentential form:

$$za_l d\hat{d}\bar{d}\hat{a}_{l+1}\bar{a}_{l+2}c \Rightarrow_{\bar{G}} za_l da_{l+1}da_{l+2}dc.$$

It can be proved that

$$\begin{aligned} L_3 = L(\bar{G}) = \{&a_1 d \ldots a_k dca_{k+1}d \ldots a_{2k}dc : \\ &d^{2k}ca_1 \ldots a_{2k} \in L, a_1, \ldots, a_{2k} \in T\} \\ \cup\ \{&a_1 d \ldots a_k cda_{k+1}d \ldots a_{2k+1}dc : \\ &d^{2k+1}ca_1 \ldots a_{2k+1} \in L, a_1, \ldots, a_{2k+1} \in T\} \\ \cup\ \{&acdc : dca \in L, a \in T\}. \end{aligned}$$

Then, by Lemma 3.9, with $k = 3$, we can erase the c's and d's so that L_1 is a propagating scattered context language. ■

Next, another important result concerning the closure properties of the family of propagating scattered context languages is established.

Theorem 3.16. *The family of propagating scattered context languages is closed under intersection, ε-free substitution, and linear erasing.*

Proof. We establish the theorem by Claims 1 through 3 stated below.

Claim 1. The family of propagating scattered context languages is closed under intersection.

Proof. Let L_1 and L_2 be propagating scattered context languages such that $L_1 \cup L_2 \subseteq T^*$, and let $c \notin T$ be a new symbol. Then, by Lemma 3.14,

$$L_3 = L_1\{c\}L_2 \cap \{wcw : w \in T^+\}$$

is a propagating scattered context language. Observe that

$$L_3 = \{wcw : w \in L_1 \cap L_2\}.$$

Let d be a new symbol, and let τ be the ε-free substitution from $\big(T \cup \{c\}\big)^*$ to $\big(T \cup \{c, d\}\big)^*$ defined as $\tau(a) = \{a, d\}$, for each $a \in T$, and $\tau(c) = c$. Let

$$L_4 = \tau(L_3) \cap \{d\}^+\{c\}T^+.$$

By Lemma 3.5, L_4 is a propagating scattered context language. Because

$$L_4 = \big\{d^k cw : |w| = k,\, w \in L_1 \cap L_2\big\},$$

by Lemma 3.15, $L_1 \cap L_2$ is a propagating scattered context language. □

Claim 2. The family of propagating scattered context languages is closed under ε-free substitution.

Proof. This claim immediately follows from the closure of the family of propagating scattered context languages under intersection and Theorem 2.6. □

Claim 3. The family of propagating scattered context languages is closed under linear erasing.

Proof. Let $L \subseteq T^*$ be a propagating scattered context language, and let h be a homomorphism from T^* to T_1^*, for which there exists an integer k such that $|w| \leq k\big|h(w)\big|$, for every $w \in L$. Without loss of generality, assume that there exists a symbol $c \in T$ such that $h(c) = \varepsilon$, and $h(a) = a$, for each $a \in T - \{c\}$.

(Otherwise, let c be a new symbol and h_1 be the homomorphism from T^* to $\big(T_1 \cup \{c\}\big)^*$ defined as $h_1(a) = h(a)$ for $h(a) \neq \varepsilon$ and $h_1(a) = c$ for $h(a) = \varepsilon$. Let h_2 be the homomorphism from $\big(T_1 \cup \{c\}\big)^*$ to T_1^* defined as $h_2(c) = \varepsilon$ and $h_2(a) = a$, for all $a \in T_1$. Clearly, $h(L) = h_2\big(h_1(L)\big)$. Obviously, $h_1(L)$ is a propagating scattered context language, and if

$$k_1 = \max\Big(\big\{|h(a)| : a \in T\big\}\Big),$$

then

$$\big|h_1(w)\big| \leq k_1 k \Big|h_2\big(h_1(w)\big)\Big|,$$

for every $w \in L$.

Let L_1 be the intersection of the language of all permutations of strings in L with the regular language

$$\Big(T\big(\{\varepsilon\} \cup \{c\} \cup \cdots \cup \{c\}^k\big)\Big)^*.$$

Let $h_3(c) = c$ and $h_3(a) = \varepsilon$, for each $a \in T$. Let $\bar{c}$ be a new symbol. Now,

$$L_2 = \left\{w_1\bar{c}w_2 : w_1, w_2 \in \left(T \cup \{c\}\right)^*, h(w_1) = h\left(\mathrm{rev}(w_2)\right), h_3(w_1) = h_3(w_2)\right\}$$

is clearly a propagating scattered context language, since

$$L_2 = h^{-1}\left(\left\{w\bar{c}\,\mathrm{rev}(w) : w \in T_1^*\right\}\right) \cap \left\{w_1\bar{c}w_2 : w_1, w_2 \in \left(T \cup \{c\}\right)^*, h_3(w_1) = h_3(w_2)\right\},$$

where both languages in the intersection are context-free. Let

$$L_3 = \mathrm{rev}(L)\bar{c}L_1 \cap L_2.$$

By Lemma 3.7, Theorem 3.12, and the closure of the family of propagating scattered context languages under intersection, L_3 is a propagating scattered context language. Let d be a new symbol, and let τ be the substitution from $\left(T \cup \{c, \bar{c}\}\right)^*$ to $\left(T \cup \{c, d, \bar{c}\}\right)^*$ defined as $\tau(\bar{c}) = \bar{c}$ and $\tau(a) = \{a, d\}$, for each $a \in T \cup \{c\}$. Let h_4 be the homomorphism from $\left(T \cup \{c, \bar{c}, d\}\right)^*$ to $\left(T \cup \{c\}\right)^*$ defined as $h_4(d) = \varepsilon$, $h_4(\bar{c}) = \varepsilon$, and $h_4(a) = a$, for each $a \in T \cup \{c\}$. Then,

$$h(L) = h\left(h_4\left(\tau(L_3) \cap \{d\}^*\{\bar{c}\}(T \cup \{c\})^*\right)\right).$$

By Lemma 3.5,

$$\tau(L_3) \cap \{d\}^*\{\bar{c}\}\left(T \cup \{c\}\right)^* \subseteq \left\{d^l cw : |w| = l, w \in L_1\right\}$$

is a propagating scattered context language, and by Lemma 3.15,

$$h_4\left(\tau(L_3) \cap \{d\}^*\{\bar{c}\}\left(T \cup \{c\}\right)^*\right)$$

is a propagating scattered context language. Thus, by Lemma 3.9, $h(L)$ is a propagating scattered context language. □

By Claims 1 through 3, the family of propagating scattered context languages is closed under intersection, ε-free substitution, and linear erasing, so the theorem holds. ■

Corollary 3.17. *If L is a recursively enumerable language, then there exists a propagating scattered context language L' and a homomorphism h such that $h(L') = L$.*

Proof. By Theorem 2.16, for every recursively enumerable language L, there exist ε-free context-free languages L_1, L_2, and a homomorphism h such that $L = h(L_1 \cap L_2)$. However, the family of propagating scattered context languages contains all ε-free context-free languages and is closed under intersection. Thus, $L' = L_1 \cap L_2$ is a propagating scattered context language such that $h(L') = L$. ■

Corollary 3.18. *The family of propagating scattered context languages is not closed under arbitrary homomorphism and quotient by a regular language.*

Proof. As demonstrated above, L_1 and L_2 can be found so that there exists a regular language R such that $L = h(L_1 \cap L_2) = (L_1 \cap L_2)/R$. ∎

Corollary 3.19. *The emptiness problem is undecidable for scattered context grammars.* ∎

3.3 Generative power

In this section, we study the generative power of scattered context grammars with and without erasing productions. We start by demonstrating that scattered context grammars are powerful enough to describe the family of recursively enumerable languages. Then, we show that the family of context-free languages is properly included in the family of propagating scattered context languages, and this family is contained in the family of context-sensitive languages. Furthermore, we compare the family of propagating scattered context languages with another two language families—family of programmed and simple matrix languages—and show that both are properly included in the family of propagating scattered context languages. Finally, we point out several open problems.

The problem of whether the family of recursively enumerable languages is characterized by scattered context grammars has a remarkable history. First, Virkkunen [15] established this characterization. Not being aware of this result, Dassow and Păun [19] stated that this characterization represented an open problem (see Figure 2.5.1 on page 146 therein). Inspired by this statement, formal language theory has demonstrated this characterization by several proof methods (see [15, 20]), which are rather complex. Based upon Corollary 3.17, this section characterizes the family of recursively enumerable languages by scattered context grammars in a trivial way.

Theorem 3.20. $\mathscr{L}(RE) = \mathscr{L}(SC)$.

Proof. Let $L \in \mathscr{L}(RE)$. By Corollary 3.17, there is a propagating scattered context grammar $G' = (V, T', P', S)$ and a homomorphism h such that $L = h\big(L(G')\big)$. Without loss of generality, assume that $\mathrm{alph}(L) \cap T' = \emptyset$. Define the scattered context grammar

$$G = \big(V \cup \mathrm{alph}(L), \mathrm{alph}(L), P \cup P', S\big),$$

where

$$P = \Big\{(a) \rightarrow \big(h(a)\big) : a \in T'\Big\}.$$

Clearly, $L(G) = L$. Therefore, $\mathscr{L}(RE) \subseteq \mathscr{L}(SC)$. Obviously, $\mathscr{L}(SC) \subseteq \mathscr{L}(RE)$, so $\mathscr{L}(RE) = \mathscr{L}(SC)$. ∎

Next, we study the generative power of propagating scattered context grammars. First, we compare their power with the power of two fundamental types of grammars underlying the Chomsky hierarchy.

Theorem 3.21. $\mathscr{L}(CF) \subset \mathscr{L}(PSC) \subseteq \mathscr{L}(CS)$.

Proof. Clearly, $\mathscr{L}(CF) \subseteq \mathscr{L}(PSC)$. As the non-context-free language $\{a^n b^n c^n : n \geq 1\}$ is generated by propagating scattered context grammars (see Example 2.42), the inclusion is proper.

Because propagating scattered context grammars do not contain erasing productions, their derivations can be simulated by context-sensitive grammars. As a result, $\mathscr{L}(PSC) \subseteq \mathscr{L}(CS)$. ∎

The following theorem shows that programmed grammars without appearance checking and without erasing productions are less powerful than propagating scattered context grammars. Let us note that we compare the language families generated by these grammars directly instead of comparing propagating scattered context grammars and propagating unordered scattered context grammars, which was the approach used in the original proof in [21]. This result is an immediate corollary of the following two lemmas.

Lemma 3.22. $\mathscr{L}(P) \subseteq \mathscr{L}(PSC)$.

Proof. Let $G = (V, T, P, S)$ be a programmed grammar without erasing productions and without appearance checking. Set $N = \{\hat{p} : p \in P\}$. Define the propagating scattered context grammar

$$\bar{G} = \big(V \cup N \cup \{\bar{S}\}, T, \bar{P}, \bar{S}\big),$$

where $\bar{P}$ is defined as follows:

1. For each $p = (S \to x, \phi) \in P$, add
   $(\bar{S}) \to (\hat{p})$ to $\bar{P}$.
2. For each $p = (A \to x, \phi) \in P$ and each $q = (B \to y, \gamma) \in P$, where $q \in \phi$, add
   (a) $(\hat{p}, B) \to (x, \hat{q})$,
   (b) $(B, \hat{p}) \to (\hat{q}, x)$ to $\bar{P}$;
   (c) if $x = x_1 B x_2$, where $x_1, x_2 \in V^*$, add
   $(\hat{p}) \to (x_1 \hat{q} x_2)$ to $\bar{P}$.
3. For each $p = (A \to x, \phi) \in P$, where $x \in T^*$, add
   $(\hat{p}) \to (x)$ to $\bar{P}$.

Every derivation starts by a production introduced in (1), and as $\bar{S}$ does not appear on the right-hand side of any production, none of these productions is used later in the derivation.

Observe that any sentential form $(x_1 A x_2, p)$ of G, where $x_1, x_2 \in V^*$, and $p = (A \rightarrow y, \phi)$, corresponds to the sentential form of $\bar{G}$ of the form $x_1 \hat{p} x_2$. Clearly, after applying a production from (1), we obtain a sentential form of this kind. Then, it is easy to see that

$$(x_1 A x_2, p) \Rightarrow_G (x_1 y x_2, q)\ [p],$$

where $q = (B \rightarrow z, \gamma) \in \phi$, if and only if

- $x_1 \hat{p} x_{21} B x_{22} \Rightarrow_{\bar{G}} x_1 y x_{21} \hat{q} x_{22}\ [\bar{p}_1]$, where $x_{21} B x_{22} = x_2$, or
- $x_{11} B x_{12} \hat{p} x_2 \Rightarrow_{\bar{G}} x_{11} \hat{q} x_{12} y x_2\ [\bar{p}_2]$, where $x_{11} B x_{12} = x_1$, or
- $x_1 \hat{p} x_2 \Rightarrow_{\bar{G}} x_1 y_1 \hat{q} y_2 x_2\ [\bar{p}_3]$, where $y_1 B y_2 = y$,

and $\bar{p}_1$, $\bar{p}_2$, and $\bar{p}_3$ are productions introduced in (2a), (2b), and (2c), respectively.

Finally, when $x_1, x_2 \in T^*$, a production from (3) generates a sentence over T^*. As a result, $w \in L(G)$ if and only if $w \in L(\bar{G})$. ■

Lemma 3.23. $\mathscr{L}(P) \neq \mathscr{L}(PSC)$.

Proof. By Theorem 2.28, all languages over one-letter alphabets in $\mathscr{L}(P)$ are regular. However, the language $\{a^{2^n} : n \geq 0\}$, which is not regular, can be generated by a propagating scattered context grammar (see Example 2.44). As a result, $\mathscr{L}(P) \neq \mathscr{L}(PSC)$. ■

Lemmas 3.22 and 3.23 imply the following theorem.

Theorem 3.24. $\mathscr{L}(P) \subset \mathscr{L}(PSC)$. ■

Finally, we compare propagating scattered context grammars with simple matrix grammars and demonstrate that the family of simple matrix languages is properly included in the family of propagating scattered context languages. As opposed to the original proof in [22], we present a constructive proof of this result by means of the following two lemmas.

Lemma 3.25. $\mathscr{L}(SM) \subseteq \mathscr{L}(PSC)$.

Proof. Let $G = (V_1, \ldots, V_n, T, P, S)$ be a simple matrix grammar. Set

$$\hat{N}_1 = \{\hat{A} : A \in V_1 - T\}, \ldots, \hat{N}_n = \{\hat{A} : A \in V_n - T\}.$$

Define the propagating scattered context grammar

$$G = \left(V_1 \cup \cdots \cup V_n \cup \hat{N}_1 \cup \cdots \cup \hat{N}_n \cup \{\bar{S}\}, T, \bar{P}, \bar{S}\right),$$

where $\bar{P}$ is constructed as follows:

1. For each

$$(S) \rightarrow (x_{11} A_{11} x_{12} A_{12} \ldots x_{1k} A_{1k} \ldots x_{n1} A_{n1} x_{n2} A_{n2} \ldots x_{nk} A_{nk} y) \in P,$$

where $y \in T^*$, $A_{ij} \in V_i - T$, $x_{ij} \in T^*$, for all $1 \le i \le n$, $1 \le j \le k$, for some $k \ge 1$, add

$$(\bar{S}) \to (x_{11}\hat{A}_{11}x_{12}A_{12}\dots x_{1k}A_{1k}\dots x_{n1}\hat{A}_{n1}x_{n2}A_{n2}\dots x_{nk}A_{nk}y) \text{ to } \bar{P}.$$

2. For each

$$(A_1, \dots, A_n) \to (x_{11}A_{11}x_{12}A_{12}\dots x_{1k}A_{1k}y_1, \dots, x_{n1}A_{n1}x_{n2}A_{n2}\dots x_{nk}A_{nk}y_n) \in P,$$

where $y_i, x_{ij} \in T^*$, $A_i, A_{ij} \in V_i - T$, for all $1 \le i \le n$, $1 \le j \le k$, for some $k \ge 1$, add

$$(\hat{A}_1, \dots, \hat{A}_n) \to (x_{11}\hat{A}_{11}x_{12}A_{12}\dots x_{1k}A_{1k}y_1, \dots, x_{n1}\hat{A}_{n1}x_{n2}A_{n2}\dots x_{nk}A_{nk}y_n) \text{ to } \bar{P}.$$

3. For each

$$(A_1, \dots, A_n) \to (x_1, \dots, x_n) \in P,$$

where $A_i \in V_i - T$, $x_i \in T^*$, for all $1 \le i \le n$, and $B_1 \in V_1 - T, \dots, B_n \in V_n - T$, add

(a) $(\hat{A}_1, B_1, \dots, \hat{A}_n, B_n) \to (x_1, \hat{B}_1, \dots, x_n, \hat{B}_n)$, and
(b) $(\hat{A}_1, \dots, \hat{A}_n) \to (x_1, \dots, x_n)$ to $\bar{P}$.

Because propagating scattered context grammars are similar to simple matrix grammars, the constructed grammar $\bar{G}$ resembles the original grammar G. One main difference between these grammars has to be pointed out, though. For every derivation step of G of the form

$$v_1A_1w_1\dots v_nA_nw_ny \Rightarrow_G v_1x_1w_1\dots v_nx_nw_ny,$$

where $y \in T^*$, $x_i, w_i \in V_i^*$, for all $1 \le i \le n$, $\bar{G}$ has to make sure that it rewrites the leftmost nonterminal in every substring $v_iA_iw_i$; that is, $v_i \in T^*$. This is accomplished by tagging the first nonterminal in each of the substrings during the derivation. By a production from (1), $\bar{G}$ tags the leftmost nonterminal in each of the substrings, and all the remaining productions rewrite only these tagged symbols. Notice that after applying a production from (2), the leftmost nonterminal in each of the substrings remains tagged. To demonstrate that also productions from (3a) preserve this condition, consider the following simulation of an application of a production

$$p = (A_1, \dots, A_n) \to (x_1, \dots, x_n) \in P,$$

where $x_1, \dots, x_n \in T^*$:

$$\begin{aligned} &v_1\hat{A}_1w_{11}B_1w_{12}\dots v_n\hat{A}_nw_{n1}B_nw_{n2}y \\ \Rightarrow_{\bar{G}}\ &v_1x_1w_{11}\hat{B}_1w_{12}\dots v_nx_nw_{n1}\hat{B}_nw_{n2}y\ [\bar{p}], \end{aligned}$$

where

$$\bar{p} = (\hat{A}_1, B_1, \dots, \hat{A}_n, B_n) \to (x_1, \hat{B}_1, \dots, x_n, \hat{B}_n)$$

is a production introduced in (3a). This production simulates p, and in addition, non-deterministically tags the leftmost nonterminal $B_i \in V_i - T$ immediately following A_i, for every $1 \leq i \leq n$. If a nonterminal is skipped—that is, $\text{alph}(w_{i1}) \cap (V_i - T) \neq \emptyset$—this skipped nonterminal cannot be tagged later in the derivation, so the derivation is unsuccessful. To finish the derivation, a production from (3b) is used, which removes the tagged symbols from the sentential form, so no further rewriting is possible.

Finally, observe that every sentential form z generated by $\bar{G}$ is divided into n parts, so $z = z_1 \ldots z_n$, where $z_i \in (\hat{N}_i \cup V_i)^*$, for all $1 \leq i \leq n$. A sentential form of this kind is introduced by a production from (1), and all the other productions preserve this form. As a result, the constructed propagating scattered context grammar properly simulates the original simple matrix grammar. ■

Lemma 3.26. $\mathscr{L}(SM) \neq \mathscr{L}(PSC)$.

Proof. By Lemma 2.25, the language $\{a^n b^n c^n : n \geq 1\}^+$ cannot be generated by any simple matrix grammar. However, this language is generated by the propagating scattered context grammar

$$G = \big(\{S, A, B, C, a, b, c\}, \{a, b, c\}, P, S\big)$$

with

$$\begin{aligned} P = \big\{&(S) \rightarrow (ABC), \\ &(A, B, C) \rightarrow (aA, bB, cC), \\ &(A, B, C) \rightarrow (a, b, cABC), \\ &(A, B, C) \rightarrow (a, b, c)\big\}. \end{aligned}$$

Therefore, $\mathscr{L}(SM) \neq \mathscr{L}(PSC)$. ■

Putting Lemmas 3.25 and 3.26 together, we obtain the following theorem.

Theorem 3.27. $\mathscr{L}(SM) \subset \mathscr{L}(PSC)$. ■

Before closing this section, we point out the following important, if not the most important, open problem.

Open Problem 3.28. Is the family $\mathscr{L}(PSC)$ properly included in $\mathscr{L}(CS)$?

On the one hand, it is well known that $\mathscr{L}(PSC) \subseteq \mathscr{L}(CS)$ (see Theorem 3.21). On the other hand, formal language theory has never determined whether this inclusion is proper.

However, concerning the generative power of propagating scattered context grammars, there exist more open problems. Not only do we not know the exact relation of $\mathscr{L}(PSC)$ and $\mathscr{L}(CS)$, but we do not even know the relation of $\mathscr{L}(PSC)$ with respect to some language families which are properly included in $\mathscr{L}(CS)$. Specifically, the relation of $\mathscr{L}(PSC)$ to the family of programmed languages with appearance checking, $\mathscr{L}(P, ac)$, and the family of E0L languages, $\mathscr{L}(E0L)$, is unknown (see [1] for more details about these language families). More precisely, it is well known that $\mathscr{L}(PSC) \not\subseteq \mathscr{L}(E0L)$ because E0L systems cannot generate the language described in Example 2.43, but it has not been determined whether $\mathscr{L}(E0L)$ is included in $\mathscr{L}(PSC)$.

Open Problem 3.29. Is the family $\mathscr{L}(P, ac)$ included in $\mathscr{L}(PSC)$?

Open Problem 3.30. Is the family $\mathscr{L}(E0L)$ included in $\mathscr{L}(PSC)$?

CHAPTER 4

Further properties

The properties discussed in the previous chapter, such as closure properties and the generative power, are usually studied for any type of grammars. In the present chapter, we establish some more specific properties concerning scattered context grammars in order to give a deeper insight into these grammars and the way they work.

4.1 Terminating left-hand sides

Consider a production $A \rightarrow x$ in a context-free grammar. Its left-hand side, A, represents a terminating symbol if a string over the terminal alphabet can be derived from A. By analogy with this well-known notion, this section introduces terminating left-hand sides of scattered context productions. That is, for a scattered context production, $(A_1, \ldots, A_n) \rightarrow (x_1, \ldots, x_n)$, its left-hand side, $A_1 \ldots A_n$, is terminating if a string over the terminal alphabet can be derived from $A_1 \ldots A_n$.

This section discusses scattered context grammars whose sentential forms contain sequences of nonterminals formed by shuffling terminating left-hand sides of their productions. It demonstrates that these grammars do not generate some context-sensitive languages. As a result, scattered context grammars restricted in this way are less powerful than unrestricted scattered context grammars. In the conclusion, we demonstrate a significance of this result and discuss some open problems.

First, we introduce the used notions formally.

Definition 4.1. For a given language $L \subseteq V^*$, shuffle(L) consists solely of strings obtained by the following two steps:

1. if $x \in L$, then $x \in$ shuffle(L);
2. if $x_1 \ldots x_n \in$ shuffle(L) and $y_1 \ldots y_n \in L$, where $x_i, y_i \in V^*$, for all $1 \leq i \leq n$ and some $n \geq 1$, then $x_1 y_1 \ldots x_n y_n \in$ shuffle(L).

Note that $L^* \subseteq$ shuffle(L).

Definition 4.2. Let $G = (V, T, P, S)$ be a scattered context grammar, and let

$$p = (A_1, \ldots, A_n) \to (x_1, \ldots, x_n) \in P.$$

The left-hand side of p, $A_1 \ldots A_n$, is *terminating* if a string over the terminal alphabet can be derived from $A_1 \ldots A_n$; formally, $\text{lhs}(p)$ is terminating if $\text{lhs}(p) \Rightarrow_G^* x$, where $x \in T^*$. Set

$$term(G) = \big\{\text{lhs}(p) : p \in P, \text{lhs}(p) \Rightarrow_G^* x, x \in T^*\big\}.$$

Define the homomorphism δ on V^* as $\delta(A) = A$, for all $A \in V - T$, and $\delta(a) = \varepsilon$, for all $a \in T$. We investigate the following two families of languages:

$$\begin{aligned}\mathscr{L}(PSC, \text{term}) = \Big\{&L(G) : G \text{ is a propagating scattered context grammar}\\ &\text{such that } \delta\big(F(G)\big) \subseteq \text{shuffle}\big(term(G)\big)\Big\},\\ \mathscr{L}(SC, \text{term}) = \Big\{&L(G) : G \text{ is a scattered context grammar}\\ &\text{such that } \delta\big(F(G)\big) \subseteq \text{shuffle}\big(term(G)\big)\Big\}.\end{aligned}$$

Example 4.3. Consider the following propagating scattered context grammar:

$$G = \big(\{S, A, B, a, b\}, \{a, b\}, P, S\big),$$

where

$$P = \big\{(S) \to (ABA), (A, B, A) \to (aA, bB, aA), (A, B, A) \to (a, b, a)\big\}.$$

Clearly, $\delta\big(F(G)\big) \subseteq \text{shuffle}\big(term(G)\big)$ and $L(G) = \{a^n b^n a^n : n \geq 1\}$. Thus,

$$\{a^n b^n a^n : n \geq 1\} \in \mathscr{L}(PSC, \text{term}).$$

Observe that the terminating left-hand side of a scattered context production is generalized from the notion of a terminating symbol in the theory of context-free grammars (see [23]). Indeed, a context-free grammar is, in effect, a scattered context grammar $G = (V, T, P, S)$ satisfying $|\text{lhs}(p)| = 1$, for each $p \in P$. That is, the left-hand side of any context-free production is formed by a single nonterminal and this nonterminal is terminating if it derives a string over the terminal alphabet.

Theorem 4.4. *For every context-free grammar G, there exists an equivalent context-free grammar $\bar{G}$ such that* $\delta\big(F(\bar{G})\big) \subseteq \text{shuffle}\big(term(\bar{G})\big)$.

Proof. Obviously, all symbols in every sentential form of G have to be terminating in order to generate a string over the terminal alphabet. Therefore, it is possible to remove all non-terminating symbols together with all productions that rewrite these symbols form G so that the resulting grammar $\bar{G}$ generates the same language. Clearly, $\delta\big(F(\bar{G})\big) \subseteq \text{shuffle}\big(term(\bar{G})\big)$. ■

Next, we demonstrate that Theorem 4.4 cannot be generalized in terms of scattered context grammars. We establish

$$\begin{aligned}\mathscr{L}(CF) &\subset \mathscr{L}(PSC, \text{term}) \subset \mathscr{L}(CS),\\ \mathscr{L}(CF) &\subset \mathscr{L}(SC, \text{term}) \quad \subset \mathscr{L}(RE).\end{aligned}$$

Finally, we discuss the impact of these results on formal language theory and formulate some open problems.

For the sake of the following lemma and its proof, set

$$K = \left\{a^{2^{2^n}} : n \geq 0\right\}.$$

Lemma 4.5. $K \notin \mathscr{L}(SC, \text{term})$.

Proof. We prove this lemma by contradiction. Assume that $K \in \mathscr{L}(SC, \text{term})$. Let $K = L(G)$, where $G = (V, T, P, S)$ is a scattered context grammar such that $\delta\big(F(G)\big) \subseteq \text{shuffle}\big(term(G)\big)$. Notice that

$$\left\{x : x \in T^+, \text{lhs}(q) \Rightarrow_G^* x, |x| > |\text{lhs}(q)|\right\} \neq \emptyset,$$

for some $q \in P$; indeed, for $q \in P$ such that $\text{lhs}(q) = S$, this set is surely non-empty because

$$\left\{x : x \in T^+, S \Rightarrow_G^* x, |x| > |S|\right\} = K$$

and K is infinite. Select $z \in T^*$ and $p \in P$ such that

$$z \in \left\{x : x \in T^+, \text{lhs}(p) \Rightarrow_G^* x, |x| > |\text{lhs}(p)|\right\},$$

and, in addition, for each $p' \in P - \{p\}$, it satisfies

$$\left\{z' : z' \in T^*, \text{lhs}(p') \Rightarrow_G^* z', |z'| \leq |z|\right\} \neq \emptyset.$$

Set $k = |z|$ and $r = 2^{2^k}$. Consider $v \in L(G)$ satisfying $r < |v|$ and

$$L(G) \cap \left\{y : y \in T^*, r < |y| < |v|\right\} = \emptyset.$$

Furthermore, consider any derivation $S \Rightarrow_G^+ v$. Since $r < |v|$, during $S \Rightarrow_G^+ v$, G makes a derivation step $u \Rightarrow_G u'$ such that $|u| \leq r < |u'|$, so we can express $S \Rightarrow_G^+ v$ as

$$S \Rightarrow_G^+ u \Rightarrow_G u' \Rightarrow_G^* v,$$

where every sentential form v' in $u' \Rightarrow_G^* v$ satisfies $|v'| > r$. As $\delta\big(F(G)\big) \subseteq \text{shuffle}\big(term(G)\big)$, we have $\delta(u) \in \text{shuffle}\big(term(G)\big)$. As $\delta(u) \in \text{shuffle}\big(term(G)\big)$ and

$$L(G) \cap \left\{y : y \in T^*, r < |y| < |v|\right\} = \emptyset,$$

we have $|v| \leq k|u|$. Because $|u| \leq r$ and $r = 2^{2^k}$, $k|u| < 2^{2^{(k+1)}}$. Thus, $2^{2^k} < |v| < 2^{2^{(k+1)}}$. Hence, $v \notin L(G)$, which contradicts $v \in L(G)$. Therefore, $K \notin \mathscr{L}(SC, \text{term})$. ■

Theorem 4.6. $\mathscr{L}(CF) \subset \mathscr{L}(PSC, \text{term}) \subset \mathscr{L}(CS)$.

Proof. Theorem 4.4 implies $\mathscr{L}(CF) \subseteq \mathscr{L}(PSC, \text{term})$. Furthermore, notice that $\mathscr{L}(PSC, \text{term}) - \mathscr{L}(CF) \neq \emptyset$; for instance, this difference contains $\{a^n b^n a^n : n \geq 1\}$. Therefore, $\mathscr{L}(CF) \subset \mathscr{L}(PSC, \text{term})$. Obviously, $\mathscr{L}(PSC, \text{term}) \subseteq \mathscr{L}(PSC)$. Recall that $\mathscr{L}(PSC) \subseteq \mathscr{L}(CS)$ and $K \in \mathscr{L}(CS)$. By the previous lemma, $K \notin \mathscr{L}(SC, \text{term})$, so $\mathscr{L}(PSC, \text{term}) \subset \mathscr{L}(CS)$. ■

Theorem 4.7. $\mathscr{L}(CF) \subset \mathscr{L}(SC, \text{term}) \subset \mathscr{L}(RE)$.

Proof. Prove this theorem by analogy with the proof of the previous theorem. ■

In the conclusion, this section brings the reader's attention to the following two open problem areas.

Open Problem 4.8. Is $\mathscr{L}(SC, \text{term}) - \mathscr{L}(CS)$ empty? If so, is $\mathscr{L}(SC, \text{term}) - \mathscr{L}(PSC, \text{term})$ empty?

Open Problem 4.9. Consider Open Problem 3.28. Notice that Theorem 4.7 allows us to narrow our attention to $\mathscr{L}(PSC) - \mathscr{L}(PSC, \text{term})$ and $\mathscr{L}(CS) - \mathscr{L}(PSC, \text{term})$ when trying to solve this important problem. Indeed, if $\mathscr{L}(PSC) - \mathscr{L}(PSC, \text{term})$ contains $\mathscr{L}(CS) - \mathscr{L}(PSC, \text{term})$, then $\mathscr{L}(CS) - \mathscr{L}(PSC) = \emptyset$. On the other hand, if $\mathscr{L}(CS) - \mathscr{L}(PSC, \text{term})$ contains a language L such that $L \notin \mathscr{L}(PSC) - \mathscr{L}(PSC, \text{term})$, then $\mathscr{L}(CS) - \mathscr{L}(PSC) \neq \emptyset$.

4.2 Generalized k-limited erasing

This section concentrates its investigation on erasing productions in scattered context grammars and their effect on the generative power of these grammars. On the one hand, scattered context grammars, which may contain erasing productions, characterize the family of recursively enumerable languages (see Theorem 3.20). On the other hand, propagating scattered context grammars, which do not contain erasing productions at all, do not generate any non-context-sensitive language (see Theorem 3.21). As a result, some scattered context grammars with erasing productions cannot be converted to equivalent propagating scattered context grammars. Therefore, establishing conditions under which this conversion is performable represents a central topic of this investigation, and the present section pays a special attention to it. More specifically, this section demonstrates that this conversion is always possible if a scattered context grammar *erases its nonterminals in a generalized k-limited way*, where $k \geq 0$; in every sentential form of a derivation, each of its substrings consisting of nonterminals from which the grammar derives empty strings later in the derivation is of length k or less. Consequently, the scattered context grammars that have erasing productions, but apply them in a generalized k-limited way, are equivalent to the scattered context grammars that do not have erasing productions at all.

In Lemma 3.9, it was demonstrated that the family of propagating scattered context languages is closed under k-restricted homomorphism, and because k-limited erasing is a special case of a k-restricted homomorphism, the family is closed under k-limited erasing as well. Note that the following definition of generalized k-limited erasing significantly differs from the way symbols are erased by k-limited erasing. Under k-limited erasing, a language can be generated by a propagating scattered context grammar if at most k symbols are deleted between any two consecutive terminals in a sentence. However, under generalized k-limited erasing, an unlimited number of symbols can be deleted between any two consecutive terminals in a sentence if the grammar erases its nonterminals in a generalized k-limited way. In this sense, the result achieved in the present section generalizes the original result concerning k-limited erasing.

To define the generalized k-limited erasing formally, some auxiliary notions are needed.

Definition 4.10. The *core grammar underlying a scattered context grammar* $G = (V, T, P, S)$ is denoted by $\mathrm{core}(G)$ and defined as the context-free grammar $\mathrm{core}(G) = (V, T, P', S)$ with

$$P' = \{A_i \to x_i : (A_1, \dots, A_i, \dots, A_n) \to (x_1, \dots, x_i, \dots, x_n) \in P, 1 \le i \le n\}.$$

Definition 4.11. Let $G = (V, T, P, S)$ be a scattered context grammar, and let $\mathrm{core}(G)$ be a core grammar underlying G. Let

$$\begin{aligned} & u_1 A_1 \dots u_n A_n u_{n+1} = v \\ \Rightarrow_G\ & u_1 x_1 \dots u_n x_n u_{n+1} = w\ [(A_1, \dots, A_n) \to (x_1, \dots, x_n)], \end{aligned}$$

where $u_i \in V^*$, for all $1 \le i \le n+1$. The *partial m-step context-free simulation* of this derivation step by $\mathrm{core}(G)$ is denoted by

$$\mathrm{cf}_m(v \Rightarrow_G w)$$

and defined as an m-step derivation of $\mathrm{core}(G)$ of the form

$$\begin{aligned} & u_1 A_1 u_2 A_2 \dots u_n A_n u_{n+1} \\ \Rightarrow_{\mathrm{core}(G)}\ & u_1 x_1 u_2 A_2 \dots u_n A_n u_{n+1} \\ \Rightarrow^{m-1}_{\mathrm{core}(G)}\ & u_1 x_1 u_2 x_2 \dots u_m x_m u_{m+1} A_{m+1} \dots u_n A_n u_{n+1}, \end{aligned}$$

where $m \le n$. The *context-free simulation* of a derivation step of G, denoted by

$$\mathrm{cf}(v \Rightarrow_G w),$$

is the partial n-step context-free simulation of this step. Let $v = v_1 \Rightarrow^*_G v_n = w$ be of the form

$$v_1 \Rightarrow_G v_2 \Rightarrow_G \cdots \Rightarrow_G v_n.$$

The context-free simulation of $v \Rightarrow_G^* w$ by core(G) is denoted by cf$(v \Rightarrow_G^* w)$ and defined as

$$v_1 \Rightarrow^*_{\mathrm{core}(G)} v_2 \Rightarrow^*_{\mathrm{core}(G)} \cdots \Rightarrow^*_{\mathrm{core}(G)} v_n$$

such that for all $1 \leq i \leq n-1$, $v_i \Rightarrow^*_{\mathrm{core}(G)} v_{i+1}$ is the context-free simulation of $v_i \Rightarrow_G v_{i+1}$.

Definition 4.12. Let $G = (V, T, P, S)$ be a scattered context grammar, and let core(G) be a core grammar underlying G. Let $S \Rightarrow_G^* x$ be of the form $S \Rightarrow_G^* uAv \Rightarrow_G^* x$. Let cf$(S \Rightarrow_G^* x)$ be the context-free simulation of $S \Rightarrow_G^* x$. Let t be the derivation tree corresponding to $S \Rightarrow^*_{\mathrm{core}(G)} x$ (regarding derivation trees and related notions, we use the terminology of [24]). Consider a subtree rooted at A in t. If the frontier of this subtree is ε, then G *erases* A in $S \Rightarrow_G^* uAv \Rightarrow_G^* x$, symbolically written as

$$\grave{A},$$

and if this frontier differs from ε, then G *does not erase* A during this derivation, symbolically written as

$$\acute{A}.$$

If $w = \acute{A}_1 \ldots \acute{A}_n$ or $w = \grave{A}_1 \ldots \grave{A}_n$, for some $n \geq 1$, we write $\acute{w}$ or $\grave{w}$, respectively.

Generalized k-limited erasing is defined next.

Definition 4.13. Let $G = (V, T, P, S)$ be a scattered context grammar, and let $k \geq 0$. G *erases its nonterminals in a generalized k-limited way*, if for every $y \in L(G)$, there exists a derivation $S \Rightarrow_G^* y$ such that every sentential form x of the derivation satisfies the following two properties:

1. every $x = uAvBw$ such that $\acute{A}$, $\acute{B}$, and $\grave{v}$, satisfies $|v| \leq k$;
2. every $x = uAw$ such that $\acute{A}$, satisfies: if $\grave{u}$, then $|u| \leq k$, and if $\grave{w}$, then $|w| \leq k$.

The family of languages generated by scattered context grammars that erase their nonterminals in a generalized k-limited way is denoted by $\mathscr{L}(SC, \varepsilon, k)$.

We illustrate these definitions by the following example.

Example 4.14. Let $G_1 = (V_1, T, P_1, S_1)$ and $G_2 = (V_2, T, P_2, S_2)$ be right-linear grammars that satisfy $(V_1 - T) \cap (V_2 - T) = \emptyset$. The following example demonstrates the use of generalized k-limited erasing to construct the grammar G satisfying

$$L(G) = \{ww : w \in L(G_1) \backslash L(G_2)\}.$$

Suppose that $S, X, Y \notin V_1 \cup V_2$. Define the homomorphism α from T^* to $\{\bar{a} : a \in T\}^*$ as $\alpha(a) = \bar{a}$, for all $a \in T$. Construct the grammar

$$G = \big(V_1 \cup V_2 \cup \{\bar{a} : a \in T\} \cup \{S, X, Y, Z\}, T, P, S\big)$$

with P defined as follows:

1. Add $(S) \to (XS_1XS_2XS_1XS_2)$ to P.
2. For each $A \to xB \in P_1 \cup P_2$, add $(A, A) \to \big(\alpha(x)B, \alpha(x)B\big)$ to P.
3. For each $A \to x \in P_1 \cup P_2$, add $(A, A) \to \big(\alpha(x)Z, \alpha(x)Z\big)$ to P.
4. For each $a \in T$, add $(X, \bar{a}, X, \bar{a}, X, \bar{a}, X, \bar{a}) \to (\varepsilon, X, \varepsilon, X, \varepsilon, X, \varepsilon, X)$ to P.
5. Add $(X, Z, X, Z, X, Z, X, Z) \to (\varepsilon, \varepsilon, Y, \varepsilon, \varepsilon, \varepsilon, Y, \varepsilon)$ to P.
6. For each $a \in T$, add $(Y, \bar{a}, Y, \bar{a}) \to (a, Y, a, Y)$ to P.
7. Add $(Y, Y) \to (\varepsilon, \varepsilon)$ to P.

Let $y \in T^*$ be the longest string such that $A \to yB \in P_1$ or $A \to y \in P_1$. Similarly, let $z \in T^*$ be the longest string such that $A \to zB \in P_2$ or $A \to z \in P_2$. Then, observe that G erases its nonterminals in a generalized $\big(|y| + |z| + 3\big)$-limited way, for all $w \in L$, $w \neq \varepsilon$.

For instance, consider

$$G_1 = \big(\{S_1, a\}, \{a, b\}, \{S_1 \to aaS_1, S_1 \to \varepsilon\}, S_1\big)$$

with $L(G_1) = \{a^{2n} : n \geq 0\}$, and

$$G_2 = \big(\{S_2, a, b\}, \{a, b\}, \{S_2 \to aaaaS_2, S_2 \to b\}, S_2\big)$$

with $L(G_2) = \{a^{4n}b : n \geq 0\}$. We construct the grammar

$$G = \big(\{S_1, S_2, S, X, Y, \bar{a}, \bar{b}, a, b\}, \{a, b\}, P, S\big)$$

with P containing the following productions:

$$\begin{aligned}
1\ &: (S) \to (XS_1XS_2XS_1XS_2),\\
2_a &: (S_1, S_1) \to (\bar{a}\bar{a}S_1, \bar{a}\bar{a}S_1),\\
2_b &: (S_2, S_2) \to (\bar{a}\bar{a}\bar{a}\bar{a}S_2, \bar{a}\bar{a}\bar{a}\bar{a}S_2),\\
3_a &: (S_1, S_1) \to (Z, Z),\\
3_b &: (S_2, S_2) \to (\bar{b}Z, \bar{b}Z),\\
4_a &: (X, \bar{a}, X, \bar{a}, X, \bar{a}, X, \bar{a}) \to (\varepsilon, X, \varepsilon, X, \varepsilon, X, \varepsilon, X),\\
4_b &: (X, \bar{b}, X, \bar{b}, X, \bar{b}, X, \bar{b}) \to (\varepsilon, X, \varepsilon, X, \varepsilon, X, \varepsilon, X),\\
5\ &: (X, Z, X, Z, X, Z, X, Z) \to (\varepsilon, \varepsilon, Y, \varepsilon, \varepsilon, \varepsilon, Y, \varepsilon),\\
6_a &: (Y, \bar{a}, Y, \bar{a}) \to (a, Y, a, Y),\\
6_b &: (Y, \bar{b}, Y, \bar{b}) \to (b, Y, b, Y),\\
7\ &: (Y, Y) \to (\varepsilon, \varepsilon).
\end{aligned}$$

This grammar generates the language

$$L(G) = L = \big\{ww : w \in L(G_1)\backslash L(G_2)\big\} = \{a^{2n}ba^{2n}b : n \geq 0\}.$$

In addition, G erases its nonterminals in a generalized 9-limited way in every derivation, which can be easily seen on the following derivation:

$$\begin{aligned}
S &\Rightarrow_G XS_1XS_2XS_1XS_2\ [1] \Rightarrow_G X\bar{a}\bar{a}S_1XS_2X\bar{a}\bar{a}S_1XS_2\ [2_a]\\
&\Rightarrow_G X\bar{a}\bar{a}S_1X\bar{a}\bar{a}\bar{a}\bar{a}S_2X\bar{a}\bar{a}S_1X\bar{a}\bar{a}\bar{a}\bar{a}S_2\ [2_b]\\
&\Rightarrow_G X\bar{a}S_1X\bar{a}\bar{a}\bar{a}S_2X\bar{a}S_1X\bar{a}\bar{a}\bar{a}S_2\ [4_a] \Rightarrow_G XS_1X\bar{a}\bar{a}S_2XS_1X\bar{a}\bar{a}S_2\ [4_a]\\
&\Rightarrow_G XZX\bar{a}\bar{a}S_2XZX\bar{a}\bar{a}S_2\ [3_a] \Rightarrow_G XZX\bar{a}\bar{a}\bar{b}ZXZX\bar{a}\bar{a}\bar{b}Z\ [3_b]\\
&\Rightarrow_G Y\bar{a}\bar{a}\bar{b}Y\bar{a}\bar{a}\bar{b}\ [5] \Rightarrow_G aY\bar{a}\bar{b}aY\bar{a}\bar{b}\ [6_a] \Rightarrow_G aaY\bar{b}aaY\bar{b}\ [6_a]\\
&\Rightarrow_G aabYaabY\ [6_b] \Rightarrow_G aabaab\ [7].
\end{aligned}$$

Notice that S_2 is not deleted in a successful derivation of $w \in L$, and the derivation can always proceed so that there are at most four $\bar{a}$'s in front of S_2 and two $\bar{a}$'s in front of S_1. Therefore, in the case when all $\bar{a}$'s, S_1 and both X's are deleted in front of S_2, $k = 9$, so the erasing is performed in a generalized 9-limited way. In fact, the two $\bar{a}$'s preceding S_2 cannot be deleted in a successful derivation of G, so the erasing is 7-limited.

As the previous example illustrates, erasing productions fulfill a useful role during the verification of a relation between substrings of a sentential form, so their involvement in a scattered context grammar is often desirable. Of course, this involvement does not rule out the existence of a propagating scattered context grammar equivalent to the scattered context grammar with erasing productions. For instance, the existence of erasing productions in the grammar in Example 4.14 might suggest that no propagating scattered context grammar generates the resulting language. However, this is not the case at all: the generated language, $\{a^{2n}ba^{2n}b : n \geq 0\}$, is clearly context-sensitive and can be easily generated by a propagating scattered context grammar. This observation brings us to the following theorem, which says that if a scattered context grammar erases its nonterminals in a generalized k-limited way, then it can be converted to an equivalent propagating scattered context grammar.

Theorem 4.15. *For every scattered context grammar G that erases its nonterminals in a generalized k-limited way, there exists a propagating scattered context grammar $\bar{G}$ such that $L(G) = L(\bar{G})$.*

Proof. Let $G = (V, T, P, S)$ be a scattered context grammar. For each

$$p = (A_1, \dots, A_i, \dots, A_n) \to (x_1, \dots, x_i, \dots, x_n) \in P,$$

let $(\!| p, i |\!)$ denote $A_i \to x_i$, for all $1 \leq i \leq n$. Let

$$\begin{aligned} \Psi &= \big\{ (\!| p, i |\!) : p \in P, 1 \leq i \leq \mathrm{len}(p) \big\}, \\ \Psi' &= \big\{ (\!| p, i |\!)' : (\!| p, i |\!) \in \Psi \big\}. \end{aligned}$$

Set

$$\bar{N}_1 = \big\{ \langle x \rangle : x \in (V - T)^* \cup (V - T)^* T (V - T)^*, |x| \leq 2k + 1 \big\}.$$

For each $\langle x \rangle \in \bar{N}_1$ and $(\!| p, i |\!) \in \Psi$, define

$$\text{lhs-replace}\big(\langle x \rangle, (\!| p, i |\!)\big) = \Big\{ \big\langle x_1 (\!| p, i |\!) x_2 \big\rangle : x_1 \,\mathrm{lhs}\big((\!| p, i |\!)\big) x_2 = x \Big\}.$$

Set

$$\bar{N}_2 = \Big\{ \langle x \rangle : \langle x \rangle \in \text{lhs-replace}\big(\langle y \rangle, (\!| p, i |\!)\big), \langle y \rangle \in \bar{N}_1, (\!| p, i |\!) \in \Psi \Big\}.$$

For each $\langle x \rangle \in \bar{N}_1$ and $(\!| p, i |\!)' \in \Psi'$, define

$$\text{insert}\big(\langle x \rangle, (\!| p, i |\!)'\big) = \Big\{ \big\langle x_1 (\!| p, i |\!)' x_2 \big\rangle : x_1 x_2 = x \Big\}.$$

Set

$$\bar{N}_2' = \Big\{\langle x\rangle : \langle x\rangle \in \text{insert}\big(\langle y\rangle, (\!|p, i|\!)'\big), \langle y\rangle \in \bar{N}_1, (\!|p, i|\!)' \in \Psi'\Big\}.$$

For each $x = \langle x_1\rangle \ldots \langle x_n\rangle \in (\bar{N}_1 \cup \bar{N}_2 \cup \bar{N}_2')^*$, for some $n \geq 1$, define

$$\text{join}(x) = x_1 \ldots x_n.$$

For each $x \in \bar{N}_1 \cup \bar{N}_2 \cup \bar{N}_2'$, define

$$\text{split}(x) = \big\{y : x = \text{join}(y)\big\}.$$

Set

$$\bar{V} = T \cup \bar{N}_1 \cup \bar{N}_2 \cup \bar{N}_2' \cup \{\bar{S}\}.$$

Define the propagating scattered context grammar $\bar{G} = (\bar{V}, T, \bar{P}, \bar{S})$ with $\bar{P}$ constructed as follows:

1. For each $p = (S) \rightarrow (x) \in P$, add
   $(\bar{S}) \rightarrow \big(\langle(\!|p, 1|\!)\rangle\big)$ to $\bar{P}$.
2. For each $\langle x\rangle \in \bar{N}_1$, each $X \in \text{insert}\big(\langle x\rangle, (\!|p, n|\!)'\big)$, where $p \in P$, $\text{len}(p) = n$, each $\langle y\rangle \in \bar{N}_1$, and each $Y \in \text{lhs-replace}\big(\langle y\rangle, (\!|q, 1|\!)\big)$, where $q \in P$, add
   (a) $\big(X, \langle y\rangle\big) \rightarrow \big(\langle x\rangle, Y\big)$, and
   (b) $\big(\langle y\rangle, X\big) \rightarrow \big(Y, \langle x\rangle\big)$ to $\bar{P}$;
   (c) if $\langle x\rangle = \langle y\rangle$, add
   $(X) \rightarrow (Y)$ to $\bar{P}$.
   (d) Add $(X) \rightarrow \big(\langle x\rangle\big)$ to $\bar{P}$.
3. For each $\langle x\rangle \in \bar{N}_1$, each $X \in \text{insert}\big(\langle x\rangle, (\!|p, i|\!)'\big)$, where $p \in P$, $i < \text{len}(p)$, each $\langle y\rangle \in \bar{N}_1$, and each $Y \in \text{lhs-replace}\big(\langle y\rangle, (\!|p, i+1|\!)\big)$, add
   (a) $\big(X, \langle y\rangle\big) \rightarrow \big(\langle x\rangle, Y\big)$ to $\bar{P}$;
   (b) if $\langle x\rangle = \langle y\rangle$, and $X = x_1(\!|p, i|\!)'x_2$, $Y = y_1(\!|p, i+1|\!)y_2$ satisfy
   $\big|x_1(\!|p, i|\!)'\big| < \big|y_1(\!|p, i+1|\!)\big|$, add $(X) \rightarrow (Y)$ to $\bar{P}$.
4. For each $\big\langle x_1(\!|p, i|\!)x_2\big\rangle \in \text{lhs-replace}\big(\langle x\rangle, (\!|p, i|\!)\big)$, $\langle x\rangle \in \bar{N}_1$, $(\!|p, i|\!) \in \Psi$, and each $Y \in \text{split}\big(x_1 \,\text{rhs}\big((\!|p, i|\!)\big)(\!|p, i|\!)'x_2\big)$, add $\big(\langle x_1(\!|p, i|\!)x_2\rangle\big) \rightarrow (Y)$ to $\bar{P}$.
5. For each $a \in T$, add $\big(\langle a\rangle\big) \rightarrow (a)$ to $\bar{P}$.

Basic Idea.
The propagating scattered context grammar $\bar{G}$ simulates G by using nonterminals of the form $\langle\ldots\rangle$. In every nonterminal of this form, during every simulated derivation step, $\bar{G}$ records a substring corresponding to the current sentential form of G. The grammar $\bar{G}$ performs its derivation so that each of the nonterminals $\langle\ldots\rangle$ contains at least one symbol not erased later in the derivation.

The production constructed in (1) only initializes the simulation process. By productions introduced in (2) through (4), $\bar{G}$ simulates the application of a scattered context production $p \in P$ in a left-to-right way. In greater detail, by using a production from (2), $\bar{G}$ non-deterministically selects a scattered context production $p \in P$. Suppose that p consists of context-free productions $r_1, \ldots, r_{i-1}, r_i, \ldots, r_n$. By using productions from (3) and (4), $\bar{G}$ simulates the application of r_1 through r_n one by one. To explain this in greater detail, suppose that $\bar{G}$ has just completed the simulation of r_{i-1}. Then, to the right of this simulation, $\bar{G}$ selects lhs(r_i) by using a production from (3). That is, this selection takes place either in a nonterminal of G in which the simulation of r_{i-1} has been performed or in one of the nonterminals appearing to the right of this nonterminal. After this selection, by using a production from (4), $\bar{G}$ performs the replacement of the selected symbol lhs(r_i) with rhs(r_i). If a terminal occurs inside of a nonterminal of $\bar{G}$, then a production from (5) allows $\bar{G}$ to change this nonterminal to the terminal contained in it.

Formal Proof.
In what follows, we denote the set of productions introduced in step i of the construction by $\bar{P}_i$, for $1 \leq i \leq 5$.

Claim 1. Every successful derivation in $\bar{G}$ can be expressed in the following way:

$$\begin{aligned} \bar{S} &\Rightarrow_{\bar{G}} \langle (\!| p, 1 |\!) \rangle \; [p_1] \\ &\Rightarrow_{\bar{G}}^{+} u \qquad [\Phi] \\ &\Rightarrow_{\bar{G}}^{+} v \qquad [\Theta], \end{aligned}$$

where $p_1 = (\bar{S}) \rightarrow (\langle (\!| p, 1 |\!) \rangle) \in \bar{P}_1$, $u = \langle a_1 \rangle \ldots \langle a_n \rangle$, $n \geq 1$, $a_1, \ldots, a_n \in T$, $v = a_1 \ldots a_n$, Φ and Θ are sequences of productions from $\bar{P}_2 \cup \bar{P}_3 \cup \bar{P}_4$, and $\bar{P}_5$, respectively.

Proof. Productions from $\bar{P}_1$ are the only productions with $\bar{S}$ on their left-hand sides. Therefore, the derivation starts with a step made by one of these productions, so

$$\begin{aligned} \bar{S} &\Rightarrow_{\bar{G}} \langle (\!| p, 1 |\!) \rangle \; [p_1] \\ &\Rightarrow_{\bar{G}}^{+} v. \end{aligned}$$

Observe that $\bar{S}$ does not appear on the right-hand side of any of the introduced productions. Therefore, productions from $\bar{P}_1$ are not used during the rest of the derivation.

The productions from $\bar{P}_5$ are the only productions with their right-hand sides over T; therefore, they have to be used to complete the derivation. Observe that none of the productions from $\bar{P}_1 \cup \bar{P}_2 \cup \bar{P}_3 \cup \bar{P}_4$ rewrites nonterminals of the form $\langle a \rangle$, where $a \in T$. As all productions from $\bar{P}_5$ are context-free, they can be applied whenever $\langle a \rangle$ appears in the sentential form. Without loss of generality, we can assume that they are applied at the end of the derivation process; therefore,

$$\begin{aligned} \bar{S} &\Rightarrow_{\bar{G}} \langle (\!| p, 1 |\!) \rangle \; [p_1] \\ &\Rightarrow_{\bar{G}}^{+} u \qquad [\Phi] \\ &\Rightarrow_{\bar{G}}^{+} v \qquad [\Theta], \end{aligned}$$

so the claim holds. □

The following notation describes the strings that may appear in a successful derivation of $\bar{G}$. Let $S \Rightarrow^*_{\bar{G}} y \Rightarrow^*_{\bar{G}} w$, $w \in L(\bar{G})$, $y \in (\bar{N}_1 \cup \bar{N}_2 \cup \bar{N}_2')^*$, and let for each $\langle z \rangle \in \text{alph}(y)$ there exists

1. $A \in \text{alph}(z)$ such that $\acute{A}$, or
2. $(\!| p, i |\!) \in \text{alph}(z)$, $(\!| p, i |\!) \in \Psi$, $A = \text{lhs}\big((\!| p, i |\!)\big)$ such that $\acute{A}$.

Then, we write

$$\check{y}.$$

Claim 2. Let

$$w_1 \in \text{split}\big(u_1 (\!| p, 1 |\!) u_2 A_2 \dots u_n A_n u_{n+1}\big),$$
$$\tau = u_1 A_1 u_2 A_2 \dots u_n A_n u_{n+1},$$

$u_1, \dots, u_{n+1} \in V^*, A_1, \dots, A_n \in V - T, A_1 = \text{lhs}((\!| p, 1 |\!)), p = (A_1, \dots, A_n) \to (x_1, \dots, x_n) \in P$, and $\check{w}_1$; then, every partial h-step context-free simulation

$$\text{cf}_h\big(\tau = u_1 A_1 u_2 A_2 \dots u_n A_n u_{n+1} \Rightarrow_G u_1 x_1 u_2 x_2 \dots u_n x_n u_{n+1}\ [p]\big)$$

of the form

$$\begin{aligned}
& u_1 A_1 u_2 A_2 u_3 A_3 \dots u_n A_n u_{n+1} = \tau \\
\Rightarrow_{\text{core}(G)}\ & u_1 x_1 u_2 A_2 u_3 A_3 \dots u_n A_n u_{n+1} \\
\Rightarrow_{\text{core}(G)}\ & u_1 x_1 u_2 x_2 u_3 A_3 \dots u_n A_n u_{n+1} \\
\Rightarrow^{h-2}_{\text{core}(G)}\ & u_1 x_1 u_2 x_2 u_3 x_3 \dots u_h x_h u_{h+1} A_{h+1} \dots u_n A_n u_{n+1}
\end{aligned}$$

is performed in core(G) if and only if

$$\begin{aligned}
& w_1 \\
\Rightarrow_{\bar{G}}\ & w_1'\ [p_1^4] \\
\Rightarrow_{\bar{G}}\ & w_2\ [p_2^3] \\
\Rightarrow_{\bar{G}}\ & w_2'\ [p_2^4] \\
& \vdots \\
\Rightarrow^{2h-5}_{\bar{G}}\ & w_h\ [p_h^3] \\
\Rightarrow_{\bar{G}}\ & w_h'\ [p_h^4]
\end{aligned}$$

is performed in $\bar{G}$, where $p_2^3, \dots, p_h^3 \in \bar{P}_3$, $p_1^4, \dots, p_h^4 \in \bar{P}_4$, and

$$\begin{aligned}
w_1' &\in \text{split}\big(u_1 x_1 (\!| p, 1 |\!)' u_2 A_2 \dots u_n A_n u_{n+1}\big), \\
w_2 &\in \text{split}\big(u_1 x_1 u_2 (\!| p, 2 |\!) u_3 \dots u_n A_n u_{n+1}\big), \\
w_2' &\in \text{split}\big(u_1 x_1 u_2 x_2 (\!| p, 2 |\!)' u_3 \dots u_n A_n u_{n+1}\big), \\
&\ \vdots \\
w_h &\in \text{split}\big(u_1 x_1 u_2 x_2 \dots u_h (\!| p, h |\!) u_{h+1} A_{h+1} \dots u_n A_n u_{n+1}\big), \\
w_h' &\in \text{split}\big(u_1 x_1 u_2 x_2 \dots u_h x_h (\!| p, h |\!)' u_{h+1} A_{h+1} \dots u_n A_n u_{n+1}\big);
\end{aligned}$$

in addition, every $w \in \{w_2, \dots, w_h, w'_1, \dots, w'_h\}$ satisfies $\check{w}$.

Proof. We start by proving the only-if part of the claim.

Only If. The only-if part is proved by induction on g for all partial g-step context-free simulations, for $g \geq 1$.

Basis. Let $g = 1$. Then,

$$u_1 A_1 u_2 A_2 \dots u_n A_n u_{n+1} \Rightarrow_{\text{core}(G)} u_1 x_1 u_2 A_2 \dots u_n A_n u_{n+1},$$

and $w_1 \in \text{split}\big(u_1 (\!| p, 1 |\!) u_2 A_2 \dots u_n A_n u_{n+1}\big)$. Notice that every production from $\bar{P}_2 \cup \bar{P}_3 \cup \bar{P}_4$ contains one symbol from

$$\text{insert}\big(\langle x \rangle, (\!| p, i |\!)'\big) \cup \text{lhs-replace}\big(\langle x \rangle, (\!| p, i |\!)\big),$$

where $\langle x \rangle \in \bar{N}_1, (\!| p, i |\!)' \in \Psi', (\!| p, i |\!) \in \Psi$, both on its left-hand side and right-hand side. Therefore, only one of these symbols occurs in every sentential form of $\bar{G}$. As

$$w_1 \in \text{split}\big(u_1 (\!| p, 1 |\!) u_2 A_2 \dots u_n A_n u_{n+1}\big),$$

only a production from $\bar{P}_4$ can be used in $\bar{G}$. The sentential form w_1 can be expressed as

$$w_1 \in \text{split}(u_{11})\big\langle u_{12} (\!| p, 1 |\!) u_{21}\big\rangle \text{split}(u_{22}),$$

where $u_{11}u_{12} = u_1$, $u_{21}u_{22} = u_2 A_2 \dots u_n A_n u_{n+1}$. Consider the following two forms of $\big\langle u_{12} (\!| p, 1 |\!) u_{21}\big\rangle$:

1. $\big\langle E^1_1 \dots E^1_{l^1} B^1 \dots E^\alpha_1 \dots \hat{E}^\alpha_m \dots E^\alpha_{l^\alpha} B^\alpha \dots E^\beta_1 \dots E^\beta_{l^\beta} B^\beta E^{\beta+1}_1 \dots E^{\beta+1}_{l^{\beta+1}}\big\rangle$ with $\hat{E}^\alpha_m = (\!| p, 1 |\!)$, $E^\alpha_m = \text{lhs}\big((\!| p, 1 |\!)\big)$, $\acute{B}^i$, for all $1 \leq i \leq \beta$, $\grave{E}^i_1, \dots, \grave{E}^i_{l^i}$, for all $1 \leq i \leq \beta + 1$. If G erases nonterminals in a generalized k-limited way, then $\bar{G}$ satisfies

$$\Big|\text{rhs}\big((\!| p, 1 |\!)\big)\Big| + l^\alpha - 1 \leq k.$$

   By using the corresponding simulating production $p^4_1 \in \bar{P}_4$, $\big\langle u_{12} (\!| p, 1 |\!) u_{21}\big\rangle$ can be rewritten and split so that we obtain $\langle y_1 \rangle \dots \langle y_o \rangle$, for some $o \geq 1$, satisfying

$$y_1 \dots y_o = E^1_1 \dots E^1_{l^1} B^1 \dots E^\alpha_1 \dots \text{rhs}\big((\!| p, 1 |\!)\big) (\!| p, 1 |\!)' \dots$$
$$\dots E^\alpha_{l^\alpha} B^\alpha \dots E^\beta_1 \dots E^\beta_{l^\beta} B^\beta E^{\beta+1}_1 \dots E^{\beta+1}_{l^{\beta+1}},$$

   where for all $1 \leq j \leq o$, there exists $B \in \{B^1, \dots, B^\beta\}$ such that $B \in \text{alph}(y_j)$. If G does not erase nonterminals in a generalized k-limited way, then some y_j, $1 \leq j \leq o$, may satisfy

$$\text{alph}(y_j) \cap \{B^1, \dots, B^\beta\} = \emptyset.$$

   However, in this case, $\langle y_j \rangle$ will be eventually rewritten to $\langle \varepsilon \rangle$, which cannot be rewritten by any production, so the derivation would be unsuccessful.

2. $\langle E_1^1 \dots E_{l^1}^1 B^1 \dots E_1^\alpha \dots E_{l^\alpha}^\alpha \hat{B}^\alpha \dots E_1^\beta \dots E_{l^\beta}^\beta B^\beta E_1^{\beta+1} \dots E_{l^{\beta+1}}^{\beta+1} \rangle$ with $\hat{B}^\alpha = \llparenthesis p, 1 \rrparenthesis$, $B^\alpha = \text{lhs}(\llparenthesis p, 1 \rrparenthesis)$, $\acute{B}^i$, for all $1 \leq i \leq \beta$, and $\grave{E}_1^i, \dots, \grave{E}_{l^i}^i$, for all $1 \leq i \leq \beta + 1$. Consider the simulated production, denoted by $\llparenthesis p, 1 \rrparenthesis$, of the form

$$B^\alpha \to C_1^1 \dots C_{p^1}^1 D^1 \dots C_1^\gamma \dots C_{p^\gamma}^\gamma D^\gamma C_1^{\gamma+1} \dots C_{p^{\gamma+1}}^{\gamma+1}$$

with $\acute{D}^i$, for all $1 \leq i \leq \gamma$, and $\grave{C}_1^i, \dots, \grave{C}_{p^i}^i$, for all $1 \leq i \leq \gamma + 1$. If G erases nonterminals in a generalized k-limited way, the production satisfies $p^2, \dots, p^\gamma \leq k$, and $p^1 + l^\alpha \leq k$, $p^{\gamma+1} + l^{\alpha+1} \leq k$. By using the corresponding simulating production $p_1^4 \in \bar{P}_4$, $\langle u_{12} \llparenthesis p, 1 \rrparenthesis u_{21} \rangle$ can be rewritten and split so that we obtain $\langle y_1 \rangle \dots \langle y_o \rangle$, for some $o \geq 1$, satisfying

$$\begin{aligned} y_1 \dots y_o = {} & E_1^1 \dots E_{l^1}^1 B^1 \dots E_1^\alpha \dots E_{l^\alpha}^\alpha \\ & C_1^1 \dots C_{p^1}^1 D^1 \dots C_1^\gamma \dots C_{p^\gamma}^\gamma D^\gamma C_1^{\gamma+1} \dots C_{p^{\gamma+1}}^{\gamma+1} \llparenthesis p, 1 \rrparenthesis' \dots \\ & \dots E_1^\beta \dots E_{l^\beta}^\beta B^\beta E_1^{\beta+1} \dots E_{l^{\beta+1}}^{\beta+1}, \end{aligned}$$

where for all $1 \leq j \leq o$, there exists $B \in \{B^1, \dots, B^\beta, D^1, \dots, D^\gamma\}$ such that $B \in \text{alph}(y_j)$. If G does not erase nonterminals in a generalized k-limited way, then some y_j, $1 \leq j \leq o$, may satisfy

$$\text{alph}(y_j) \cap \{B^1, \dots, B^\beta, D^1, \dots, D^\gamma\} = \emptyset.$$

Similarly to the form (1), $\langle y_j \rangle$ will be eventually rewritten to $\langle \varepsilon \rangle$, so the derivation would be unsuccessful.

Therefore, some production $p_1^4 \in \bar{P}_4$ is applicable, so we obtain

$$w_1 \Rightarrow_{\bar{G}} w_1' \; [p_1^4]$$

with

$$w_1' \in \text{split}(u_{11}) \, \text{split}\big(u_{12} x_1 \llparenthesis p, 1 \rrparenthesis' u_{21}\big) \, \text{split}(u_{22}),$$

so $w_1' \in \text{split}\big(u_{11} u_{12} x_1 \llparenthesis p, 1 \rrparenthesis' u_{21} u_{22}\big)$, and

$$w_1' \in \text{split}\big(u_1 x_1 \llparenthesis p, 1 \rrparenthesis' u_2 A_2 \dots u_n A_n u_{n+1}\big).$$

Induction Hypothesis. Suppose that the claim holds for all partial k-step context-free simulations, where $k \leq g$, for some $g \geq 1$.

Induction Step. Consider a partial $(g+1)$-step context-free simulation

$$x \Rightarrow_{\text{core}(G)}^{g+1} z,$$

where $z \in V^*$. As $g + 1 \geq 2$, there exists $y \in V^*$ such that

$$x \Rightarrow^{g}_{\mathrm{core}(G)} y \Rightarrow_{\mathrm{core}(G)} z\ [A_{g+1} \rightarrow x_{g+1}],$$

where $y = u_1x_1u_2x_2 \ldots u_gx_gu_{g+1}A_{g+1} \ldots u_nA_nu_{n+1}$, and by the induction hypothesis,

$$w_1 \Rightarrow^{2g-1}_{\bar{G}} w'_g.$$

We perform the partial $(g + 1)$-step context-free simulation of a production p, so $g < \mathrm{len}(p)$ and

$$w'_g \in \mathrm{split}\big(u_1x_1u_2x_2 \ldots u_gx_g(\!| p, g |\!)' u_{g+1}A_{g+1} \ldots u_nA_nu_{n+1}\big);$$

therefore, only productions from $\bar{P}_3$ can be used. The sentential form w'_g has either of the following two forms:

- $\mathrm{split}(r_1)\langle r_2(\!| p, g |\!)' r_3\rangle\, \mathrm{split}(r_4A_{g+1}r_5)$ such that $y = r_1r_2r_3r_4A_{g+1}r_5$. In this case, a production from (3a) can be used and after its application, we obtain

$$w_{g+1} = \mathrm{split}(r_1)\langle r_2r_3\rangle\, \mathrm{split}\big(r_4(\!| p, g + 1 |\!) r_5\big).$$

- $\mathrm{split}(r_1)\langle r_2(\!| p, g |\!)' u_{g+1}A_{g+1}r_3\rangle\, \mathrm{split}(r_4)$ such that $y = r_1r_2u_{g+1}A_{g+1}r_3r_4$. In this case, a production from (3b) can be used and after its application, we obtain

$$w_{g+1} = \mathrm{split}(r_1)\langle r_2u_{g+1}(\!| p, g + 1 |\!) r_3\rangle\, \mathrm{split}(r_4).$$

Thus, this derivation step can be expressed as

$$w'_g \Rightarrow_{\bar{G}} w_{g+1}\ [p^3_{g+1}],$$

where $p^3_{g+1} \in \bar{P}_3$, and

$$w_{g+1} \in \mathrm{split}\big(u_1x_1u_2x_2 \ldots u_gx_gu_{g+1}(\!| p, g + 1 |\!) \ldots u_nA_nu_{n+1}\big).$$

If $\breve{w}'_g$, the form of the productions from $\bar{P}_3$ implies that w_{g+1} satisfies $\breve{w}_{g+1}$ as well. At this point, only productions from $p^4_{g+1} \in \bar{P}_4$ can be used. The proof of

$$w_{g+1} \Rightarrow_{\bar{G}} w'_{g+1}\ [p^4_{g+1}]$$

is analogous to the proof of

$$w_1 \Rightarrow_{\bar{G}} w'_1\ [p^4_1]$$

described in the Basis and is left to the reader. As a result,

$$w'_{g+1} \in \mathrm{split}\big(u_1x_1u_2x_2 \ldots u_{g+1}x_{g+1}(\!| p, g + 1 |\!)' u_{g+2}A_{g+2} \ldots u_nA_nu_{n+1}\big),$$

satisfying $\breve{w}'_{g+1}$.

If. The if part is proved by induction on g for all g-step derivations in $\bar{G}$, for $g \geq 1$.

Basis. Let $g = 1$. Then, $w_1 \Rightarrow_{\bar{G}} w'_1\ [p_1^4]$ and $\tau = u_1 A_1 \ldots u_n A_n u_{n+1}$. Clearly,

$$u_1 A_1 \ldots u_n A_n u_{n+1} \Rightarrow_{\text{core}(G)} u_1 x_1 \ldots u_n A_n u_{n+1}\ [A_1 \rightarrow x_1].$$

Induction Hypothesis. Suppose that the claim holds for all k-step derivations, where $k \leq g$, for some $g \geq 1$.

Induction Step. Consider a derivation

$$w_1 \Rightarrow_{\bar{G}}^{2(g+1)-1} w'_{g+1},$$

where

$$w'_{g+1} \in \text{split}\big(u_1 x_1 \ldots u_{g+1} x_{g+1} \llparenthesis p, g+1 \rrparenthesis' u_{g+2} A_{g+2} \ldots u_n A_n u_{n+1}\big).$$

Since $2(g+1) - 1 \geq 3$, there exists a derivation

$$w_1 \Rightarrow_{\bar{G}}^{2g-1} w'_g \Rightarrow_{\bar{G}} w_{g+1} \Rightarrow_{\bar{G}} w'_{g+1},$$

where

$$w_{g+1} \in \text{split}\big(u_1 x_1 \ldots u_g x_g u_{g+1} \llparenthesis p, g+1 \rrparenthesis u_{g+2} A_{g+2} \ldots u_n A_n u_{n+1}\big).$$

By the induction hypothesis, there is a derivation

$$u_1 A_1 \ldots u_n A_n u_{n+1} \Rightarrow_{\text{core}(G)}^{g} u_1 x_1 \ldots u_g x_g u_{g+1} A_{g+1} \ldots u_n A_n u_{n+1}.$$

Clearly,

$$\begin{aligned} &u_1 x_1 \ldots u_g x_g u_{g+1} A_{g+1} u_{g+2} A_{g+2} \ldots u_n A_n u_{n+1} \\ \Rightarrow_{\text{core}(G)}\ &u_1 x_1 \ldots u_g x_g u_{g+1} x_{g+1} u_{g+2} A_{g+2} \ldots u_n A_n u_{n+1}\ [A_{g+1} \rightarrow x_{g+1}]. \end{aligned}$$

□

Claim 3. The result from Claim 2 holds for a context-free simulation.

Proof. As the context-free simulation of the whole scattered context production $(A_1, \ldots, A_n) \rightarrow (x_1, \ldots, x_n)$ is a partial context-free simulation of the length n, Claim 2 holds for a context-free simulation as well. □

We use the following notation to describe the simulation of a derivation step in G by productions of $\bar{G}$ as demonstrated by Claims 2 and 3. Let

$$\begin{aligned} &u_1 A_1 \ldots u_n A_n u_{n+1} \\ \Rightarrow_G\ &u_1 x_1 \ldots u_n x_n u_{n+1}\ [p], \end{aligned}$$

for some $p = (A_1, \ldots, A_n) \rightarrow (x_1, \ldots, x_n) \in P$. Then, $\Rrightarrow$ denotes the simulation of this derivation step in $\bar{G}$. We write

$$w_1 \Rrightarrow w'_n\ [p],$$

or, shortly, $w_1 \Rrightarrow w'_n$. Therefore, $w_1 \Rightarrow_{\bar{G}}^{2n-1} w'_n$ from Claim 2 is equivalent to $w_1 \Rrightarrow w'_n$.

Claim 4. Let $x_1 \in V^*$ and $\bar{x}'_1 \in \mathrm{split}\big(x'_{11}\llparenthesis p_1, 1\rrparenthesis x'_{12}\big)$, where $x'_{11}\,\mathrm{lhs}\big(\llparenthesis p_1, 1\rrparenthesis\big)\, x'_{12} = x_1$, $\llparenthesis p_1, 1\rrparenthesis \in \Psi$, and $\check{\bar{x}}'_1$; then, every derivation

$$\begin{aligned} & x_1 \\ \Rightarrow_G\ & x_2\ [p_1] \\ & \vdots \\ \Rightarrow_G\ & x_{m+1}\ [p_m] \end{aligned}$$

is performed in G if and only if

$$\begin{aligned} & \bar{x}'_1 & \\ \Rrightarrow\ & \bar{x}_1 & [p_1] \\ \Rightarrow_{\bar{G}}\ & \bar{x}'_2 & [p'_2] \\ \Rrightarrow\ & \bar{x}_2 & [p_2] \\ \Rightarrow_{\bar{G}}\ & \bar{x}'_3 & [p'_3] \\ & \vdots & \\ \Rrightarrow\ & \bar{x}_m & [p_m] \\ \Rightarrow_{\bar{G}}\ & \bar{x}'_{m+1} & [p'_{m+1}] \end{aligned}$$

is performed in $\bar{G}$, where $x_2, \ldots, x_{m+1} \in V^*$, $p_1, \ldots, p_m \in P$, $p'_2, \ldots, p'_{m+1} \in \bar{P}_2$,

$$\bar{x}_i \in \mathrm{split}\big(x_{i1}\llparenthesis p_i, \mathrm{len}(p_i)\rrparenthesis' x_{i2}\big),$$
$$\bar{x}'_j \in \mathrm{split}\big(x'_{j1}\llparenthesis p_j, 1\rrparenthesis x'_{j2}\big),$$

for all $1 \le i \le m$, $2 \le j \le m$, and

- $\bar{x}'_{m+1} \in \mathrm{split}\big(x'_{(m+1)1}\llparenthesis p_{m+1}, 1\rrparenthesis x'_{(m+1)2}\big)$, for $x_{m+1} \notin T^*$, or
- $\bar{x}'_{m+1} \in \mathrm{split}(x_{m+1})$, for $x_{m+1} \in T^*$,

where $x_{i1}x_{i2} = x_i$, for all $1 \le i \le m$, $x'_{j1}\,\mathrm{lhs}\big(\llparenthesis p_j, 1\rrparenthesis\big) x'_{j2} = x_j$, for all $2 \le j \le m+1$, and every $\bar{x} \in \{\bar{x}_1, \ldots, \bar{x}_m, \bar{x}'_2, \ldots, \bar{x}'_{m+1}\}$ satisfies $\check{\bar{x}}$.

Proof. We start by proving the only-if part of the claim.

Only If. The only-if part is proved by induction on g for all g-step derivations in G, for $g \ge 0$.

Basis. Let $g = 0$. Then, $x_1 \Rightarrow_G^0 x_1$ and $\bar{x}'_1 \Rightarrow_{\bar{G}}^0 \bar{x}'_1$.

Induction Hypothesis. Suppose that the claim holds for all k-step derivations, where $k \le g$, for some $g \ge 0$.

Induction Step. Consider a derivation

$$x_1 \Rightarrow_G^{g+1} x_{g+2}.$$

Since $g + 1 \geq 1$, there exists a derivation

$$x_1 \Rightarrow_G^g x_{g+1} \Rightarrow_G x_{g+2}.$$

By the induction hypothesis, there is a derivation

$$\bar{x}'_1 \Rrightarrow \bar{x}_1 \Rightarrow_{\bar{G}} \bar{x}'_2 \Rrightarrow \bar{x}_2 \Rightarrow_{\bar{G}} \dots \Rrightarrow \bar{x}_g \Rightarrow_{\bar{G}} \bar{x}'_{g+1}.$$

Because we are performing $(g + 1)$-step derivation, $x_{g+1} \notin T^*$. The sentential forms $\bar{x}_g$ and $\bar{x}'_{g+1}$ in the g-step simulation have to satisfy

$$\begin{aligned} \bar{x}_g &\in \text{split}\big(x_{g1} (\!| p_g, \text{len}(p_g) |\!)' x_{g2}\big), \\ \bar{x}'_{g+1} &\in \text{split}\big(x'_{(g+1)1} (\!| p_{g+1}, 1 |\!) x'_{(g+1)2}\big), \end{aligned}$$

where $x_g = x_{g1} x_{g2}$,

$$x_{g+1} = x'_{(g+1)1} \, \text{lhs}\big((\!| p_{g+1}, 1 |\!)\big) x'_{(g+1)2},$$

and $\check{\bar{x}}'_{g+1}$. Then, by Claim 3,

$$\bar{x}'_{g+1} \Rrightarrow \bar{x}_{g+1},$$

where

$$\bar{x}_{g+1} \in \text{split}\big(x_{(g+1)1} (\!| p_{g+1}, \text{len}(p_{g+1}) |\!)' x_{(g+1)2}\big),$$

$x_{(g+1)1} x_{(g+1)2} = x_{g+1}$, and $\check{\bar{x}}_{g+1}$. As

$$\bar{x}_{g+1} \in \text{split}\big(x_{(g+1)1} (\!| p_{g+1}, \text{len}(p_{g+1}) |\!)' x_{(g+1)2}\big),$$

$(\!| p, i |\!)' = (\!| p_{g+1}, \text{len}(p_{g+1}) |\!)' \in \Psi'$, and $i = \text{len}(p)$, only productions from $\bar{P}_2$ can be used. Let

$$x_{g+2} = u_{(g+2)1} A_{(g+2)1} \dots u_{(g+2)j} A_{(g+2)j} u_{(g+2)(j+1)},$$

where $u_{(g+2)1}, \dots, u_{(g+2)(j+1)} \in V^*$, $A_{(g+2)1}, \dots, A_{(g+2)j} \in V - T$, for some $j \geq 1$. We distinguish the following three forms of $\bar{x}_{g+1}$:

1. $\text{split}(r_1)\big\langle r_2 (\!| p_{g+1}, \text{len}(p_{g+1}) |\!)' r_3\big\rangle \text{split}(r_4 A_{(g+2)1} r_5)$ such that

   $$x_{g+2} = r_1 r_2 r_3 r_4 A_{(g+2)1} r_5.$$

   Then, a production constructed in (2a) can be used, and by its application, we obtain a sentential form

   $$\bar{x}'_{g+2} = \text{split}(r_1)\langle r_2 r_3\rangle \, \text{split}\big(r_4 (\!| p_{g+2}, 1 |\!) r_5\big).$$

2. $\text{split}(r_1 A_{(g+2)1} r_2)\big\langle r_3 (\!| p_{g+1}, \text{len}(p_{g+1}) |\!)' r_4\big\rangle \text{split}(r_5)$ such that

   $$x_{g+2} = r_1 A_{(g+2)1} r_2 r_3 r_4 r_5.$$

   Then, a production constructed in (2b) can be used, and by its application, we obtain a sentential form

   $$\bar{x}'_{g+2} = \text{split}\big(r_1 (\!| p_{g+2}, 1 |\!) r_2\big)\langle r_3 r_4\rangle \, \text{split}(r_5).$$

3. (a) $\text{split}(r_1)\langle r_2 (\!| p_{g+1}, \text{len}(p_{g+1}) |\!)' r_3 A_{(g+2)1} r_4 \rangle \, \text{split}(r_5)$ such that

$$x_{g+2} = r_1 r_2 r_3 A_{(g+2)1} r_4 r_5.$$

Then, a production constructed in (2c) can be used, and by its application, we obtain a sentential form

$$\bar{x}'_{g+2} = \text{split}(r_1)\langle r_2 r_3 (\!| p_{g+2}, 1 |\!) r_4 \rangle \, \text{split}(r_5).$$

(b) $\text{split}(r_1)\langle r_2 A_{(g+2)1} r_3 (\!| p_{g+1}, \text{len}(p_{g+1}) |\!)' r_4 \rangle \, \text{split}(r_5)$ such that

$$x_{g+2} = r_1 r_2 A_{(g+2)1} r_3 r_4 r_5.$$

Then, a production constructed in (2c) can be used, and by its application, we obtain a sentential form

$$\bar{x}'_{g+2} = \text{split}(r_1)\langle r_2 (\!| p_{g+2}, 1 |\!) r_3 r_4 \rangle \, \text{split}(r_5).$$

In the case when $x_{g+2} \in T^*$, $\bar{x}_{g+1}$ has the form

$$\text{split}(r_1)\langle r_2 (\!| p_{g+1}, \text{len}(p_{g+1}) |\!)' r_3 \rangle \, \text{split}(r_4),$$

where $x_{g+2} = r_1 r_2 r_3 r_4 \in T^*$. Then, a production constructed in (2d) can be used, and by its application, we obtain a sentential form

$$\bar{x}'_{g+2} = \text{split}(r_1)\langle r_2 r_3 \rangle \, \text{split}(r_4).$$

Notice that a production from (2d) is applicable also in the case when $x_{g+2} \notin T^*$ (cases 1 through 3 above). This production removes the symbol from Ψ' from the sentential form. However, as all productions from (2) through (4) require a symbol from Ψ or Ψ', its application for $x_{g+2} \notin T^*$ does not lead to a successful derivation.

As a result, there is a derivation

$$\bar{x}_{g+1} \Rightarrow_{\bar{G}} \bar{x}'_{g+2} \; [p'_{g+1}],$$

where

- $\bar{x}'_{g+2} \in \text{split}\big(x'_{(g+2)1} (\!| p_{g+2}, 1 |\!) x'_{(g+2)2}\big)$, for $x_{g+2} \notin T^*$, or
- $\bar{x}'_{g+2} \in \text{split}(x_{g+2})$, for $x_{g+2} \in T^*$,

with $x'_{(g+2)1} \, \text{lhs}\big((\!| p_{g+2}, 1 |\!)\big) x'_{(g+2)2} = x_{g+2}$, satisfying $\check{\bar{x}}'_{g+2}$.

If. The if part is proved by induction on the number g of simulation steps in a derivation of $\bar{G}$, for $g \geq 0$.

Basis. Let $g = 0$. Then, $\bar{x}'_1 \Rightarrow^0_{\bar{G}} \bar{x}'_1$ and $x_1 \Rightarrow^0_G x_1$.

Induction Hypothesis. Suppose that the claim holds for all derivations of $\bar{G}$ containing k simulation steps, where $k \leq g$, for some $g \geq 0$.

Induction Step. Consider a derivation

$$\bar{x}'_1 \Rrightarrow \bar{x}_1 \Rightarrow_{\bar{G}} \dots \Rrightarrow \bar{x}_{g+1} \Rightarrow_{\bar{G}} \bar{x}'_{g+2}.$$

Since $g + 1 \geq 1$, there exists a derivation

$$\bar{x}'_1 \Rrightarrow \bar{x}_1 \Rightarrow_{\bar{G}} \dots \Rrightarrow \bar{x}_g \Rightarrow_{\bar{G}} \bar{x}'_{g+1} \Rrightarrow \bar{x}_{g+1} \Rightarrow_{\bar{G}} \bar{x}'_{g+2}.$$

By the induction hypothesis, there is a derivation

$$x_1 \Rightarrow_G^g x_{g+1}.$$

As

$$\bar{x}'_{g+1} \in \mathrm{split}\big(x'_{(g+1)1} (\!| p_{g+1}, 1 |\!) x'_{(g+1)2}\big),$$
$$x_{g+1} = x'_{(g+1)1}\, \mathrm{lhs}\big((\!| p_{g+1}, 1 |\!)\big) x'_{(g+1)2},$$

and

$$\bar{x}'_{g+1} \Rrightarrow \bar{x}_{g+1} \Rightarrow_{\bar{G}} \bar{x}'_{g+2},$$

then, by Claim 3, there is also a derivation

$$x_{g+1} \Rightarrow_G x_{g+2}$$

such that

$$\bar{x}'_{g+2} \in \mathrm{split}\big(x'_{(g+2)1} (\!| p_{g+2}, 1 |\!) x'_{(g+2)2}\big),$$
$$x_{g+2} = x'_{(g+2)1}\, \mathrm{lhs}\big((\!| p_{g+2}, 1 |\!)\big) x'_{(g+2)2},$$

or $\bar{x}'_{g+2} \in \mathrm{split}(x_{g+2})$. □

From Claim 1,

$$\bar{S} \Rightarrow_{\bar{G}} \big\langle (\!| p, 1 |\!) \big\rangle.$$

As $\big\langle (\!| p, 1 |\!) \big\rangle \in \mathrm{split}\big((\!| p, 1 |\!)\big)$ and $S = \mathrm{lhs}\big((\!| p, 1 |\!)\big)$, the simulation of G as described in Claim 4 can be performed, so

$$\big\langle (\!| p, 1 |\!) \big\rangle \Rightarrow_{\bar{G}}^* u\ [\Phi],$$

where Φ is a sequence of productions from $\bar{P}_2 \cup \bar{P}_3 \cup \bar{P}_4$. If a successful derivation is simulated, then we obtain $u = \langle a_1 \rangle \dots \langle a_n \rangle$, where $n \geq 1$ and $a_1, \dots, a_n \in T$. Finally, by using productions from $\bar{P}_5$, we obtain

$$u \Rightarrow_{\bar{G}}^+ v,$$

where $v = a_1 \dots a_n$. Therefore, every string during whose generation G erases nonterminals in a generalized k-limited way can be generated by a propagating scattered context grammar $\bar{G}$. ■

Corollary 4.16. *$\mathscr{L}(PSC) = \mathscr{L}(SC, \varepsilon, i)$, for all $i \geq 0$.* ■

In this section, we have proved that every scattered context grammar that erases its nonterminals in a generalized k-limited way can be converted to an equivalent propagating scattered context grammar. This main result of this section gives rise to several open problems, two of which deserve our special attention.

Open Problem 4.17. Is it true that a scattered context grammar G can be converted to a propagating scattered context grammar $\bar{G}$ if and only if G erases its nonterminals in a generalized k-limited way?

In terms of decidability, we want to answer the next question, which closes the present section.

Open Problem 4.18. Let k be any non-negative integer and G be any scattered context grammar. Is there an algorithm that decides whether G erases its nonterminals in a generalized k-limited way?

CHAPTER 5

Restrictions and extensions

This chapter introduces several restricted and extended versions of scattered context grammars. Two types of these modifications are discussed—modifications that only change the definition of the derivation step, and modifications of the whole concept of scattered context grammars. Most importantly, we investigate the generative power of scattered context grammars modified in this way.

5.1 n-Limited derivations

As formal language theory has always studied various left restrictions placed on grammatical derivations, we investigate this classical topic in terms of propagating scattered context grammars in this section as well. More specifically, we discuss the language families generated by propagating scattered context grammars and propagating unordered scattered context grammars whose derivations are n-limited, where n is a positive integer. In these derivations, a scattered context production is always applied within the first n occurrences of nonterminals in the current sentential form. We demonstrate that this restriction gives rise to an infinite hierarchy of language families. In addition, we prove that every family of this hierarchy is properly included in the family of context-sensitive languages. Based upon this proper inclusion, we obtain several conclusions and formulate new open problems. Perhaps most importantly, we point out that the language family generated by propagating scattered context grammars that make derivations in the above n-limited way is properly contained in the context-sensitive language family, so in this sense, we partially solve Open Problem 3.28. First, we define n-limited derivations formally.

Definition 5.1. Let $G = (V, T, P, S)$ be a propagating scattered context grammar. If

$$(A_1, \dots, A_k) \to (x_1, \dots, x_k) \in P,$$

$u = u_1 A_1 \dots u_k A_k u_{k+1}$, and $v = u_1 x_1 \dots u_k x_k u_{k+1}$, where $u_i \in V^*$, for all $1 \leq i \leq k + 1$, and $u \Rightarrow_G v$ satisfies

$$|u_1 A_1 \dots u_k A_k|_{V-T} \leq n,$$

then the derivation step is *n-limited*, symbolically written as

$$u \ {}_{lim}{\overset{n}{\Rightarrow}}_G \ v.$$

An *n-limited derivation*, denoted by $x \ {}_{lim}{\overset{n}{\Rightarrow}}_G^* \ y$, is a derivation in which every derivation step $u \ {}_{lim}{\overset{j}{\Rightarrow}}_G \ v$ satisfies $j \leq n$. Define the *language of degree n* generated by G as

$$L(G, lim, n) = \{x : x \in T^*, S \ {}_{lim}{\overset{n}{\Rightarrow}}_G^* \ x\}.$$

The family of languages of degree n generated by propagating scattered context grammars is denoted by $\mathscr{L}(PSC, lim, n)$, and

$$\mathscr{L}(PSC, lim, \infty) = \bigcup_{i=1}^{\infty} \mathscr{L}(PSC, lim, i).$$

Analogously, we define n-limited derivations for propagating unordered scattered context grammars. The family of languages of degree n generated by propagating unordered scattered context grammars is denoted by $\mathscr{L}(PSC, un, lim, n)$, and

$$\mathscr{L}(PSC, un, lim, \infty) = \bigcup_{i=1}^{\infty} \mathscr{L}(PSC, un, lim, i).$$

We prove the main result, $\mathscr{L}(PSC, lim, n) = \mathscr{L}(ST, n)$, for all $n \geq 1$, by demonstrating that $\mathscr{L}(ST, n) \subseteq \mathscr{L}(PSC, lim, n)$ and $\mathscr{L}(PSC, lim, n) \subseteq \mathscr{L}(ST, n)$ in Lemmas 5.2 and 5.3, respectively.

Lemma 5.2. $\mathscr{L}(ST, n) \subseteq \mathscr{L}(PSC, lim, n)$, *for all* $n \geq 1$.

Proof. Let $G = (V, T, K, P, S, p_0)$ be a state grammar of degree n. Set

$$\begin{aligned}
N_1 &= \{\langle A, p, k\rangle : A \in V - T, p \in K, 1 \leq k \leq n\},\\
N_2 &= \{\langle \hat{A}, p, k\rangle : A \in V - T, p \in K, 1 \leq k \leq n\},\\
N_3 &= \{\langle A', p, n-1\rangle : A \in V - T, p \in K\},\\
N_4 &= \{\hat{A} : A \in V - T\}.
\end{aligned}$$

Set $\alpha(p) = \{A : (A, p) \rightarrow (x, q) \in P\}$, for each $p \in K$. Define the propagating scattered context grammar

$$\bar{G} = \big(V \cup N_1 \cup N_2 \cup N_3 \cup N_4 \cup \{\bar{S}\}, T, \bar{P}, \bar{S}\big)$$

with $\bar{P}$ constructed as follows (throughout the construction, we add intuitive explanation of the purpose of the constructed productions):

1. Add $(\bar{S}) \rightarrow (\langle \hat{S}, p_0, 1\rangle)$ to $\bar{P}$.
2. For each $A_1, \ldots, A_k \in V - T$, where $1 \leq k \leq n$, each

$$(A_r, p) \rightarrow (x_1 B_1 \ldots x_t B_t x_{t+1}, q) \in P,$$

where $1 \le r \le k$, $B_1, \ldots, B_t \in V - T$, $x_1, \ldots, x_{t+1} \in T^*$, for some $t \ge 0$, $A_i \notin \alpha(p)$, for every $1 \le i < r$ ($A_1, \ldots, A_k$ denote the first k nonterminals in the sentential form; k is the number of nonterminals present in the sentential form if it contains fewer than n nonterminals, otherwise $k = n$; A_r is the nonterminal whose rewriting is simulated; t is the number of nonterminals appearing on the right-hand side of the simulated production),

(a) and $r + t - 1 > n$, add

(i) (used when the sentential form contains more than n nonterminals)

$$\begin{aligned}&(\langle A_1, p, n\rangle, \ldots, \langle A_{r-1}, p, n\rangle, \langle A_r, p, n\rangle,\\ &\langle A_{r+1}, p, n\rangle, \ldots, \langle A_n, p, n\rangle)\\ \to\ &(\langle A_1, q, n\rangle, \ldots, \langle A_{r-1}, q, n\rangle,\\ &x_1\langle B_1, q, n\rangle \ldots x_{n-r+1}\langle B_{n-r+1}, q, n\rangle\\ &x_{n-r+2}B_{n-r+2} \ldots x_t B_t x_{t+1}, A_{r+1}, \ldots, A_n)\end{aligned}$$

to $\bar{P}$;

(ii) (used when the sentential form contains at most n nonterminals and A_r is not the last nonterminal)
if $r < k$, add

$$\begin{aligned}&(\langle A_1, p, k\rangle, \ldots, \langle A_{r-1}, p, k\rangle, \langle A_r, p, k\rangle,\\ &\langle A_{r+1}, p, k\rangle, \ldots, \langle A_{k-1}, p, k\rangle, \langle \hat{A}_k, p, k\rangle)\\ \to\ &(\langle A_1, q, n\rangle, \ldots, \langle A_{r-1}, q, n\rangle,\\ &x_1\langle B_1, q, n\rangle \ldots x_{n-r+1}\langle B_{n-r+1}, q, n\rangle\\ &x_{n-r+2}B_{n-r+2} \ldots x_t B_t x_{t+1}, A_{r+1}, \ldots, A_{k-1}, \hat{A}_k)\end{aligned}$$

to $\bar{P}$;

(iii) (used when the sentential form contains at most n nonterminals and A_r is the last nonterminal)
if $r = k$, add

$$\begin{aligned}&(\langle A_1, p, k\rangle, \ldots, \langle A_{k-1}, p, k\rangle, \langle \hat{A}_k, p, k\rangle)\\ \to\ &(\langle A_1, q, n\rangle, \ldots, \langle A_{k-1}, q, n\rangle,\\ &x_1\langle B_1, q, n\rangle \ldots x_{n-k+1}\langle B_{n-k+1}, q, n\rangle\\ &x_{n-k+2}B_{n-k+2} \ldots x_{t-1}B_{t-1}x_t\hat{B}_t x_{t+1})\end{aligned}$$

to $\bar{P}$;

(b) and $r + t - 1 \le n$, $k + t - 1 > n$, add

(i) (used when the sentential form contains more than n nonterminals)

$$\begin{aligned}&(\langle A_1, p, n\rangle, \ldots, \langle A_{r-1}, p, n\rangle, \langle A_r, p, n\rangle,\\ &\ \langle A_{r+1}, p, n\rangle, \ldots, \langle A_{n-t+1}, p, n\rangle,\\ &\ \langle A_{n-t+2}, p, n\rangle, \ldots, \langle A_n, p, n\rangle)\\ \rightarrow\ &(\langle A_1, q, n\rangle, \ldots, \langle A_{r-1}, q, n\rangle, x_1\langle B_1, q, n\rangle \ldots x_t\langle B_t, q, n\rangle x_{t+1},\\ &\ \langle A_{r+1}, q, n\rangle, \ldots, \langle A_{n-t+1}, q, n\rangle, A_{n-t+2}, \ldots, A_n)\end{aligned}$$

to $\bar{P}$;

(ii) (used when the sentential form contains at most n nonterminals and A_r is not the last nonterminal)
if $r < k$, add

$$\begin{aligned}&(\langle A_1, p, k\rangle, \ldots, \langle A_{r-1}, p, k\rangle, \langle A_r, p, k\rangle,\\ &\ \langle A_{r+1}, p, k\rangle, \ldots, \langle A_{n-t+1}, p, k\rangle,\\ &\ \langle A_{n-t+2}, p, k\rangle, \ldots, \langle A_{k-1}, p, k\rangle, \langle \hat{A}_k, p, k\rangle)\\ \rightarrow\ &(\langle A_1, q, n\rangle, \ldots, \langle A_{r-1}, q, n\rangle, x_1\langle B_1, q, n\rangle \ldots x_t\langle B_t, q, n\rangle x_{t+1},\\ &\ \langle A_{r+1}, q, n\rangle, \ldots, \langle A_{n-t+1}, q, n\rangle, A_{n-t+2}, \ldots, A_{k-1}, \hat{A}_k)\end{aligned}$$

to $\bar{P}$;

(c) and $k + t - 1 \leq n$, and

(i) if $t = 0$, add

(A) (used when the sentential form contains more than n nonterminals and A_r is rewritten to $x_1 \in T^*$)

$$\begin{aligned}&(\langle A_1, p, n\rangle, \ldots, \langle A_{r-1}, p, n\rangle, \langle A_r, p, n\rangle,\\ &\ \langle A_{r+1}, p, n\rangle, \ldots, \langle A_n, p, n\rangle)\\ \rightarrow\ &(\langle A'_1, q, n-1\rangle, \ldots, \langle A'_{r-1}, q, n-1\rangle, x_1,\\ &\ \langle A'_{r+1}, q, n-1\rangle, \ldots, \langle A'_n, q, n-1\rangle),\end{aligned}$$

(B) (used immediately after (2.c.i.A))

$$\begin{aligned}&(\langle A'_1, q, n-1\rangle, \ldots, \langle A'_{r-1}, q, n-1\rangle,\\ &\ \langle A'_{r+1}, q, n-1\rangle, \ldots, \langle A'_n, q, n-1\rangle, A_{n+1})\\ \rightarrow\ &(\langle A_1, q, n\rangle, \ldots, \langle A_{r-1}, q, n\rangle,\\ &\ \langle A_{r+1}, q, n\rangle, \ldots, \langle A_n, q, n\rangle, \langle A_{n+1}, q, n\rangle),\end{aligned}$$

where $A_{n+1} \in (V - T) \cup N_4$, to $\bar{P}$;

(ii) (used when the sentential form contains at most n nonterminals and A_r is not the last nonterminal) if $r < k$, add

$$\begin{aligned}
&\big(\langle A_1, p, k\rangle, \ldots, \langle A_{r-1}, p, k\rangle,\\
&\langle A_r, p, k\rangle, \langle A_{r+1}, p, k\rangle, \ldots, \langle A_{k-1}, p, k\rangle, \langle \hat{A}_k, p, k\rangle\big)\\
\rightarrow &\big(\langle A_1, q, k+t-1\rangle, \ldots, \langle A_{r-1}, q, k+t-1\rangle,\\
&x_1\langle B_1, q, k+t-1\rangle \ldots x_t\langle B_t, q, k+t-1\rangle x_{t+1},\\
&\langle A_{r+1}, q, k+t-1\rangle, \ldots, \langle A_{k-1}, q, k+t-1\rangle,\\
&\langle \hat{A}_k, q, k+t-1\rangle\big)
\end{aligned}$$

to $\bar{P}$;

(iii) (used when the sentential form contains at most n nonterminals and A_r is the last nonterminal)
if $r = k$

(A) and $k > 1$ or $t \neq 0$, add

$$\begin{aligned}
&\big(\langle A_1, p, k\rangle, \ldots, \langle A_{k-1}, p, k\rangle, \langle \hat{A}_k, p, k\rangle\big)\\
\rightarrow &\big(\langle A_1, q, k+t-1\rangle, \ldots, \langle A_{k-1}, q, k+t-1\rangle,\\
&x_1\langle B_1, q, k+t-1\rangle \ldots x_{t-1}\langle B_{t-1}, q, k+t-1\rangle\\
&x_t\langle \hat{B}_t, q, k+t-1\rangle x_{t+1}\big)
\end{aligned}$$

to $\bar{P}$;

(B) (simulates the last derivation step of G)
and $k = 1$, $t = 0$, add
$\big(\langle \hat{A}_1, p, 1\rangle\big) \rightarrow (x_1)$ to $\bar{P}$.

Basic Idea.
For every sentential form (x, p) of G, strings u and v can be found so that $x = uv$ and either $|u|_{V-T} = n$ and $|v|_{V-T} \geq 1$ or $|u|_{V-T} = k$, where $k \leq n$, and $|v|_{V-T} = 0$. As a result, only nonterminals occurring in u can be rewritten by a production of G. As n is a finite number, it is possible to construct a propagating scattered context grammar $\bar{G}$ that rewrites all nonterminals occurring in u in every derivation step. In this way, $\bar{G}$ simulates the rewriting of the leftmost nonterminal for a given state by considering all possible forms of u and constructing productions of $\bar{G}$ accordingly. The constructed grammar simulates every sentential form of G by its division into two parts. The first part contains only nonterminals from $N_1 \cup N_2$, which can be rewritten by the constructed productions. The other part contains nonterminals from $(V - T) \cup N_4$, which no production rewrites (with the exception of the productions from (2.c.i.B) whose application is explained next).

By rewriting a nonterminal in the first part, the number of nonterminals appearing in the first part might exceed n. To prevent this, the constructed productions move the extra nonterminals from the end of the first part to the beginning of the second part (see all productions from (2.a) and (2.b)), so the number of nonterminals appearing in the first part is no more than n.

Apart from adding nonterminals, a nonterminal can be removed from the first part as well. This happens when a nonterminal is rewritten to a string over T. In this case, a special action is in order when the second part contains some nonterminals. For this purpose, the grammar records the last nonterminal of the sentential form. If the last nonterminal appears within the first part, it is represented by a symbol from N_2, and if it occurs in the second part, it is represented by a symbol from N_4. Now, consider the case when a nonterminal from the first part is rewritten to a string over T and the second part contains some nonterminals; in other words, a symbol from N_2 does not appear at the end of the first part. In this case, the first nonterminal of the second part is removed, converted to a symbol from N_1 (or N_2 if it is the last nonterminal), and added to the end of the first part (see the productions introduced in (2.c.i.A) and (2.c.i.B)). Therefore, the number of nonterminals that appear in the first part remains n. If a symbol from N_2 appears at the end of the first part, the second part can be ignored because it does not contain any nonterminal. In this way, the grammar guarantees that if the first part of the sentential form contains fewer than n nonterminals, the second part does not contain any nonterminal at all. Productions from (2.c.ii) and (2.c.iii) are used when the second part remains empty after the sentential form is rewritten.

Every production changes the current state p incorporated into every nonterminal of the first part to the new state q. In addition, each of these nonterminals records the number of nonterminals, k, occurring in the first part of the sentential form and this number is updated after every single derivation step. Therefore, productions that simulate the rewriting in a different state and productions that rewrite a different number of nonterminals are not applicable.

Formal Proof.
By examining the constructed productions, we see that the derivations of G and $\bar{G}$ resemble each other very much. In most cases, one production of $\bar{G}$ simulates one production of G. However, when a production from (2.c.i.A) is applied, this application is followed by (2.c.i.B), so in this case, one derivation step in G corresponds to two derivation steps in $\bar{G}$. Formally, we define the term *sf-correspondence* between the sentential forms of G and $\bar{G}$ by the following recursive definition, and use this term in the formulation of Claim 1:

1. The sentential form (S, p_0) of G sf-corresponds to the sentential form $\langle \hat{S}, p_0, 1\rangle$ in $\bar{G}$.
2. Let $(x, p) \Rightarrow_G (y, q)\ [\alpha]$, where (x, p) sf-corresponds to some $\bar{x}$ in $\bar{G}$.
   - If $(x, p) \Rightarrow_G (y, q)\ [\alpha]$ satisfies $|x|_{V-T} > n$, $k + t - 1 \le n$, and $t = 0$, then (y, q) sf-corresponds to $\bar{z}$ in $\bar{G}$, where $\bar{x} \Rightarrow_{\bar{G}}^2 \bar{z}\ [\bar{\alpha}_1\bar{\alpha}_2]$, $\bar{\alpha}_1$ and $\bar{\alpha}_2$ are productions from (2.c.i.A) and (2.c.i.B), respectively, whose construction is based on α.
   - Otherwise, (y, q) sf-corresponds to $\bar{y}$ in $\bar{G}$, where $\bar{x} \Rightarrow_{\bar{G}} \bar{y}\ [\bar{\alpha}]$ and the construction of $\bar{\alpha}$ is based on α.

Claim 1. Every sentential form $(y_1A_1 \dots y_mA_my_{m+1}, p)$ of G, where $y_1, \dots, y_{m+1} \in T^*$, $p \in K$, $A_1, \dots, A_m \in V - T$, for some $m \ge 0$, sf-corresponds to one of the following sentential forms in $\bar{G}$:

1. $y_1\langle A_1, p, m\rangle \dots y_{m-1}\langle A_{m-1}, p, m\rangle y_m\langle \hat{A}_m, p, m\rangle y_{m+1}$, for $m \leq n$;
2. $y_1\langle A_1, p, n\rangle \dots y_n\langle A_n, p, n\rangle y_{n+1}A_{n+1} \dots y_{m-1}A_{m-1}y_m\hat{A}_m y_{m+1}$, for $m > n$.

Proof. Every derivation in $\bar{G}$ starts by the production from (1), and this production is not used during the rest of the derivation process, so

$$S \Rightarrow_{\bar{G}} \langle \hat{S}, p_0, 1\rangle.$$

The rest of the claim is proved by induction on length h of derivations, for $h \geq 0$.

Basis. Let $h = 0$. Then, $(S, p_0) \Rightarrow_G^0 (S, p_0)$ corresponds to $\langle \hat{S}, p_0, 1\rangle \Rightarrow_{\bar{G}}^0 \langle \hat{S}, p_0, 1\rangle$.

Induction Hypothesis. Suppose that the claim holds for all derivations of length h or less, for some $h \geq 0$.

Induction Step. First, consider a sentential form $(y_1A_1 \dots y_mA_my_{m+1}, p)$ of G, where $m \leq n$, and a production

$$(A_r, p) \to (x_1B_1 \dots x_tB_tx_{t+1}, q) \in P,$$

where $1 \leq r \leq m$, $B_1, \dots, B_t \in V - T$, $x_1, \dots, x_{t+1} \in T^*$, for some $t \geq 0$, that is applicable to the above sentential form (that is, $A_i \notin \alpha(p)$, for every $1 \leq i < r$). Then,

$$\begin{aligned}&(y_1A_1 \dots y_{r-1}A_{r-1}y_rA_ry_{r+1}A_{r+1} \dots y_mA_my_{m+1}, p)\\ \Rightarrow_G\ &(y_1A_1 \dots y_{r-1}A_{r-1}y_rx_1B_1 \dots x_tB_tx_{t+1}y_{r+1}A_{r+1} \dots y_mA_my_{m+1}, q).\end{aligned}$$

By the induction hypothesis, for $m \leq n$, the sentential form of $\bar{G}$ sf-corresponding to

$$(y_1A_1 \dots y_{r-1}A_{r-1}y_rA_ry_{r+1}A_{r+1} \dots y_mA_my_{m+1}, p)$$

is of the form

$$y_1\langle A_1, p, m\rangle \dots y_r\langle A_r, p, m\rangle \dots y_{m-1}\langle A_{m-1}, p, m\rangle y_m\langle \hat{A}_m, p, m\rangle y_{m+1}.$$

Now, one of the productions from (2.a.ii), (2.a.iii), (2.b.ii), (2.c.ii), or (2.c.iii) is applicable depending on the simulated production, m, and n:

- If $r + t - 1 > n$ and $r < m$, then a production introduced in (2.a.ii) is applied, so

$$\begin{aligned}&y_1\langle A_1, p, m\rangle \dots y_{r-1}\langle A_{r-1}, p, m\rangle y_r\langle A_r, p, m\rangle\\ &y_{r+1}\langle A_{r+1}, p, m\rangle \dots y_{m-1}\langle A_{m-1}, p, m\rangle y_m\langle \hat{A}_m, p, m\rangle y_{m+1}\\ {}_{lim}^{\ n}\Rightarrow_{\bar{G}}\ &y_1\langle A_1, q, n\rangle \dots y_{r-1}\langle A_{r-1}, q, n\rangle y_r\\ &x_1\langle B_1, q, n\rangle \dots x_{n-r+1}\langle B_{n-r+1}, q, n\rangle x_{n-r+2}B_{n-r+2} \dots x_tB_tx_{t+1}\\ &y_{r+1}A_{r+1} \dots y_{m-1}A_{m-1}y_m\hat{A}_m y_{m+1}.\end{aligned}$$

- If $r + t - 1 > n$ and $r = m$, then a production introduced in (2.a.iii) is applied, so

$$\begin{aligned} & y_1\langle A_1, p, m\rangle \dots y_{m-1}\langle A_{m-1}, p, m\rangle y_m\langle \hat{A}_m, p, m\rangle y_{m+1} \\ {}_{lim}^{\;\,n}\!\Rightarrow_{\bar{G}}\; & y_1\langle A_1, q, n\rangle \dots y_{m-1}\langle A_{m-1}, q, n\rangle y_m \\ & x_1\langle B_1, q, n\rangle \dots x_{n-m+1}\langle B_{n-m+1}, q, n\rangle \\ & x_{n-m+2}B_{n-m+2} \dots x_{t-1}B_{t-1}x_t\hat{B}_t x_{t+1}. \end{aligned}$$

- If $r + t - 1 \leq n$, $m + t - 1 > n$, and $r < m$, then a production introduced in (2.b.ii) is applied, so

$$\begin{aligned} & y_1\langle A_1, p, m\rangle \dots y_{r-1}\langle A_{r-1}, p, m\rangle y_r\langle A_r, p, m\rangle \\ & y_{r+1}\langle A_{r+1}, p, m\rangle \dots y_{m-1}\langle A_{m-1}, p, m\rangle y_m\langle \hat{A}_m, p, m\rangle y_{m+1} \\ {}_{lim}^{\;\,n}\!\Rightarrow_{\bar{G}}\; & y_1\langle A_1, q, n\rangle \dots y_{r-1}\langle A_{r-1}, q, n\rangle y_r x_1\langle B_1, q, n\rangle \dots x_t\langle B_t, q, n\rangle x_{t+1} \\ & y_{r+1}\langle A_{r+1}, q, n\rangle \dots y_{n-t+1}\langle A_{n-t+1}, q, n\rangle \\ & y_{n-t+2}A_{n-t+2} \dots y_{m-1}A_{m-1}y_m\hat{A}_m y_{m+1}. \end{aligned}$$

- If $m + t - 1 \leq n$ and $r < m$, then a production introduced in (2.c.ii) is applied, so

$$\begin{aligned} & y_1\langle A_1, p, m\rangle \dots y_{r-1}\langle A_{r-1}, p, m\rangle y_r\langle A_r, p, m\rangle \\ & y_{r+1}\langle A_{r+1}, p, m\rangle \dots y_{m-1}\langle A_{m-1}, p, m\rangle y_m\langle \hat{A}_m, p, m\rangle y_{m+1} \\ {}_{lim}^{\;\,n}\!\Rightarrow_{\bar{G}}\; & y_1\langle A_1, q, m+t-1\rangle \dots y_{r-1}\langle A_{r-1}, q, m+t-1\rangle y_r \\ & x_1\langle B_1, q, m+t-1\rangle \dots x_t\langle B_t, q, m+t-1\rangle x_{t+1} \\ & y_{r+1}\langle A_{r+1}, q, m+t-1\rangle \dots y_{m-1}\langle A_{m-1}, q, m+t-1\rangle \\ & y_m\langle \hat{A}_m, q, m+t-1\rangle y_{m+1}. \end{aligned}$$

- If $m + t - 1 \leq n$ and $r = m$, and $m > 1$ or $t \neq 0$, then a production introduced in (2.c.iii.A) is applied, so

$$\begin{aligned} & y_1\langle A_1, p, m\rangle \dots y_{m-1}\langle A_{m-1}, p, m\rangle y_m\langle \hat{A}_m, p, m\rangle y_{m+1} \\ {}_{lim}^{\;\,n}\!\Rightarrow_{\bar{G}}\; & y_1\langle A_1, q, m+t-1\rangle \dots y_{m-1}\langle A_{m-1}, q, m+t-1\rangle y_m \\ & x_1\langle B_1, q, m+t-1\rangle \dots x_{t-1}\langle B_{t-1}, q, m+t-1\rangle \\ & x_t\langle \hat{B}_t, q, m+t-1\rangle x_{t+1}y_{m+1}. \end{aligned}$$

- If $m = 1$, $t = 0$, then a production introduced in (2.c.iii.B) is applied, so

$$y_1\langle \hat{A}_1, p, 1\rangle y_2 \;{}_{lim}^{\;\,n}\!\Rightarrow_{\bar{G}}\; y_1x_1y_2.$$

  Observe that this production removes the last symbol from $N_1 \cup N_2$ from the sentential form and that this symbol appears on the left-hand side of every production introduced in (2). As a result, this production can be used only during the very last derivation step.

Second, consider a sentential form $(y_1A_1 \dots y_mA_my_{m+1}, p)$ of G, where $m > n$, and a production

$$(A_r, p) \rightarrow (x_1B_1 \dots x_tB_tx_{t+1}, q) \in P,$$

where $1 \leq r \leq m$, $B_1, \ldots, B_t \in V - T$, $x_1, \ldots, x_{t+1} \in T^*$, for some $t \geq 0$, that is applicable to the above sentential form. Then,

$$\begin{aligned}&(y_1 A_1 \ldots y_{r-1} A_{r-1} y_r A_r y_{r+1} A_{r+1} \ldots y_n A_n \ldots y_m A_m y_{m+1}, p)\\ \Rightarrow_G\ &(y_1 A_1 \ldots y_{r-1} A_{r-1} y_r x_1 B_1 \ldots x_t B_t x_{t+1}\\ &y_{r+1} A_{r+1} \ldots y_n A_n \ldots y_m A_m y_{m+1}, q).\end{aligned}$$

By the induction hypothesis, for $m > n$, the sentential form of $\bar{G}$ sf-corresponding to

$$(y_1 A_1 \ldots y_{r-1} A_{r-1} y_r A_r y_{r+1} A_{r+1} \ldots y_n A_n \ldots y_m A_m y_{m+1}, p)$$

is of the form

$$y_1 \langle A_1, p, n\rangle \ldots y_r \langle A_r, p, n\rangle \ldots y_n \langle A_n, p, n\rangle y_{n+1} A_{n+1} \ldots y_{m-1} A_{m-1} y_m \hat{A}_m y_{m+1}.$$

Now, one of the productions from (2.a.i), (2.b.i), and (2.c.i.A) is applicable depending on the simulated production, m, and n:

- If $r + t - 1 > n$, then a production introduced in (2.a.i) is applied, so

$$\begin{aligned}&y_1 \langle A_1, p, n\rangle \ldots y_{r-1} \langle A_{r-1}, p, n\rangle y_r \langle A_r, p, n\rangle\\ &y_{r+1} \langle A_{r+1}, p, n\rangle \ldots y_n \langle A_n, p, n\rangle\\ &y_{n+1} A_{n+1} \ldots y_{m-1} A_{m-1} y_m \hat{A}_m y_{m+1}\\ {}_{lim}^{\;n}\!\!\Rightarrow_{\bar{G}}\ &y_1 \langle A_1, q, n\rangle \ldots y_{r-1} \langle A_{r-1}, q, n\rangle y_r\\ &x_1 \langle B_1, q, n\rangle \ldots x_{n-r+1} \langle B_{n-r+1}, q, n\rangle x_{n-r+2} B_{n-r+2} \ldots x_t B_t x_{t+1}\\ &y_{r+1} A_{r+1} \ldots y_n A_n y_{n+1} A_{n+1} \ldots y_{m-1} A_{m-1} y_m \hat{A}_m y_{m+1}.\end{aligned}$$

- If $r + t - 1 \leq n$ and $m + t - 1 > n$, then a production introduced in (2.b.i) is applied, so

$$\begin{aligned}&y_1 \langle A_1, p, n\rangle \ldots y_{r-1} \langle A_{r-1}, p, n\rangle y_r \langle A_r, p, n\rangle\\ &y_{r+1} \langle A_{r+1}, p, n\rangle \ldots y_{n-t+1} \langle A_{n-t+1}, p, n\rangle\\ &y_{n-t+2} \langle A_{n-t+2}, p, n\rangle \ldots y_n \langle A_n, p, n\rangle\\ &y_{n+1} A_{n+1} \ldots y_{m-1} A_{m-1} y_m \hat{A}_m y_{m+1}\\ {}_{lim}^{\;n}\!\!\Rightarrow_{\bar{G}}\ &y_1 \langle A_1, q, n\rangle \ldots y_{r-1} \langle A_{r-1}, q, n\rangle y_r\\ &x_1 \langle B_1, q, n\rangle \ldots x_t \langle B_t, q, n\rangle x_{t+1}\\ &y_{r+1} \langle A_{r+1}, q, n\rangle \ldots y_{n-t+1} \langle A_{n-t+1}, q, n\rangle\\ &y_{n-t+2} A_{n-t+2} \ldots y_n A_n y_{n+1} A_{n+1} \ldots y_{m-1} A_{m-1} y_m \hat{A}_m y_{m+1}.\end{aligned}$$

- If $m + t - 1 \leq n$ and $t = 0$, then a production introduced in (2.c.i.A) is applied, so

$$\begin{aligned}&y_1 \langle A_1, p, n\rangle \ldots y_{r-1} \langle A_{r-1}, p, n\rangle y_r \langle A_r, p, n\rangle\\ &y_{r+1} \langle A_{r+1}, p, n\rangle \ldots y_n \langle A_n, p, n\rangle\\ &y_{n+1} A_{n+1} \ldots y_{m-1} A_{m-1} y_m \hat{A}_m y_{m+1}\\ {}_{lim}^{\;n}\!\!\Rightarrow_{\bar{G}}\ &y_1 \langle A'_1, q, n-1\rangle \ldots y_{r-1} \langle A'_{r-1}, q, n-1\rangle y_r x_1\\ &y_{r+1} \langle A'_{r+1}, q, n-1\rangle \ldots y_n \langle A'_n, q, n-1\rangle\\ &y_{n+1} A_{n+1} \ldots y_{m-1} A_{m-1} y_m \hat{A}_m y_{m+1}.\end{aligned}$$

Recall that the last nonterminal in every sentential form of $\bar{G}$ is from $N_2 \cup N_4$. As $\langle A_n, p, n\rangle \notin N_2 \cup N_4$, there is at least one nonterminal in the sentential form following $\langle A_n, p, n\rangle$. Therefore, a production from (2.c.i.B) can be used. This production rewrites a nonterminal $A \in (V - T) \cup N_4$ in its last component. Because we generate the language of degree n, $A = A_{n+1}$, so

- either

$$\begin{aligned} & y_1\langle A'_1, q, n-1\rangle \dots y_{r-1}\langle A'_{r-1}, q, n-1\rangle y_r x_1 \\ & y_{r+1}\langle A'_{r+1}, q, n-1\rangle \dots y_n\langle A'_n, q, n-1\rangle \\ & y_{n+1}A_{n+1}y_{n+2}A_{n+2}\dots y_{m-1}A_{m-1}y_m\hat{A}_m y_{m+1} \\ {}_{lim}{}^{n}\!\Rightarrow_{\bar{G}}\ & y_1\langle A_1, q, n\rangle \dots y_{r-1}\langle A_{r-1}, q, n\rangle y_r x_1 \\ & y_{r+1}\langle A_{r+1}, q, n\rangle \dots y_n\langle A_n, q, n\rangle \\ & y_{n+1}\langle A_{n+1}, q, n\rangle y_{n+2}A_{n+2}\dots y_{m-1}A_{m-1}y_m\hat{A}_m y_{m+1}, \end{aligned}$$

  for $A_{n+1} \in V - T$,
- or

$$\begin{aligned} & y_1\langle A'_1, q, n-1\rangle \dots y_{r-1}\langle A'_{r-1}, q, n-1\rangle y_r x_1 \\ & y_{r-1}\langle A'_{r+1}, q, n-1\rangle \dots y_n\langle A'_n, q, n-1\rangle y_{n+1}\hat{A}_{n+1}y_{n+2} \\ {}_{lim}{}^{n}\!\Rightarrow_{\bar{G}}\ & y_1\langle A_1, q, n\rangle \dots y_{r-1}\langle A_{r-1}, q, n\rangle y_r x_1 \\ & y_{r+1}\langle A_{r+1}, q, n\rangle \dots y_n\langle A_n, q, n\rangle y_{n+1}\langle \hat{A}_{n+1}, q, n\rangle y_{n+2}, \end{aligned}$$

  for $\hat{A}_{n+1} \in N_4$.

To see that for a given sentential form and a production of G, there exists only one of the above derivations in $\bar{G}$, let us make the following observations:

- Notice that every sentential form of G determines the number of nonterminals m, first $k \leq n$ nonterminals, and the state p. Furthermore, a production of G determines the new state q, $B_1, \dots, B_t$, and the constants r and t. Observe that for any sentential form and a production like these, there exists only one production in $\bar{G}$ that simulates this production.
- The simulating production rewrites all nonterminals from $N_1 \cup N_2$ appearing in the sentential form of $\bar{G}$. Indeed, as k is included in each of these nonterminals, no production rewriting fewer than k nonterminals can be used.
- The last nonterminal of the sentential form in $\bar{G}$ is always from $N_2 \cup N_4$.
- A production of G is properly simulated by the corresponding production of $\bar{G}$—that is, all the constructed productions satisfy $A_i \notin \alpha(p)$, for every $1 \leq i < r$, and p is changed to q in all nonterminals from $N_1 \cup N_2$. In addition, in every nonterminal from $N_1 \cup N_2$, k is properly updated.

Finally, notice that if a sentential form of $\bar{G}$ is of the form (1) or (2) as described in Claim 1, the sentential form obtained after performing a derivation step is of one of these forms as well. As the right-hand side of the production introduced in (1) of the construction is of the form (1), every sentential form obtained during the derivation process satisfies the properties given in Claim 1. □

From Claim 1 and the derivations described in its proof, it is easy to see that $\bar{G}$ rewrites at most n first nonterminals in a sentential form and that $L(G, n) = L(\bar{G}, lim, n)$. ■

Lemma 5.3. *$\mathscr{L}(PSC, lim, n) \subseteq \mathscr{L}(ST, n)$, for all $n \geq 1$.*

Proof. Let $L(G, lim, n)$ be a language of degree n generated by a propagating scattered context grammar $G = (V, T, P, S)$. Set

$$N = \{\langle A, i\rangle : A \in V - T, 1 \leq i \leq n\}.$$

Furthermore, set $K_1 = \{\langle p, i\rangle : p \in P, 0 \leq i < n\}$ and

$$K_2 = \{\langle p, i, j\rangle : p = (A_1, \dots, A_k) \to (x_1, \dots, x_k) \in P, 0 \leq i \leq n, 0 \leq j \leq k\}.$$

Define the state grammar

$$\bar{G} = (V \cup N \cup \{\bar{S}\}, T, K_1 \cup K_2 \cup \{p_0\}, \bar{P}, \bar{S}, p_0)$$

with $\bar{P}$ constructed as follows:

1. For each $p = (S) \to (x) \in P$, add
   $(\bar{S}, p_0) \to (S, \langle p, 0\rangle)$ to $\bar{P}$.
2. For each $A \in V - T$, $p = (A_1, \dots, A_k) \to (x_1, \dots, x_k) \in P, 0 \leq i < n$, add

   (a) $(A, \langle p, i\rangle) \to (\langle A, i+1\rangle, \langle p, i+1\rangle)$,
   (b) $(A, \langle p, i\rangle) \to (\langle A, i+1\rangle, \langle p, i+1, k\rangle)$ to $\bar{P}$.

3. For each $p = (A_1, \dots, A_j, \dots, A_k) \to (x_1, \dots, x_j, \dots, x_k) \in P, q \in P, A \in V - T, 1 \leq i \leq n, 0 \leq j \leq k$, add

   (a) $(\langle A, i\rangle, \langle p, i, j\rangle) \to (A, \langle p, i-1, j\rangle)$,
   (b) if $j \geq 1$, add
   $(\langle A_j, i\rangle, \langle p, i, j\rangle) \to (x_j, \langle p, i-1, j-1\rangle)$ to $\bar{P}$.
   (c) Add $(A, \langle p, 0, 0\rangle) \to (A, \langle q, 0\rangle)$ to $\bar{P}$.

Basic Idea.
Every derivation step of G is simulated in two phases in $\bar{G}$. In the first phase, performed by productions from (2), $\bar{G}$ assigns a sequence number to the first m nonterminals in the sentential form, where $m \leq n$ is selected non-deterministically. The form of the constructed productions guarantees that no nonterminal is skipped during this phase. $\bar{G}$ enters the second phase by a production from (2b). In the second phase, $\bar{G}$ simulates the scattered context production backwards; it starts by simulating the last context-free component of the scattered context production and ends by simulating its first context-free component. The previously numbered nonterminals are processed backwards from this point on; as before, none of them can be skipped. The state of $\bar{G}$ consists of three components. First, it contains the

scattered context production that is being simulated; second, it contains the position of the nonterminal within the sentential form that is being rewritten; finally, it contains the position of the context-free component within the scattered context production whose rewriting is being simulated. If the current nonterminal coincides with the left-hand side of the currently simulated context-free component, the simulation can be performed by a production from (3b). Every nonterminal can be skipped by a production from (3a), which only removes the sequence number assigned during the first phase. Finally, when the simulation of the whole scattered context production is completed (the last component of the state equals 0) and the sequence numbers are removed from all nonterminals (the second component of the state equals 0), the simulation of the following scattered context production can be initiated by a production from (3c). Otherwise, the simulation is unsuccessful and the derivation is blocked.

Formal Proof.
The derivation starts in $\bar{G}$ by a production introduced in (1), and because no production contains $\bar{S}$ on its right-hand side, none of the productions from (1) is used during the rest of the derivation.

Consider a sentential form $u_1 A_1 \dots u_k A_k u_{k+1}$ of G, where $u_1, \dots, u_{k+1} \in V^*$, and a production

$$p = (A_1, \dots, A_k) \to (x_1, \dots, x_k) \in P.$$

Obviously, for a sentential form satisfying $|u_1 A_1 \dots u_k A_k|_{V-T} \leq n$,

$$u_1 A_1 \dots u_k A_k u_{k+1} \ {}_{lim}\!\overset{n}{\Rightarrow}_G \ u_1 x_1 \dots u_k x_k u_{k+1} \ [p].$$

Consider now a sentential form

$$\big(u_1 A_1 \dots u_k A_k u_{k+1}, \langle p, 0 \rangle\big)$$

of $\bar{G}$ corresponding to the above sentential form of G. Notice that $\big(S, \langle q, 0 \rangle\big)$, where $q = (S) \to (x) \in P$, obtained by the application of a production from (1) is a sentential form of this kind as well. To describe the derivation of G, we express

$$\big(u_1 A_1 \dots u_k A_k u_{k+1}, \langle p, 0 \rangle\big)$$

as

$$\big(w_1 B_1 \dots w_m B_m \dots w_n B_n \dots w_t B_t w_{t+1}, \langle p, 0 \rangle\big),$$

where $w_1, \dots, w_{t+1} \in T^*$, $B_1, \dots, B_t \in V - T$, $t = |u_1 A_1 \dots u_k A_k u_{k+1}|_{V-T}$, $B_{l_i} = A_i$, for some $1 \leq l_i \leq m$, for all $1 \leq i \leq k$, and $l_j < l_{j+1}$, for all $1 \leq j \leq k-1$. (Discussion of other possible kinds of this sentential form, for example when $t < n$, is left to the reader.) Then, the derivation performed by productions from (2a) can be expressed as

$$\begin{aligned}
&\big(w_1 B_1 \dots w_m B_m \dots w_t B_t w_{t+1}, \langle p, 0\rangle\big)\\
\Rightarrow_{\bar{G}}\ &\big(w_1 \langle B_1, 1\rangle w_2 B_2 \dots w_m B_m \dots w_t B_t w_{t+1}, \langle p, 1\rangle\big)\\
&\vdots\\
\Rightarrow_{\bar{G}}\ &\big(w_1 \langle B_1, 1\rangle \dots w_{m-1}\langle B_{m-1}, m-1\rangle w_m B_m \dots w_t B_t w_{t+1}, \langle p, m-1\rangle\big).
\end{aligned}$$

Finally, a production from (2b) is used, so

$$\begin{aligned}
&\big(w_1 \langle B_1, 1\rangle \dots w_{m-1}\langle B_{m-1}, m-1\rangle w_m B_m \dots w_t B_t w_{t+1}, \langle p, m-1\rangle\big)\\
\Rightarrow_{\bar{G}}\ &\big(w_1 \langle B_1, 1\rangle \dots w_m\langle B_m, m\rangle w_{m+1} B_{m+1} \dots w_t B_t w_{t+1}, \langle p, m, k\rangle\big).
\end{aligned}$$

Next, productions from (3) simulate all context-free components of p in reverse order. The simulation of $A_k \to x_k$ is performed as follows:

$$\begin{aligned}
&\big(w_1 \langle B_1, 1\rangle \dots w_m\langle B_m, m\rangle w_{m+1} B_{m+1} \dots w_t B_t w_{t+1}, \langle p, m, k\rangle\big)\\
\Rightarrow_{\bar{G}}\ &\big(w_1 \langle B_1, 1\rangle \dots w_{m-1}\langle B_{m-1}, m-1\rangle w_m B_m \dots w_t B_t w_{t+1}, \langle p, m-1, k\rangle\big)\\
&\vdots\\
\Rightarrow_{\bar{G}}\ &\big(w_1 \langle B_1, 1\rangle \dots w_{l_k}\langle B_{l_k}, l_k\rangle w_{l_k+1} B_{l_k+1} \dots w_t B_t w_{t+1}, \langle p, l_k, k\rangle\big)\\
\Rightarrow_{\bar{G}}\ &\big(w_1 \langle B_1, 1\rangle \dots w_{l_k-1}\langle B_{l_k-1}, l_k-1\rangle\\
&\quad w_{l_k} x_k w_{l_k+1} B_{l_k+1} \dots w_t B_t w_{t+1}, \langle p, l_k-1, k-1\rangle\big).
\end{aligned}$$

The context-free components $A_{k-1} \to x_{k-1}, \dots, A_1 \to x_1$ are simulated analogously until a sentential form

$$\big(u_1 x_1 \dots u_k x_k u_{k+1}, \langle p, 0, 0\rangle\big)$$

is obtained. Notice that when a state $\langle p, 0, i\rangle$, where $i \geq 1$, is reached, the derivation is blocked. This means that either in the non-deterministic part of the derivation the value of m was chosen too low so the whole scattered context production cannot be simulated or more than n first nonterminals need to be rewritten to simulate the scattered context production. Finally, a production from (3c) finishes the simulation of p and starts the simulation of some $q \in P$:

$$\begin{aligned}
&\big(u_1 x_1 \dots u_k x_k u_{k+1}, \langle p, 0, 0\rangle\big)\\
\Rightarrow_{\bar{G}}\ &\big(u_1 x_1 \dots u_k x_k u_{k+1}, \langle q, 0\rangle\big).
\end{aligned}$$

This simulation continues until we obtain the sentential form $\big(w, \langle r, 0, 0\rangle\big)$, where $w \in T^*$ and $r \in P$. ■

As $\mathscr{L}(ST, n) \subseteq \mathscr{L}(PSC, lim, n)$ and $\mathscr{L}(PSC, lim, n) \subseteq \mathscr{L}(ST, n)$, for all $n \geq 1$, we obtain the following result.

Theorem 5.4. $\mathscr{L}(PSC, lim, n) = \mathscr{L}(ST, n)$, *for all* $n \geq 1$. ■

Next, we reformulate Theorem 5.4 in terms of $\mathscr{L}(PSC, un, lim, n)$.

Theorem 5.5. *$\mathscr{L}(PSC, un, lim, n) = \mathscr{L}(ST, n)$, for all $n \geq 1$.*

Proof. To prove this theorem, we demonstrate that $\mathscr{L}(ST, n) \subseteq \mathscr{L}(PSC, un, lim, n)$ and $\mathscr{L}(PSC, un, lim, n) \subseteq \mathscr{L}(ST, n)$, for all $n \geq 1$.

The first inclusion can be proved similarly to the proof of Lemma 5.2. However, in this case, the constructed grammar must also record the sequence number of each of the first n nonterminals in the sentential form in order to guarantee that the right component of the unordered scattered context production is used; without this record, any permutation of the unordered scattered context production could be applied. Therefore, the elements of the sets N_1, N_2, and N_3 have to be changed to contain one more component that determines the order of the nonterminal in the sentential form. In addition, each of the constructed productions has to be modified so that it preserves the correct sequence numbers of these nonterminals in every sentential form. This can be easily accomplished because each of these productions rewrites all the nonterminals from $N_1 \cup N_2 \cup N_3$ in the sentential form. The rest of the proof is analogous to the proof of Lemma 5.2 and, therefore, left to the reader.

The second inclusion, $\mathscr{L}(PSC, un, lim, n) \subseteq \mathscr{L}(ST, n)$, can be proved as follows. For any propagating unordered scattered context grammar G of degree n, we can construct a propagating scattered context grammar $\bar{G}$ of the same degree such that $L(G, lim, n) = L(\bar{G}, lim, n)$. Indeed, if we construct $\bar{G}$ so that it contains all possible permutations of every production of G, we obtain a grammar satisfying these properties. Therefore, $L(G, lim, n) = L(\bar{G}, lim, n)$ and $\mathscr{L}(PSC, un, lim, n) \subseteq \mathscr{L}(PSC, lim, n)$. As $\mathscr{L}(PSC, lim, n) = \mathscr{L}(ST, n)$, we obtain $\mathscr{L}(PSC, un, lim, n) \subseteq \mathscr{L}(ST, n)$. ∎

Recall that

$$\mathscr{L}(CF) = \mathscr{L}(ST, 1) \subset \mathscr{L}(ST, 2) \subset \cdots \subset \mathscr{L}(ST, \infty) \subset \mathscr{L}(ST) = \mathscr{L}(CS),$$

where every $\mathscr{L}(ST, n)$, for some $n \geq 1$, is an abstract family of languages (see Theorems 2.32 and 2.33). These properties together with Theorems 5.4 and 5.5 imply the following two corollaries.

Corollary 5.6.

$$\begin{aligned} &\mathscr{L}(PSC, un, lim, 1) = \mathscr{L}(PSC, lim, 1) = \mathscr{L}(ST, 1) = \mathscr{L}(CF) \\ \subset\, &\mathscr{L}(PSC, un, lim, 2) = \mathscr{L}(PSC, lim, 2) = \mathscr{L}(ST, 2) \\ &\vdots \\ \subset\, &\mathscr{L}(PSC, un, lim, \infty) = \mathscr{L}(PSC, lim, \infty) = \mathscr{L}(ST, \infty) \\ \subset\, &\mathscr{L}(CS). \end{aligned}$$

∎

Corollary 5.7. *Every $\mathscr{L}(PSC, lim, n)$ and $\mathscr{L}(PSC, un, lim, n)$, where $n \geq 1$, is an abstract family of languages.* ∎

We have demonstrated that limiting derivations performed by propagating scattered context grammars and propagating unordered scattered context grammars to the first n nonterminals gives rise to an infinite hierarchy of languages. This result is of some practical interest in terms of compilers. When constructing a compiler based on a grammatical model, we usually need to restrict this model in order to make the compiler more effective. The presented result shows that if the model is based on propagating scattered context grammars, by limiting the width of the window in which the context dependency is checked, we also limit the power of the resulting compiler. In certain situations, such as parsing of streamed data, limiting the context dependency checks to a finite window is necessary because the exact length of the input is unknown.

From a theoretical point of view, the achieved results are interesting too. It is known that $\mathscr{L}(PSC, un) \subset \mathscr{L}(PSC)$ (see Corollary 5.20). However, when using n-limited derivations, $\mathscr{L}(PSC, un, lim, n) = \mathscr{L}(PSC, lim, n)$. On the other hand, the definition of n-limited derivations induces the following problem.

Open Problem 5.8. Can we construct ordinary propagating scattered context grammars that automatically perform only n-limited derivations—that is, they make these derivations without any explicitly required n-limited derivation restriction placed on them? If so, can we establish the results of this section for them? How would this modification influence the generative power of propagating unordered scattered context grammars?

5.2 Leftmost derivations

While the previous section discussed a left restriction placed on sentential forms, the present section studies a left restriction placed on the use of productions in propagating scattered context grammars. In essence, this restriction requires that in the current sentential form, every production p is applied so that p rewrites the leftmost possible occurrences of the nonterminals corresponding to its left-hand side. We prove that propagating scattered context grammars restricted in this way are equivalent to context-sensitive grammars. This result is of some interest for two reasons. First, in terms of ordinary propagating scattered context grammars, this equivalence represents a famous long-standing open problem (see Open Problem 3.28). Second, regarding all four grammars underlying the Chomsky hierarchy, analogical restriction does not affect their generative power at all.

From a historical perspective, the equivalence mentioned above was originally established in [15] by a rather complicated and difficult-to-follow proof. Later on, the same result was proved by Masopust and Techet [25] in a simpler way. Naturally, we base this section on the latter.

Definition 5.9. A *propagating scattered context grammar that uses leftmost* or *rightmost derivations* is a propagating scattered context grammar $G = (V, T, P, S)$ whose language is defined as

$$L(G, lm) = \{x : x \in T^*, S \;{}_{lm}\!\Rightarrow_G^* x\}, \text{ or}$$
$$L(G, rm) = \{x : x \in T^*, S \;{}_{rm}\!\Rightarrow_G^* x\},$$

respectively. The family of languages generated by propagating scattered context grammars that use leftmost or rightmost derivations is denoted by $\mathscr{L}(PSC, lm)$ or $\mathscr{L}(PSC, rm)$, respectively.

The following theorem demonstrates that propagating scattered context grammars that perform their derivations in a leftmost way are equivalent to context-sensitive grammars.

Theorem 5.10. $\mathscr{L}(PSC, lm) = \mathscr{L}(CS)$.

Proof. As propagating scattered context grammars do not contain erasing productions, their derivations can be simulated by context-sensitive grammars. As a result, $\mathscr{L}(PSC, lm) \subseteq \mathscr{L}(CS)$. In what follows, we demonstrate that also $\mathscr{L}(CS) \subseteq \mathscr{L}(PSC, lm)$ holds true by demonstrating that for every context-sensitive grammar in Kuroda normal form, there exists an equivalent propagating scattered context grammar that uses leftmost derivations.

Let $G = (V, T, P, S)$ be a context-sensitive grammar in Kuroda normal form (see Definition 2.17). Set

$$N_1 = (V - T) \cup \{\bar{a} : a \in T\}$$

(suppose that $(V - T) \cap \{\bar{a} : a \in T\} = \emptyset$), and $\hat{N}_1 = \{\hat{A} : A \in N_1\}$. Let $n = |N_1|$; then, we denote the elements of N_1 as $\{A_1, \ldots, A_n\}$. Define the homomorphism α from V^* to N_1^* as $\alpha(A) = A$, for each $A \in V - T$, and $\alpha(a) = \bar{a}$, for each $a \in T$. Set

$$\begin{aligned} N_2' &= \{A' : A \in V - T\}, \\ N_3 &= \big\{\langle ab\rangle : a, b \in V\big\}, \\ N_4' &= \big\{\langle Aa\rangle' : A \in V - T, a \in V\big\}, \\ N_5 &= \big\{\langle a, 0\rangle, \langle ab, 0\rangle : a, b \in V\big\} \\ &\cup \big\{\langle a, i, j\rangle : a \in V - T, 1 \le i \le 3, 1 \le j \le n\big\} \\ &\cup \big\{\langle ab, 4\rangle : a, b \in T\big\}. \end{aligned}$$

Without loss of generality, assume that the sets N_1, $\hat{N}_1$, N_2', N_3, N_4', N_5, $\{\bar{S}, X\}$, and T are pairwise disjoint. Define the propagating scattered context grammar

$$\bar{G} = \big(N_1 \cup \hat{N}_1 \cup N_2' \cup N_3 \cup N_4' \cup N_5 \cup \{\bar{S}, X\} \cup T, T, \bar{P}, \bar{S}\big),$$

where $\bar{P}$ is constructed as follows:

1. (a) For each $a \in L(G)$, where $a \in T$, add $(\bar{S}) \to (a)$ to $\bar{P}$.
   (b) For each $S \Rightarrow_G ab$, where $a, b \in V$, add $(\bar{S}) \to (\langle ab, 0\rangle X)$ to $\bar{P}$.
2. For each $a, b, c \in V$, add

   (a) $(\langle a, 0\rangle, \alpha(b)) \to (\alpha(a), \langle b, 0\rangle)$,

(b) $(\alpha(a), \langle b, 0\rangle) \rightarrow (\langle a, 0\rangle, \alpha(b))$,
(c) $(\langle a, 0\rangle, \langle bc\rangle) \rightarrow (\alpha(a), \langle bc, 0\rangle)$,
(d) $(\alpha(a), \langle bc, 0\rangle) \rightarrow (\langle a, 0\rangle, \langle bc\rangle)$ to $\bar{P}$.

3. For each $A \rightarrow a \in P$ and $b \in V$, add

(a) $(\langle A, 0\rangle) \rightarrow (\langle a, 0\rangle)$,
(b) $(\langle Ab, 0\rangle) \rightarrow (\langle ab, 0\rangle)$,
(c) $(\langle bA, 0\rangle) \rightarrow (\langle ba, 0\rangle)$ to $\bar{P}$.

4. For each $A \rightarrow BC \in P$ and $a \in V$, add

(a) $(\langle A, 0\rangle) \rightarrow (B\langle C, 0\rangle)$,
(b) $(\langle Aa, 0\rangle) \rightarrow (B\langle Ca, 0\rangle)$,
(c) $(\langle aA, 0\rangle) \rightarrow (\alpha(a)\langle BC, 0\rangle)$ to $\bar{P}$.

5. For each $AB \rightarrow CD \in P, a \in V, E \in N_3 \cup N_4', F' \in \{B', \langle Ba\rangle'\}, 1 \leq i \leq n$, and $1 \leq j \leq n-1$, add

(a) $(\langle AB, 0\rangle) \rightarrow (\langle CD, 0\rangle)$,
(b) (i) $(\langle A, 0\rangle, B, X) \rightarrow (\langle A, 1, 1\rangle, B', A_1)$,
(ii) $(\langle A, 0\rangle, \langle Ba\rangle, X) \rightarrow (\langle A, 1, 1\rangle, \langle Ba\rangle', A_1)$,
(c) (i) $(\langle A, 1, i\rangle, A_i) \rightarrow (\langle A, 2, i\rangle, \hat{A}_i)$,
(ii) $(\langle A, 2, i\rangle, F', \hat{A}_i) \rightarrow (\langle A, 3, i\rangle, F', A_i)$,
(iii) $(\langle A, 3, j\rangle, E, A_j) \rightarrow (\langle A, 1, j+1\rangle, E, A_{j+1})$,
(d) (i) $(\langle A, 3, n\rangle, B', E, A_n) \rightarrow (\langle C, 0\rangle, D, E, X)$,
(ii) $(\langle A, 3, n\rangle, \langle Ba\rangle', A_n) \rightarrow (\langle C, 0\rangle, \langle Da\rangle, X)$ to $\bar{P}$.

6. For each $a, b, c \in T$, add

(a) $(\langle ab, 0\rangle) \rightarrow (\langle ab, 4\rangle)$,
(b) $(\bar{c}, \langle ab, 4\rangle) \rightarrow (c, \langle ab, 4\rangle)$,
(c) $(\langle ab, 4\rangle, X) \rightarrow (a, b)$ to $\bar{P}$.

Basic Idea.
Productions introduced in (1) initiate the derivation. Productions from (2) select the nonterminal to be rewritten. Productions from (3), (4), and (5) simulate productions of G of the form $A \rightarrow a$, $A \rightarrow BC$, and $AB \rightarrow CD$, respectively. Finally, productions from (6) finish the derivation.

Formal Proof.
Every derivation starts either by a production introduced in (1a) to generate sentences $a \in L(G)$, where $a \in T$, or by a production introduced in (1b) to generate sentences $x \in L(G)$, where $|x| \geq 2$. As $\bar{S}$ does not occur on the right-hand side of any production, productions from (1) are not used during the rest of the derivation.

Consider a sentential form $a_1 \dots a_k$ of G, where $a_1, \dots, a_k \in V$, for some $k \geq 2$. In $\bar{G}$, this sentential form corresponds

- either to
$$b_1 \dots b_{r-1}\langle a_r, 0\rangle b_{r+1}b_{r+2}\dots b_{k-2}\langle a_{k-1}a_k\rangle X,$$
where $b_i = \alpha(a_i)$, for all
$$i \in \{1, 2, \dots, r-1, r+1, r+2, \dots, k-2\},$$
for some $1 \leq r \leq k-2$,
- or to
$$b_1 \dots b_{k-2}\langle a_{k-1}a_k, 0\rangle X;$$
where $b_i = \alpha(a_i)$, for all $1 \leq i \leq k-2$ (observe that every right-hand side of a production from (1b) represents a sentential form of this kind).

To simulate a production of G, the leftmost nonterminal from its left-hand side has to be selected in the sentential form of $\bar{G}$. This is made by appending 0 to the selected symbol by productions from (2). Specifically, for a symbol $a \in V$, (2a) selects the leftmost symbol a immediately following the currently selected symbol, and (2b) selects the leftmost symbol a preceding the currently selected symbol. Productions from (2c) and (2d) select and deselect the penultimate nonterminal in a sentential form of $\bar{G}$, which consists of two symbols from V. Observe that in this way, any symbol (except for the final X) in every sentential form of $\bar{G}$ can be selected. Furthermore, observe that during a derivation, always one symbol is selected.

After the nonterminal is selected, the application of the production of G can be simulated. Productions of the form $A \rightarrow a$ are simulated by (3a) for every selected nonterminal $a_1, \dots, a_{k-2}$, and by (3b), (3c) if the penultimate nonterminal (which contains a_{k-1}, a_k) of the sentential form of $\bar{G}$ is selected. Analogously, productions of the form $A \rightarrow BC$ are simulated by productions from (4).

Productions from (5a) simulate applications of productions of the form $AB \rightarrow CD$ within the penultimate nonterminal of a sentential form of $\bar{G}$. In what follows, we demonstrate how productions from (5b), (5c), and (5d) are used if this production is simulated within $a_1 \dots a_{k-2}$. Suppose that the sentential form in $\bar{G}$ has the form

$$b_1 \dots b_{r-1}\langle a_r, 0\rangle b_{r+1}b_{r+2}\dots b_{k-2}\langle a_{k-1}a_k\rangle X,$$

and we simulate the application of $a_r a_{r+1} \rightarrow c_r c_{r+1} \in P$. Recall that $N_1 = \{A_1, \dots, A_n\}$ denotes the set of all symbols that may occur in $b_{r+1}b_{r+2}\dots b_{k-2}$. First, to select $b_{r+1} = \alpha(a_{r+1})$, the production

$$\big(\langle a_r, 0\rangle, b_{r+1}, X\big) \rightarrow \big(\langle a_r, 1, 1\rangle, b'_{r+1}, A_1\big)$$

from (5bi) is applied in a successful derivation, so

$$\begin{aligned} & b_1 \dots b_{r-1}\langle a_r, 0\rangle b_{r+1}b_{r+2}\dots b_{k-2}\langle a_{k-1}a_k\rangle X \\ {}_{lm}\Rightarrow_{\bar{G}} \; & b_1 \dots b_{r-1}\langle a_r, 1, 1\rangle b'_{r+1}b_{r+2}b_{r+3}\dots b_{k-2}\langle a_{k-1}a_k\rangle A_1. \end{aligned}$$

Observe that if b_{r+1} does not immediately follow $\langle a_r, 0\rangle$, the leftmost

$$b \in \text{alph}(b_{r+2}b_{r+3} \dots b_{k-2})$$

satisfying $b = b_{r+1}$ is selected by the production from (5bi). The purpose of productions from (5c) is to verify that the nonterminal immediately following $\langle a_r, 0\rangle$ has been selected. First, the production

$$\big(\langle a_r, 1, 1\rangle, A_1\big) \to \big(\langle a_r, 2, 1\rangle, \hat{A}_1\big)$$

from (5ci) is applied to tag the first A_1 following $\langle a_r, 1, 1\rangle$, so

$$\begin{aligned} & b_1 \dots b_{r-1}\langle a_r, 1, 1\rangle b'_{r+1} b_{r+2}b_{r+3} \dots b_{k-2}\langle a_{k-1}a_k\rangle A_1 \\ {}_{lm}\Rightarrow_{\bar{G}}\ & b_1 \dots b_{r-1}\langle a_r, 2, 1\rangle b'_{r+1} y_1 \langle a_{k-1}a_k\rangle d_1, \end{aligned}$$

where

- either $d_1 = A_1$,

  $$y_1 = b_{r+2}b_{r+3} \dots b_{m-1}\hat{A}_1 b_{m+1}b_{m+2} \dots b_{k-2},$$

  satisfying $A_1 \notin \text{alph}(b_{r+2}b_{r+3} \dots b_{m-1})$, for some $1 \le m \le k-2$,
- or $d_1 = \hat{A}_1$,

  $$y_1 = b_{r+2}b_{r+3} \dots b_{k-2},$$

  satisfying $A_1 \notin \text{alph}(y_1)$.

Then, the production

$$\big(\langle a_r, 2, 1\rangle, b'_{r+1}, \hat{A}_1\big) \to \big(\langle a_r, 3, 1\rangle, b'_{r+1}, A_1\big)$$

from (5cii) is applied to untag the first symbol $\hat{A}_1$ following b'_{r+1}, so

$$\begin{aligned} & b_1 \dots b_{r-1}\langle a_r, 2, 1\rangle b'_{r+1} y_1 \langle a_{k-1}a_k\rangle d_1 \\ {}_{lm}\Rightarrow_{\bar{G}}\ & b_1 \dots b_{r-1}\langle a_r, 3, 1\rangle b'_{r+1} b_{r+2}b_{r+3} \dots b_{k-2}\langle a_{k-1}a_k\rangle A_1. \end{aligned}$$

This means that if A_1 occurs between $\langle a_r, 2, 1\rangle$ and b'_{r+1}, it is tagged by the production from (5ci), but it cannot be untagged by any production from (5cii), so the derivation is blocked. Finally, the production

$$\big(\langle a_r, 3, 1\rangle, \langle a_{k-1}a_k\rangle, A_1\big) \to \big(\langle a_r, 1, 2\rangle, \langle a_{k-1}a_k\rangle, A_2\big)$$

from (5ciii) is applied, so

$$\begin{aligned} & b_1 \dots b_{r-1}\langle a_r, 3, 1\rangle b'_{r+1} b_{r+2}b_{r+3} \dots b_{k-2}\langle a_{k-1}a_k\rangle A_1 \\ {}_{lm}\Rightarrow_{\bar{G}}\ & b_1 \dots b_{r-1}\langle a_r, 1, 2\rangle b'_{r+1} b_{r+2}b_{r+3} \dots b_{k-2}\langle a_{k-1}a_k\rangle A_2, \end{aligned}$$

and the same verification can be performed for A_2. This verification proceeds for all symbols from N_1, so this part of the derivation can be expressed as

$$\begin{aligned} & u_1 && {}_{lm}\Rightarrow_{\bar{G}} v_1\ [p_{11}] && {}_{lm}\Rightarrow_{\bar{G}} w_1\ [p_{12}] \\ {}_{lm}\Rightarrow_{\bar{G}}\ & u_2\ [p_{13}] && {}_{lm}\Rightarrow_{\bar{G}} v_2\ [p_{21}] && {}_{lm}\Rightarrow_{\bar{G}} w_2\ [p_{22}] \\ & \vdots && && \\ {}_{lm}\Rightarrow_{\bar{G}}\ & u_n\ [p_{(n-1)3}] && {}_{lm}\Rightarrow_{\bar{G}} v_n\ [p_{n1}] && {}_{lm}\Rightarrow_{\bar{G}} w_n\ [p_{n2}] \end{aligned}$$

with

$$\begin{aligned}u_i &= b_1 \dots b_{r-1}\langle a_r, 1, i\rangle b'_{r+1} b_{r+2} b_{r+3} \dots b_{k-2}\langle a_{k-1}a_k\rangle A_i,\\ v_i &= b_1 \dots b_{r-1}\langle a_r, 2, i\rangle b'_{r+1} y_i \langle a_{k-1}a_k\rangle d_i,\\ w_i &= b_1 \dots b_{r-1}\langle a_r, 3, i\rangle b'_{r+1} b_{r+2} b_{r+3} \dots b_{k-2}\langle a_{k-1}a_k\rangle A_i,\end{aligned}$$

where p_{i1}, p_{i2}, and p_{j3} are productions from (5ci), (5cii), and (5ciii), respectively, for all $1 \leq i \leq n$, $1 \leq j \leq n-1$, and

- either $d_i = A_i$,

  $$y_i = b_{r+2} b_{r+3} \dots b_{i_{m-1}} \hat{A}_i b_{i_{m+1}} b_{i_{m+2}} \dots b_{k-2},$$

  satisfying $A_i \notin \text{alph}(b_{r+2} b_{r+3} \dots b_{i_{m-1}})$, for some $1 \leq i_m \leq k-2$,
- or $d_i = \hat{A}_i$,

  $$y_i = b_{r+2} b_{r+3} \dots b_{k-2},$$

  satisfying $A_i \notin \text{alph}(y_i)$.

After the verification is finished, the application of $a_r a_{r+1} \to c_r c_{r+1} \in P$ is simulated by

$$\big(\langle a_r, 3, n\rangle, b'_{r+1}, \langle a_{k-1}a_k\rangle, A_n\big) \to \big(\langle c_r, 0\rangle, c_{r+1}, \langle a_{k-1}a_k\rangle, X\big)$$

from (5di), so

$$\begin{aligned}& b_1 \dots b_{r-1}\langle a_r, 3, n\rangle b'_{r+1} b_{r+2} b_{r+3} \dots b_{k-2}\langle a_{k-1}a_k\rangle A_n\\ {}_{lm}\Rightarrow_{\bar{G}}\ & b_1 \dots b_{r-1}\langle c_r, 0\rangle c_{r+1} b_{r+2} b_{r+3} \dots b_{k-2}\langle a_{k-1}a_k\rangle X.\end{aligned}$$

Observe that in order to simulate a production of the form $AB \to CD$ within $a_{k-2}a_{k-1}$, productions from (5bii) and (5dii) have to be used instead of productions from (5bi) and (5di) in the simulation described above. The details of this simulation are left to the reader.

Finally, consider a sentence $a_1 \dots a_k \in T^+$ of G. After the simulation is completed, this sentence corresponds in $\bar{G}$

- either to

  $$\bar{a}_1 \dots \bar{a}_{r-1}\langle a_r, 0\rangle \bar{a}_{r+1} \bar{a}_{r+2} \dots \bar{a}_{k-2}\langle a_{k-1}a_k\rangle X$$

- or to

  $$\bar{a}_1 \dots \bar{a}_{k-2}\langle a_{k-1}a_k, 0\rangle X.$$

To enter the final phase in $\bar{G}$, we need the sentential form to be in the second above described form. This can be achieved by applying a production from (2c) to the first sentential form. The rest of the derivation can be expressed as

$$\begin{aligned}& \bar{a}_1 \dots \bar{a}_{k-2}\langle a_{k-1}a_k, 0\rangle X & \\ {}_{lm}\Rightarrow_{\bar{G}}\ & \bar{a}_1 \dots \bar{a}_{k-2}\langle a_{k-1}a_k, 4\rangle X & [p_{6a}]\\ {}_{lm}\Rightarrow_{\bar{G}}^{k-2}\ & a_1 \dots a_{k-2}\langle a_{k-1}a_k, 4\rangle X & [\Xi_{6b}]\\ {}_{lm}\Rightarrow_{\bar{G}}\ & a_1 \dots a_{k-2} a_{k-1} a_k & [p_{6c}],\end{aligned}$$

where p_{6a} and p_{6c} are productions introduced in (6a) and (6c), respectively, and Ξ_{6b} is a sequence of $k-2$ productions from (6b). As a result, $x \in L(\bar{G}, lm)$ if and only if $x \in L(G)$. Therefore, $\mathscr{L}(CS) \subseteq \mathscr{L}(PSC, lm)$.

As $\mathscr{L}(PSC, lm) \subseteq \mathscr{L}(CS)$ and $\mathscr{L}(CS) \subseteq \mathscr{L}(PSC, lm)$, we get $\mathscr{L}(PSC, lm) = \mathscr{L}(CS)$, so the theorem holds. ■

The following corollary reformulates Theorem 5.10 in terms of right derivations.

Corollary 5.11. $\mathscr{L}(PSC, rm) = \mathscr{L}(CS)$.

Proof. This corollary can be proved by a straightforward modification of the proof of Theorem 5.10 and its proof is, therefore, left to the reader. ■

5.3 Maximal and minimal derivations

In this section, we introduce two natural and simple modifications of propagating scattered context grammars. As a matter of fact, both modifications only change the way propagating scattered context grammars perform their derivations while keeping their grammatical concept unchanged. More specifically, during every derivation step, these modified versions select an applicable production containing the maximal or, in contrast, the minimal number of nonterminals on its left-hand side. We prove that both of these versions generate the family of context-sensitive languages.

Definition 5.12. Let $G = (V, T, P, S)$ be a scattered context grammar. Define the *maximal derivation step* as

$$u \ {}_{max}{\Rightarrow}_G \ v \ [p]$$

if and only if $u \Rightarrow_G v \ [p]$ and there is no $r \in P$ satisfying $\text{len}(r) > \text{len}(p)$ such that $u \Rightarrow_G w \ [r]$. Similarly, define the *minimal derivation step* as

$$u \ {}_{min}{\Rightarrow}_G \ v \ [p]$$

if and only if $u \Rightarrow_G v \ [p]$ and there is no $r \in P$ satisfying $\text{len}(r) < \text{len}(p)$ such that $u \Rightarrow_G w \ [r]$. Define the transitive closure and the reflexive and transitive closure of ${}_{max}{\Rightarrow}_G$ and ${}_{min}{\Rightarrow}_G$ in the standard way. The *language of a scattered context grammar G that uses maximal* or *minimal derivations* is denoted by $L(G, max)$ or $L(G, min)$, and defined as

$$L(G, max) = \{x : x \in T^*, S \ {}_{max}{\Rightarrow}_G^* \ x\}, \text{ or}$$
$$L(G, min) = \{x : x \in T^*, S \ {}_{min}{\Rightarrow}_G^* \ x\},$$

respectively. The corresponding language families are denoted by $\mathscr{L}(PSC, max)$ and $\mathscr{L}(PSC, min)$.

Next, we demonstrate that propagating scattered context grammars that use either maximal or minimal derivations characterize the family of context-sensitive languages.

Theorem 5.13. $\mathscr{L}(CS) = \mathscr{L}(PSC, max)$.

Proof. Let L be a context-sensitive language. As state grammars characterize the family of context-sensitive languages (see Theorem 2.32), we suppose that L is described by a state grammar $\bar{G} = (\bar{V}, T, K, \bar{P}, \bar{S}, p_0)$. Set

$$Y = \{\langle A, q \rangle : A \in \bar{V} - T, q \in K\}$$

and $Z = \{\bar{a} : a \in T\}$. Define the homomorphism α form $\bar{V}^*$ to $((\bar{V} - T) \cup Z)^*$ as $\alpha(A) = A$, for all $A \in \bar{V} - T$, and $\alpha(a) = \bar{a}$, for all $a \in T$. Set $V = \bar{V} \cup Y \cup Z \cup \{S, X\}$. Define the propagating scattered context grammar $G = (V, T, P, S)$, where P is constructed as follows:

1. For each $x \in L(\bar{G})$, where $|x| \leq 2$, add $(S) \to (x)$ to P.
2. For each

$$(x, q) \in \Big\{(x, q) : (\bar{S}, p_0) \Rightarrow^+_{\bar{G}} (x, q), \text{ for some } q \in K, \\ \text{and } 3 \leq |x| \leq \max\big(\{3\} \cup \{|y| : (B, p) \to (y, p') \in \bar{P}\}\big)\Big\},$$

where

   (a) $x \in T^*$, add $(S) \to (x)$ to P;
   (b) $x = x_1 A x_2$, $A \in \bar{V} - T$, $x_1, x_2 \in \bar{V}^*$, add $(S) \to (\alpha(x_1)\langle A, q\rangle\alpha(x_2))$ to P.

3. For each $(A, p) \to (x, q)$, $(B, p) \to (y, r) \in \bar{P}$, $C \in \bar{V}$, $\Gamma_{21} \in \text{perm}(2, 1)$, and

$$z = \text{reorder}\big((B, \langle A, p\rangle, \alpha(C)), \Gamma_{21}\big),$$

add $z \to (X, X, X)$ to P.

4. For each $(A, p) \to (x, q) \in \bar{P}$, $B \in \bar{V} - T$, $C \in \bar{V}$, $\Gamma_{11} \in \text{perm}(1, 1)$, and

$$y = \text{reorder}\big((\langle A, p\rangle, \alpha(C)), \Gamma_{11}\big),$$

add

   (a) $(B, \langle A, p\rangle) \to (\langle B, q\rangle, \alpha(x))$,
   (b) $(\langle A, p\rangle, B) \to (\alpha(x), \langle B, q\rangle)$ to P;
   (c) if $x = vBw$, $v, w \in \bar{V}^*$, for each

$$z = \text{reorder}\big((\alpha(v)\langle B, q\rangle\alpha(w), \alpha(C)), \Gamma_{11}\big),$$

   add $y \to z$ to P;
   (d) for each

$$u = \text{reorder}\big((\alpha(x), \alpha(C)), \Gamma_{11}\big),$$

   add $y \to u$ to P.

5. For each $a \in T$, add
   $(\bar{a}) \to (a)$ to P.

Basic Idea.
The state grammar $\bar{G}$ is simulated by the propagating scattered context grammar G that performs maximal derivations. Productions introduced in (1) are used to generate a sentence $w \in L(\bar{G})$, where $|w| \leq 2$, while productions introduced in (2) start the simulation of a derivation of a sentence $w \in \bar{G}$, where $|w| \geq 3$. Let $(A, p) \to (x, q)$ be a production of $\bar{G}$ that is applicable to a sentential form $(w_1 A w_2, p)$ generated by $\bar{G}$. The sentential form $(w_1 A w_2, p)$ in $\bar{G}$ corresponds to the sentential form $\alpha(w_1)\langle A, p\rangle\alpha(w_2)$ in G. Consider the application of a production $(A, p) \to (x, q)$ in $\bar{G}$. G simulates this application as follows. First, G checks whether the production is applied to the leftmost nonterminal of the sentential form for the given state p. If not, a production from (3) is applicable. This production is applied because it has the highest priority of all productions, and its application introduces the symbol X into the sentential form, which blocks the derivation. The successful derivation proceeds by applying a production from (4a), (4b), and (4c), which non-deterministically selects the next nonterminal to be rewritten, and appends the new state to it. The production that finishes the derivation of a sentence in $\bar{G}$ is simulated by a production from (4d), which removes the compound nonterminal $\langle \ldots \rangle$ from the sentential form. Finally, every symbol $\bar{a}$, where $a \in T$, is rewritten to a.

Formal Proof.
We establish the theorem by Claims 1 through 4 stated below.

Claim 1. Every $x \in L(\bar{G})$, where $|x| \leq 2$, is generated by G as follows:

$$S \ {}_{max}\!\Rightarrow_G x \ [p_1],$$

where p_1 is one of the productions introduced in (1). □

Claim 2. Every

$$(\bar{S}, p_0) \Rightarrow^+_{\bar{G}} (x, q),$$

where $q \in K$, $x \in T^+$, and

$$3 \leq |x| \leq \max\Big(\{3\} \cup \big\{|y| : (B, p) \to (y, p') \in \bar{P}\big\}\Big),$$

is generated by G as follows:

$$S \ {}_{max}\!\Rightarrow_G x \ [p_{2a}],$$

where p_{2a} is one of the productions introduced in (2a). □

Claim 3. Every

$$(\bar{S}, p_0) \Rightarrow^+_{\bar{G}} (x, q) \Rightarrow^+_{\bar{G}} (u, r),$$

where $q, r \in K, u \in T^+, x = v_0 A w_0, A \in \bar{V} - T, v_0, w_0 \in \bar{V}^*$, and

$$3 \leq |x| \leq \max\Big(\{3\} \cup \big\{|y| : (B, p) \rightarrow (y, p') \in \bar{P}\big\}\Big),$$

can only be generated by G as follows:

$$\begin{aligned} S \ {}_{max}\Rightarrow_G \ & \alpha(v_0)\langle A, q\rangle\alpha(w_0) \ [p_{2b}] \\ {}_{max}\Rightarrow_G^* \ & y \quad [\Xi_4] \\ {}_{max}\Rightarrow_G \ & z \quad [p_{4d}] \\ {}_{max}\Rightarrow_G^{|u|} \ & u \quad [\Xi_5], \end{aligned}$$

where $y \in Z^*YZ^*, z = \alpha(u)$; p_{2b} and p_{4d} denote one of the productions introduced in (2b) and (4d), respectively, Ξ_4 is a sequence of productions from (4a), (4b), and (4c), and Ξ_5 is a sequence of productions from (5).

Proof. Observe that the productions from (1) and (2) are the only productions containing S on their left-hand sides and no other productions contain S on their right-hand sides. To generate a sentence u, $|u| \geq 3$, the derivation has to start as

$$S \ {}_{max}\Rightarrow_G \ \alpha(v_0)\langle A, q\rangle\alpha(w_0) \ [p_{2b}],$$

and productions from (1) and (2) are not used during the rest of the derivation.

Further, observe that none of the productions introduced in (3) can be applied during a successful derivation because no production rewrites the nonterminal X that appears on the right-hand side of every production from (3).

To generate a sentence over T, all symbols from $\bar{V} - T$ have to be removed from the sentential form, and only productions from (4) can perform this removal because only these productions contain symbols from $\bar{V} - T$ on their left-hand sides. Furthermore, productions (4a), (4b), and (4c) contain one symbol from Y both on their left-hand sides and their right-hand sides while productions from (4d) contain a symbol from Y only on their left-hand sides. Therefore, after the application of a production from (4d), none of the productions from (4) is applicable. Because for each production p_4 and p_5 introduced in (4) and (5), respectively, it holds that $\mathrm{len}(p_4) > \mathrm{len}(p_5)$, no production from (5) is used while some production from (4) is applicable. As a result, the corresponding part of the derivation can be expressed as follows:

$$\begin{aligned} \alpha(v_0)\langle A, q\rangle\alpha(w_0) \ {}_{max}\Rightarrow_G^* \ & y \ [\Xi_4] \\ {}_{max}\Rightarrow_G \ & z \ [p_{4d}]. \end{aligned}$$

At this point, $z = \alpha(u)$ in a successful derivation. Productions from (5) replace every $\bar{a} \in \mathrm{alph}(z)$ with a in $|u|$ steps, so we obtain

$$z \ {}_{max}\Rightarrow_G^{|u|} \ u \ [\Xi_5].$$

Putting together all the previous observations, we obtain Claim 3. □

Claim 4. In a successful derivation, every

$$
\begin{aligned}
&\alpha(v_0)\langle B_0, q_0\rangle\alpha(w_0) \\
{}_{max}\Rightarrow_G\ &\alpha(v_1)\langle B_1, q_1\rangle\alpha(w_1)\ [p_0] \\
&\vdots \\
{}_{max}\Rightarrow_G\ &\alpha(v_n)\langle B_n, q_n\rangle\alpha(w_n)\ [p_{n-1}]
\end{aligned}
$$

is performed in G if and only if

$$
\begin{aligned}
&(v_0 B_0 w_0, q_0) \\
\Rightarrow_{\bar{G}}\ &(v_1 B_1 w_1, q_1)\ \big[(B_0, q_0) \to (x_1, q_1)\big] \\
&\vdots \\
\Rightarrow_{\bar{G}}\ &(v_n B_n w_n, q_n)\ \big[(B_{n-1}, q_{n-1}) \to (x_n, q_n)\big]
\end{aligned}
$$

is performed in $\bar{G}$, where $v_i, w_i \in \bar{V}^*$, $B_i \in \bar{V} - T$, $q_i \in K$, for all $0 \le i \le n$, for some $n \ge 0$, $x_1, \ldots, x_n \in \bar{V}^+$, and $p_0, \ldots, p_{n-1}$ are productions introduced in (4a), (4b), and (4c).

Proof. We start by proving the only-if part of the claim.

Only If. We show that

$$\alpha(v_0)\langle B_0, q_0\rangle\alpha(w_0)\ {}_{max}\Rightarrow_G^m\ \alpha(v_m)\langle B_m, q_m\rangle\alpha(w_m)$$

implies

$$(v_0 B_0 w_0, q_0) \Rightarrow_{\bar{G}}^m (v_m B_m w_m, q_m)$$

by induction on $m \ge 0$.

Basis. Let $m = 0$. Then,

$$\alpha(v_0)\langle B_0, q_0\rangle\alpha(w_0)\ {}_{max}\Rightarrow_G^0\ \alpha(v_0)\langle B_0, q_0\rangle\alpha(w_0)$$

and clearly,

$$(v_0 B_0 w_0, q_0) \Rightarrow_{\bar{G}}^0 (v_0 B_0 w_0, q_0).$$

Induction Hypothesis. Suppose that the claim holds for all k-step derivations, where $k \le m$, for some $m \ge 0$.

Induction Step. Let us consider a derivation

$$\alpha(v_0)\langle B_0, q_0\rangle\alpha(w_0)\ {}_{max}\Rightarrow_G^{m+1}\ \alpha(v_{m+1})\langle B_{m+1}, q_{m+1}\rangle\alpha(w_{m+1}).$$

Since $m + 1 \ge 1$, there is some

$$\alpha(v_m)\langle B_m, q_m\rangle\alpha(w_m) \in \big((\bar{V} - T) \cup Z\big)^* Y \big((\bar{V} - T) \cup Z\big)^*$$

and a production p_m such that

$$
\begin{aligned}
\alpha(v_0)\langle B_0, q_0\rangle\alpha(w_0)\ &{}_{max}\Rightarrow_G^m\ \alpha(v_m)\langle B_m, q_m\rangle\alpha(w_m) \\
&{}_{max}\Rightarrow_G\ \alpha(v_{m+1})\langle B_{m+1}, q_{m+1}\rangle\alpha(w_{m+1})\ [p_m].
\end{aligned}
$$

By the induction hypothesis, there is a derivation

$$(v_0 B_0 w_0, q_0) \Rightarrow^m_{\bar{G}} (v_m B_m w_m, q_m).$$

As p_m is a production introduced in (4a) through (4c), it has one of the following forms depending on the placement of B_{m+1}:

- $\big(B_{m+1}, \langle B_m, q_m\rangle\big) \rightarrow \big(\langle B_{m+1}, q_{m+1}\rangle, \alpha(x_{m+1})\big)$, for $v_m = v'_m B_{m+1} v''_m$;
- $\big(\langle B_m, q_m\rangle, B_{m+1}\big) \rightarrow \big(\alpha(x_{m+1}), \langle B_{m+1}, q_{m+1}\rangle\big)$, for $w_m = w'_m B_{m+1} w''_m$;
- $\big(\langle B_m, q_m\rangle, \alpha(A)\big) \rightarrow \big(\alpha(x'_{m+1})\langle B_{m+1}, q_{m+1}\rangle\alpha(x''_{m+1}), \alpha(A)\big)$, or $\big(\alpha(A), \langle B_m, q_m\rangle\big) \rightarrow \big(\alpha(A), \alpha(x'_{m+1})\langle B_{m+1}, q_{m+1}\rangle\alpha(x''_{m+1})\big)$, for $x_{m+1} = x'_{m+1} B_{m+1} x''_{m+1}$,

where $A \in \bar{V}$ and $x_{m+1}, x'_{m+1}, x''_{m+1} \in \bar{V}^*$. Their construction is based on $\bar{P}$, so there is a production $(B_m, q_m) \rightarrow (x_{m+1}, q_{m+1}) \in \bar{P}$.

Simulating a derivation of G by $\bar{G}$, we now prove that for the given state q_m, the leftmost nonterminal in the sentential form is rewritten in G. We make this proof by contradiction. Suppose that there is a production $p'_m \in P$ from (4) that rewrites some $B'_m \in \bar{V} - T$ in a state q_m, and $B'_m \in \text{alph}(v_m)$. Then, there exists $(B'_m, q_m) \rightarrow (x'_{m+1}, q'_{m+1}) \in \bar{P}$ and, as a result, there also exist productions from (3), which are based on $(B_m, q_m) \rightarrow (x_{m+1}, q_{m+1})$ and $(B'_m, q_m) \rightarrow (x'_{m+1}, q'_{m+1})$. These productions have the following forms:

$$\big(B'_m, \langle B_m, q_m\rangle, \alpha(A)\big) \rightarrow (X, X, X),$$
$$\big(B'_m, \alpha(A), \langle B_m, q_m\rangle\big) \rightarrow (X, X, X),$$
$$\big(\alpha(A), B'_m, \langle B_m, q_m\rangle\big) \rightarrow (X, X, X),$$

where $A \in \bar{V}$. Because $\big|\alpha(v_m)\langle B_m, q_m\rangle\alpha(w_m)\big| \geq 3$, one of these productions is applicable. As productions introduced in (3) have higher priority than productions introduced in (4), one of them is applied, which introduces X to the sentential form. However, this symbol can never be removed from the sentential form, so the derivation is unsuccessful in this case.

As a result, the leftmost nonterminal in the state q_m is rewritten in G, so $(B_m, q_m) \rightarrow (x_{m+1}, q_{m+1})$ is used in $\bar{G}$, and we obtain

$$(v_m B_m w_m, q_m) \Rightarrow_{\bar{G}} (v_{m+1} B_{m+1} w_{m+1}, q_{m+1}) \big[(B_m, q_m) \rightarrow (x_{m+1}, q_{m+1})\big].$$

If. We demonstrate that

$$(v_0 B_0 w_0, q_0) \Rightarrow^m_{\bar{G}} (v_m B_m w_m, q_m)$$

implies

$$\alpha(v_0)\langle B_0, q_0\rangle\alpha(w_0) \;{}_{max}\!\Rightarrow^m_G \alpha(v_m)\langle B_m, q_m\rangle\alpha(w_m)$$

by induction on m.

Basis. Let $m = 0$. Then,

$$(v_0 B_0 w_0, q_0) \Rightarrow^0_{\bar{G}} (v_0 B_0 w_0, q_0).$$

Clearly,

$$\alpha(v_0)\langle B_0, q_0\rangle\alpha(w_0) \ {}_{max}{\Rightarrow}^0_G \ \alpha(v_0)\langle B_0, q_0\rangle\alpha(w_0).$$

Induction Hypothesis. Suppose that the claim holds for all k-step derivations, where $k \leq m$, for some $m \geq 0$.

Induction Step. Consider a derivation

$$(v_0 B_0 w_0, q_0) \Rightarrow^{m+1}_{\bar{G}} (v_{m+1} B_{m+1} w_{m+1}, q_{m+1}).$$

Since $m + 1 \geq 1$, there is some $(v_m B_m w_m, q_m)$, where $v_m, w_m \in \bar{V}^*, B_m \in \bar{V} - T$, and a production $(B_m, q_m) \to (x_{m+1}, q_{m+1})$ such that

$$\begin{aligned}(v_0 B_0 w_0, q_0) &\Rightarrow^m_{\bar{G}} (v_m B_m w_m, q_m)\\ &\Rightarrow_{\bar{G}} (v_{m+1} B_{m+1} w_{m+1}, q_{m+1}) \left[(B_m, q_m) \to (x_{m+1}, q_{m+1})\right].\end{aligned}$$

By the induction hypothesis, there is a derivation

$$\alpha(v_0)\langle B_0, q_0\rangle\alpha(w_0) \ {}_{max}{\Rightarrow}^m_G \ \alpha(v_m)\langle B_m, q_m\rangle\alpha(w_m).$$

Because $(B_m, q_m) \to (x_{m+1}, q_{m+1})$ rewrites the leftmost rewritable symbol B_m in a given state q_m, there is no production $(B'_m, q_m) \to (x'_{m+1}, q'_{m+1})$ satisfying $B'_m \in \text{alph}(v_m)$. As a result, none of the productions from (3) is applicable.

For each $(B_m, q_m) \to (x_{m+1}, q_{m+1}) \in \bar{P}$, there are productions of the following forms in G whose application depends on the placement of B_{m+1}:

- $\big(B_{m+1}, \langle B_m, q_m\rangle\big) \to \big(\langle B_{m+1}, q_{m+1}\rangle, \alpha(x_{m+1})\big)$, for $v_m = v'_m B_{m+1} v''_m$;
- $\big(\langle B_m, q_m\rangle, B_{m+1}\big) \to \big(\alpha(x_{m+1}), \langle B_{m+1}, q_{m+1}\rangle\big)$, for $w_m = w'_m B_{m+1} w''_m$;
- $\big(\langle B_m, q_m\rangle, \alpha(A)\big) \to \big(\alpha(x'_{m+1})\langle B_{m+1}, q_{m+1}\rangle\alpha(x''_{m+1}), \alpha(A)\big)$, or
  $\big(\alpha(A), \langle B_m, q_m\rangle\big) \to \big(\alpha(A), \alpha(x'_{m+1})\langle B_{m+1}, q_{m+1}\rangle\alpha(x''_{m+1})\big)$,
  for $x_{m+1} = x'_{m+1} B_{m+1} x''_{m+1}$,

where $A \in \bar{V}$ and $x_{m+1}, x'_{m+1}, x''_{m+1} \in \bar{V}^*$. As $\left|\alpha(v_m)\langle B_m, q_m\rangle\alpha(w_m)\right| \geq 3$, one of them is applicable in G, so we obtain

$$\alpha(v_m)\langle B_m, q_m\rangle\alpha(w_m) \ {}_{max}{\Rightarrow}_G \ \alpha(v_{m+1})\langle B_{m+1}, q_{m+1}\rangle\alpha(w_{m+1}).$$

□

By Claims 1 through 4, it follows that $\mathscr{L}(CS) \subseteq \mathscr{L}(PSC, max)$. As propagating scattered context grammars do not contain erasing productions, their derivations can be simulated by context-sensitive grammars. As a result, $\mathscr{L}(PSC, max) \subseteq \mathscr{L}(CS)$. Therefore, $\mathscr{L}(CS) = \mathscr{L}(PSC, max)$. ■

Theorem 5.14. $\mathscr{L}(CS) = \mathscr{L}(PSC, min)$.

Proof. Let L be a context-sensitive language described by a state grammar $\bar{G} = (\bar{V}, T, K, \bar{P}, \bar{S}, p_0)$. Set

$$Y = \{\langle A, q\rangle : A \in \bar{V} - T, q \in K\}$$

and $Z = \{\bar{a} : a \in T\}$. Define the homomorphism α form $\bar{V}^*$ to $\big((\bar{V} - T) \cup Z\big)^*$ as $\alpha(A) = A$, for all $A \in \bar{V} - T$, and $\alpha(a) = \bar{a}$, for all $a \in T$. Set $V = \bar{V} \cup Y \cup Z \cup \{S, X\}$. Define the propagating scattered context grammar $G' = (V, T, P', S)$, where P' is constructed as follows:

1. For each $x \in L(\bar{G})$, where $|x| \leq 3$, add $(S) \rightarrow (x)$ to P'.
2. For each

$$(x, q) \in \Big\{(x, q) : (\bar{S}, p_0) \Rightarrow^+_{\bar{G}} (x, q), \text{ for some } q \in K, \\ \text{and } 4 \leq |x| \leq \max\big(\{4\} \cup \{|y| : (B, p) \rightarrow (y, p') \in \bar{P}\}\big)\Big\},$$

where

(a) $x \in T^*$, add $(S) \rightarrow (x)$ to P';
(b) $x = x_1 A x_2$, $A \in \bar{V} - T$, and $x_1, x_2 \in \bar{V}^*$, add $(S) \rightarrow \big(\alpha(x_1)\langle A, q\rangle\alpha(x_2)\big)$ to P'.

3. For each $(A, p) \rightarrow (x, q)$ and $(B, p) \rightarrow (y, r) \in \bar{P}$, add $\big(B, \langle A, p\rangle\big) \rightarrow (X, X)$ to P'.
4. For each $(A, p) \rightarrow (x, q) \in \bar{P}$, $B \in \bar{V} - T$, D, $E \in \bar{V}$, $\Gamma_{21} \in \text{perm}(2, 1)$, $\Gamma_{12} \in \text{perm}(1, 2)$, and

$$\begin{aligned} u &= \text{reorder}\Big(\big(B, \langle A, p\rangle, \alpha(D)\big), \Gamma_{21}\Big), \\ u' &= \text{reorder}\Big(\big(\langle B, q\rangle, \alpha(x), \alpha(D)\big), \Gamma_{21}\Big), \\ r &= \text{reorder}\Big(\big(\langle A, p\rangle, B, \alpha(D)\big), \Gamma_{21}\Big), \\ r' &= \text{reorder}\Big(\big(\alpha(x), \langle B, q\rangle, \alpha(D)\big), \Gamma_{21}\Big), \\ y &= \text{reorder}\Big(\big(\langle A, p\rangle, \alpha(D), \alpha(E)\big), \Gamma_{12}\Big), \end{aligned}$$

add

(a) $u \rightarrow u'$,
(b) $r \rightarrow r'$ to P';
(c) if $x = vBw$ and $v, w \in \bar{V}^*$, for each

$$z = \text{reorder}\Big(\big(\alpha(v)\langle B, q\rangle\alpha(w), \alpha(D), \alpha(E)\big), \Gamma_{12}\Big),$$

add $y \rightarrow z$ to P'.

(d) For each

$$u = \text{reorder}\Big(\big(\alpha(x), \alpha(D), \alpha(E)\big), \Gamma_{12}\Big),$$

add $y \rightarrow u$ to P'.

5. For each $a, b, c, d \in T$, add
   (a) $(\bar{a}, \bar{b}, \bar{c}, \bar{d}) \rightarrow (a, \bar{b}, \bar{c}, \bar{d})$,
   (b) $(\bar{a}, \bar{b}, \bar{c}, \bar{d}) \rightarrow (a, b, c, d)$ to P'.

Claim 1. Every

$$(\bar{S}, p_0) \Rightarrow^{+}_{\bar{G}} (x, q) \Rightarrow^{+}_{\bar{G}} (u, r),$$

where $q, r \in K$, $u \in T^{+}$, $x = v_0 A w_0$, $A \in \bar{V} - T$, $v_0, w_0 \in \bar{V}^{*}$,

$$4 \leq |x| \leq \max\Big(\{4\} \cup \big\{|y| : (B, p) \rightarrow (y, p') \in \bar{P}\big\}\Big),$$

can only be generated by G' as follows:

$$\begin{aligned} S\ {}_{min}{\Rightarrow}_{G}\ & \alpha(v_0)\langle A, q\rangle\alpha(w_0)\ [p_{2b}] \\ {}_{min}{\Rightarrow}^{*}_{G}\ & y \quad [\Xi_4] \\ {}_{min}{\Rightarrow}_{G}\ & z \quad [p_{4d}] \\ {}_{min}{\Rightarrow}^{|u|-4}_{G}\ & v \quad [\Xi_5] \\ {}_{min}{\Rightarrow}_{G}\ & u \quad [p_{5b}], \end{aligned}$$

where $y \in Z^{*}YZ^{*}$, $z = \alpha(u)$, $v \in (T \cup Z)^{+}$, p_{2b}, p_{4d}, and p_{5b} represent productions introduced in (2b), (4d), and (5b), respectively, Ξ_4 is a sequence of productions from (4a), (4b), and (4c), and Ξ_5 is a sequence of productions from (5a).

Proof. The proof of the form of the beginning of the derivation,

$$\begin{aligned} S\ {}_{min}{\Rightarrow}_{G}\ & \alpha(v_0)\langle A, q\rangle\alpha(w_0)\ [p_{2b}] \\ {}_{min}{\Rightarrow}^{*}_{G}\ & y \quad [\Xi_4] \\ {}_{min}{\Rightarrow}_{G}\ & z \quad [p_{4d}], \end{aligned}$$

is analogous to the proof of Claim 3 (in terms of minimal derivations) and, therefore, left to the reader.

Recall that z satisfies $z = \alpha(u)$. Each of the productions from (5a) replaces one occurrence of $\bar{a}$ with a, for some $a \in T$, and finally, the application of a production from (5b) replaces the remaining four nonterminals with their terminal variants. Therefore,

$$\begin{aligned} z\ {}_{min}{\Rightarrow}^{|u|-4}_{G}\ & v\ [\Xi_5] \\ {}_{min}{\Rightarrow}_{G}\ & u\ [p_{5b}], \end{aligned}$$

so the claim holds. □

Notice that $\text{len}(p_3) < \text{len}(p_4) < \text{len}(p_5)$, for each production p_3, p_4, and p_5 introduced in (3), (4), and (5), respectively, so the priorities of the productions from the individual steps are the same as in the case of grammars that use maximal derivations. As a result, Claim 1, 2, and 4 can be straightforwardly rephrased in terms of minimal derivations, and we leave this simple task to the reader. Therefore, $\mathscr{L}(CS) \subseteq \mathscr{L}(PSC, min)$, and for the same reason as in the proof of Theorem 5.13, $\mathscr{L}(PSC, min) \subseteq \mathscr{L}(CS)$. Thus, $\mathscr{L}(CS) = \mathscr{L}(PSC, min)$. ■

Before closing this section, let us point out a potential use of the obtained results in the future. Simply and briefly stated, we have demonstrated that both of the modified versions of propagating scattered context grammars, which make either maximal or minimal derivations, characterize the family of context-sensitive languages. Consequently, if in the future formal language theory proves that these versions are as powerful as ordinary propagating scattered context grammars, it also achieves "yes" as the answer to the long-standing open problem whether context-sensitive and propagating scattered context grammars are equivalent.

5.4 Unordered scattered context grammars

Unordered scattered context grammars belong to the most natural modifications of scattered context grammars. As indicated by their name, the order of the context-free components in an unordered scattered context production is unimportant; that is, these components can be applied by simultaneously rewriting their left-hand sides no matter in what order these left-hand sides appear in the current sentential form. This important modification was independently introduced and studied in [21] and [26]. After their introduction, Virkkunen [15] and Fernau [27] discussed special derivation forms of these grammars.

Definition 5.15. An *unordered scattered context grammar* is a quadruple $G = (V, T, P, S)$, where V, T, P, and S are defined as in the case of a scattered context grammar. If there is a permutation $\pi \in \text{perm}(n)$, for some $n \geq 1$, such that

$$p = \text{reorder}\big((A_1, \dots, A_n), \pi\big) \to \text{reorder}\big((x_1, \dots, x_n), \pi\big) \in P,$$

and

$$u = u_1 A_1 \dots u_n A_n u_{n+1},$$
$$v = u_1 x_1 \dots u_n x_n u_{n+1},$$

where $u_i \in V^*$, for all $1 \leq i \leq n+1$, then G makes a derivation step from u to v according to p, symbolically written as

$$u \Rightarrow_G v\ [p],$$

or, simply, $u \Rightarrow_G v$. In the standard way, define the transitive closure and the reflexive and transitive closure of $\Rightarrow_G$, and the language generated by G. If every production

$$(A_1, \dots, A_k) \to (x_1, \dots, x_k) \in P$$

satisfies $x_i \in V^+$, for all $1 \leq i \leq k$, G is a *propagating unordered scattered context grammar*. The language families generated by unordered scattered context grammars and propagating unordered scattered context grammars are denoted by $\mathscr{L}(SC, un)$ and $\mathscr{L}(PSC, un)$, respectively.

Example 5.16 (see [19]). Consider the unordered scattered context grammar

$$G = \big(\{S, A, a, b, c\}, \{a, b, c\}, P, S\big),$$

where

$$\begin{aligned} P = \big\{&(S) \to (AAA), \\ &(A, A, A) \to (aA, bA, cA), \\ &(A, A, A) \to (\varepsilon, \varepsilon, \varepsilon)\big\}. \end{aligned}$$

This grammar generates the language

$$L(G) = \big\{x_1 \dots x_{3n} : n \geq 0, \{x_j, x_{n+j}, x_{2n+j}\} = \{a, b, c\}, \text{ for all } 1 \leq j \leq n\big\}$$

while the generated language of the scattered context grammar with the same set of productions is $\{a^n b^n c^n : n \geq 0\}$.

Propagating unordered scattered context grammars are as powerful as programmed grammars without erasing productions and appearance checking as demonstrated both in [21] and [26]. Next, we establish two lemmas that straightforwardly imply this result.

Lemma 5.17. $\mathscr{L}(P) \subseteq \mathscr{L}(PSC, un)$.

Proof. Observe that the construction used in the proof of Lemma 3.22 can be used to prove this lemma as well; however, the constructed grammar $\bar{G}$ is a propagating unordered scattered context grammar in this case. ■

Lemma 5.18. $\mathscr{L}(PSC, un) \subseteq \mathscr{L}(P)$.

Proof. Let $G = (V, T, P, S)$ be a propagating unordered scattered context grammar. Set

$$N = \big\{\langle x_i \rangle : (A_1, \dots, A_n) \to (x_1, \dots, x_n) \in P, 1 \leq i \leq n\big\}.$$

Define the programmed grammar $\bar{G} = (V \cup N, T, \bar{P}, S)$, where $\bar{P}$ is defined as follows:

1. Let Q_2 denote the set of all productions introduced in step (2) of this construction (see below). For each

$$p = (A_1, \dots, A_n) \to (x_1, \dots, x_n) \in P,$$

add

$$\begin{aligned}
p_1 &= \big(A_1 \rightarrow \langle x_1\rangle, \{p_2\}\big),\\
&\ \ \vdots\\
p_{n-1} &= \big(A_{n-1} \rightarrow \langle x_{n-1}\rangle, \{p_n\}\big),\\
p_n &= \big(A_n \rightarrow \langle x_n\rangle, \{r_1\}\big),\\
r_1 &= \big(\langle x_1\rangle \rightarrow x_1, \{r_2\}\big),\\
&\ \ \vdots\\
r_{n-1} &= \big(\langle x_{n-1}\rangle \rightarrow x_{n-1}, \{r_n\}\big),\\
r_n &= \big(\langle x_n\rangle \rightarrow x_n, Q_2\big) \text{ to } \bar{P}.
\end{aligned}$$

2. Let Q_1 denote the set of all productions of the form $p_1 = \big(A_1 \rightarrow \langle x_1\rangle, \{p_2\}\big)$ introduced in step (1) of this construction. For each $A \in V - T$, add

$$(A \rightarrow A, Q_1) \text{ to } \bar{P}.$$

To give an insight into the construction above, we informally explain how $\bar{G}$ simulates the application of a production from G. The application of every production of the form $(A_1, \ldots, A_n) \rightarrow (x_1, \ldots, x_n)$ is simulated by $2n$ derivation steps in $\bar{G}$. First, all left-hand sides of its context-free components, $A_1, \ldots, A_n$, are rewritten to $\langle x_1\rangle, \ldots, \langle x_n\rangle$, respectively, which are symbols that encode the real right-hand sides of the context-free productions. As a result, in this phase of the simulation, $\bar{G}$ cannot rewrite $x_1, \ldots, x_n$, which would lead to an illegal simulation. Second, all the symbols $\langle x_1\rangle, \ldots, \langle x_n\rangle$ are rewritten back to the original right-hand sides, $x_1, \ldots, x_n$, respectively. Finally, to start the simulation of the following production of G, a production from (2) is used, which non-deterministically selects the next production of the propagating unordered scattered context grammar to be simulated. The simulation is successfully completed when the resulting sentential form w does not contain any nonterminal. Clearly, $w \in L(\bar{G})$ if and only if $w \in L(G)$. ■

Putting together Lemmas 5.17 and 5.18, we obtain the following theorem.

Theorem 5.19. $\mathscr{L}(PSC, un) = \mathscr{L}(P)$. ■

From Theorems 3.24 and 5.19, we obtain the following corollary.

Corollary 5.20. $\mathscr{L}(PSC, un) \subset \mathscr{L}(PSC)$. ■

Obviously, the constructions described in Lemmas 3.22 and 5.18 can be applied to unordered scattered context grammars with erasing productions as well. In this way, we obtain the following corollary.

Corollary 5.21. $\mathscr{L}(SC, un) = \mathscr{L}(P, \varepsilon)$. ■

From Theorem 3.20, and Corollaries 5.21 and 2.29, we obtain the following corollary.

Corollary 5.22. $\mathscr{L}(SC, un) \subset \mathscr{L}(SC)$. ■

In the conclusion of this section, we summarize the most important results achieved in the papers dealing with unordered scattered context grammars. A normal form similar to 2-limited unordered scattered context grammars was established in [26] by using a technique that resembles the proof of Theorem 3.4. Unordered scattered context grammars in which productions are applied in the leftmost way were studied in [15]. This paper demonstrates that these grammars are less powerful than phrase-structure grammars, but more powerful than ordinary unordered scattered context grammars. Finally, Fernau [27] summarizes all results concerning regulated versions of scattered context grammars. In essence, this study demonstrates that all well-known mechanisms of derivation regulation, such as appearance checking or unconditional transfer, applied to scattered context grammars result in the generative power that coincides with the power of programmed grammars regulated in the same way. To put it more generally, under regulating restrictions, unordered scattered context grammars behave just like most regulated grammars do.

5.5 Linear scattered context grammars

Indisputably, linear and right-linear grammars represent more than significant special cases of context-free grammars. As context-free grammars underlie scattered context grammars, it is natural and important to discuss special cases of scattered context grammars based upon linear and right-linear grammars—the subject of the present section. These special cases of scattered context grammars first apply a context-free starting production to generate an initial string consisting of n nonterminals, where n is a positive integer. After this initial application, however, only scattered context productions with linear or right-linear components are applied. First, this section proves that linear versions of scattered context grammars with n-nonterminal initial strings are as powerful as linear simple matrix grammars of degree n. Then, it demonstrates that right-linear versions of scattered context grammars with n-nonterminal initial strings are equivalent to right-linear simple matrix grammars of degree n. In addition, the present section derives several corollaries from these two main results and discusses the generative power of scattered context grammars with context-sensitive and phrase-structure productions.

We start by defining linear and right-linear scattered context grammars formally.

Definition 5.23. A *linear scattered context grammar* is a scattered context grammar $G = (V, T, P, S)$, where P is a finite set of productions of the following two forms:

1. $(S) \rightarrow (x_1 A_1 \ldots x_k A_k x_{k+1})$, where $A_i \in (V - T) - \{S\}, x_j \in T^*$, for all $1 \leq i \leq k, 1 \leq j \leq k + 1$;
2. $(A_1, \ldots, A_k) \rightarrow (z_1, \ldots, z_k)$, where $A_i \in (V - T) - \{S\}$, and
   - either $z_i = x_i B_i y_i$, where $x_i, y_i \in T^*$, $B_i \in (V - T) - \{S\}$,
   - or $z_i \in T^*$, for all $1 \leq i \leq k$ and some $k \geq 1$.

A linear scattered context grammar is *of degree n* if $(S) \rightarrow (x_1 A_1 \dots x_n A_n x_{n+1}) \in P$ satisfies $n \geq m$, for all $(S) \rightarrow (y_1 A_1 \dots y_m A_m y_{m+1}) \in P$. The family of languages generated by linear scattered context grammars of degree n is denoted by $\mathscr{L}(SC, LIN, n)$, and

$$\mathscr{L}(SC, LIN) = \bigcup_{n=1}^{\infty} \mathscr{L}(SC, LIN, n).$$

Definition 5.24. A *right-linear scattered context grammar* is a linear scattered context grammar $G = (V, T, P, S)$, where P is a finite set of productions of the following two forms:

1. $(S) \rightarrow (x_1 A_1 \dots x_k A_k)$, where $A_i \in (V - T) - \{S\}$, $x_i \in T^*$, for all $1 \leq i \leq k$ and some $k \geq 1$;
2. $(A_1, \dots, A_k) \rightarrow (z_1, \dots, z_k)$, where $A_i \in (V - T) - \{S\}$, and

- either $z_i = x_i B_i$, where $x_i \in T^*$, $B_i \in (V - T) - \{S\}$,
- or $z_i \in T^*$, for all $1 \leq i \leq k$ and some $k \geq 1$.

The family of languages generated by right-linear scattered context grammars of degree n is denoted by $\mathscr{L}(SC, RLIN, n)$, and

$$\mathscr{L}(SC, RLIN) = \bigcup_{n=1}^{\infty} \mathscr{L}(SC, RLIN, n).$$

To prove that $\mathscr{L}(SM, LIN, n) = \mathscr{L}(SC, LIN, n)$, for every $n \geq 1$, we first give two preliminary lemmas.

Lemma 5.25. *For every* $n \geq 1$, $\mathscr{L}(SM, LIN, n) \subseteq \mathscr{L}(SC, LIN, n)$.

Proof. Let $\bar{G} = (\bar{V}_1, \dots, \bar{V}_n, T, \bar{P}, \bar{S})$ be a linear simple matrix grammar of degree n. Set $N = \{\langle p, i\rangle : p \in \bar{P}, 1 \leq i \leq n\}$. Define the linear scattered context grammar of degree n,

$$G = \left(\bar{V}_1 \cup \dots \cup \bar{V}_n \cup N \cup \{S\}, T, P, S\right),$$

where P is defined as follows:

1. For each $(\bar{S}) \rightarrow (x_1 A_1 \dots x_n A_n x_{n+1}) \in \bar{P}$, where $x_i \in T^*$, for all $1 \leq i \leq n+1$, and $p = (A_1, \dots, A_n) \rightarrow (y_1, \dots, y_n) \in \bar{P}$, add $(S) \rightarrow \left(x_1 \langle p, 1\rangle x_2 A_2 \dots x_n A_n x_{n+1}\right)$ to P.
2. For each $p = (A_1, \dots, A_i, \dots, A_n) \rightarrow (x_1 B_1 y_1, \dots, x_i B_i y_i, \dots, x_n B_n y_n) \in \bar{P}$, where $x_j, y_j \in T^*$, $A_j, B_j \in \bar{V}_j - T$, for all $1 \leq j \leq n$, and

   (a) for each $i < n$, add $\left(\langle p, i\rangle, A_{i+1}\right) \rightarrow \left(x_i B_i y_i, \langle p, i+1\rangle\right)$ to P;

(b) for each $q = (B_1, \ldots, B_n) \rightarrow (z_1, \ldots, z_n) \in \bar{P}$, add

(i) $\big(B_1, \langle p, n\rangle\big) \rightarrow \big(\langle q, 1\rangle, x_n B_n y_n\big)$ to P;

(ii) if $n = 1$, add
$\big(\langle p, 1\rangle\big) \rightarrow \big(x_1\langle q, 1\rangle y_1\big)$ to P.

3. For each $p = (A_1, \ldots, A_i, \ldots, A_n) \rightarrow (x_1, \ldots, x_i, \ldots, x_n) \in \bar{P}$, where $x_j \in T^*$, for all $1 \leq j \leq n$, and

(a) for each $i < n$, add
$\big(\langle p, i\rangle, A_{i+1}\big) \rightarrow \big(x_i, \langle p, i+1\rangle\big)$ to P;

(b) add $\big(\langle p, n\rangle\big) \rightarrow (x_n)$ to P.

Every production introduced in (1) simulates the initial production of $\bar{G}$ and, in addition, selects the next production p to be simulated. After its application, we obtain the sentential form of the form

$$w_1\langle p, 1\rangle w_2 A_2 \ldots w_n A_n w_{n+1},$$

where $w_i \in T^*$, for all $1 \leq i \leq n$, and

$$p = (A_1, \ldots, A_n) \rightarrow (z_1, \ldots, z_n) \in \bar{P}.$$

Consider any derivation

$$w_1 A_1 w_2 A_2 \ldots w_n A_n w_{n+1} \Rightarrow_{\bar{G}} w_1 x_1 B_1 y_1 \ldots w_n x_n B_n y_n w_{n+1}\ [p],$$

where

$$p = (A_1, \ldots, A_n) \rightarrow (x_1 B_1 y_1, \ldots, x_n B_n y_n),$$

$x_i, y_i \in T^*$, and $A_i, B_i \in \bar{V}_i - T$, for all $1 \leq i \leq n$. This derivation is simulated by G in n derivation steps by first applying a production from (2a) $n - 1$ times and, finally, applying a production from (2bi), so

$$\begin{aligned} & w_1\langle p, 1\rangle w_2 A_2 \ldots w_n A_n w_{n+1} \\ \Rightarrow_G\ & w_1 x_1 B_1 y_1 w_2\langle p, 2\rangle \ldots w_n A_n w_{n+1} \\ & \vdots \\ \Rightarrow_G\ & w_1 x_1 B_1 y_1 w_2 x_2 B_2 y_2 \ldots w_n\langle p, n\rangle w_{n+1} \\ \Rightarrow_G\ & w_1 x_1\langle q, 1\rangle y_1 w_2 x_2 B_2 y_2 \ldots w_n x_n B_n y_n w_{n+1}, \end{aligned}$$

where

$$q = (B_1, \ldots, B_n) \rightarrow (z_1, \ldots, z_n) \in \bar{P}.$$

Observe that no nonterminal A_i can be skipped by a production from (2a) because the sentential form contains exactly n nonterminals and the form of the productions from (2a) requires their n applications during every simulation. For the same reason, a production from (2bi) has to select the first nonterminal in a sentential form of G. If $n = 1$, a production from (2bii) is used instead of a production from (2a) or (2bi). Finally, a production of the form $(A_1, \ldots, A_n) \rightarrow (x_1, \ldots, x_n) \in \bar{P}$, where $x_i \in T^*$, for all $1 \leq i \leq n$, is simulated by productions from (3a) and (3b) that perform the simulation analogously to the productions from (2a) and (2bi), respectively. By removing the symbol from N from the sentential form, (3b) finishes the derivation. ■

As the number of components in every production of G constructed in the proof of Lemma 5.25 is at most 2, we state the following corollary.

Corollary 5.26. *For every linear simple matrix grammar $\bar{G}$ of degree n, there is a linear scattered context grammar G of degree n such that $L(\bar{G}) = L(G)$, and* $\text{mcs}(G) = 1$. ■

Lemma 5.27. *For every $n \geq 1$, $\mathscr{L}(SC, LIN, n) \subseteq \mathscr{L}(SM, LIN, n)$.*

Proof. Let $\bar{G} = (\bar{V}, T, \bar{P}, \bar{S})$ be a linear scattered context grammar of degree n. Set

$$V_1 = \Big\{\langle a, 1\rangle : a \in \big(\bar{V} - \{\bar{S}\}\big) \cup \{\varepsilon\}\Big\} \cup T,$$
$$\vdots$$
$$V_n = \Big\{\langle a, n\rangle : a \in \big(\bar{V} - \{\bar{S}\}\big) \cup \{\varepsilon\}\Big\} \cup T.$$

For all $1 \leq i \leq n$, set $\alpha(xay, i) = x\langle a, i\rangle y$, where $a \in \bar{V} - \{\bar{S}\}$, $x, y \in T^*$, and $\alpha(\varepsilon, i) = \langle \varepsilon, i\rangle$. Define the linear simple matrix grammar $G = (V_1, \dots, V_n, T, P, S)$ of degree n, where P is defined as follows:

1. For each $(\bar{S}) \to (x_1 A_1 \dots x_k A_k x_{k+1}) \in \bar{P}$, where $k \leq n$, add $(S) \to \big(x_1\langle A_1, 1\rangle \dots x_k\langle A_k, k\rangle x_{k+1}\langle \varepsilon, k+1\rangle \dots \langle \varepsilon, n\rangle\big)$ to P.
2. For each $(A_1, \dots, A_k) \to (z_1, \dots, z_k) \in \bar{P}$, where $k \leq n$, $A_i \in (\bar{V} - T) - \{\bar{S}\}$, for all $1 \leq i \leq k$, $c_1, \dots, c_{n-k} \in \big(\bar{V} - \{\bar{S}\}\big) \cup \{\varepsilon\}$, $\Gamma \in \text{perm}(k, n-k)$, and
$$(d_1, \dots, d_n) = \text{reorder}\big((A_1, \dots, A_k, c_1, \dots, c_{n-k}), \Gamma\big),$$
$$(u_1, \dots, u_n) = \text{reorder}\big((z_1, \dots, z_k, c_1, \dots, c_{n-k}), \Gamma\big),$$
add $\big(\langle d_1, 1\rangle, \dots, \langle d_n, n\rangle\big) \to \big(\alpha(u_1, 1), \dots, \alpha(u_n, n)\big)$ to P.
3. For each $a_i \in T \cup \{\varepsilon\}$, for all $1 \leq i \leq n$, add $\big(\langle a_1, 1\rangle, \dots, \langle a_n, n\rangle\big) \to \big(a_1, \dots, a_n\big)$ to P.

Productions from (1) simulate productions of $\bar{G}$ of the form

$$(\bar{S}) \to (x_1 A_1 \dots x_k A_k x_{k+1}),$$

where $k \leq n$, so that each $A_i \in (\bar{V} - T) - \{\bar{S}\}$ is converted to $\langle A_i, i\rangle \in V_i - T$, for all $1 \leq i \leq k$, and the string $\langle \varepsilon, k+1\rangle \dots \langle \varepsilon, n\rangle$, which is erased in the last step of the derivation, is added to the end of the resulting sentential form so that the sentential form contains n nonterminals. Consider the sentential form of the form

$$w_1\langle B_1, 1\rangle \dots w_m\langle B_m, m\rangle w_{m+1}\langle \varepsilon, m+1\rangle \dots \langle \varepsilon, n\rangle,$$

where $w_j \in T^*$ and $\langle B_i, i\rangle \in V_i - T$, for all $1 \leq j \leq m+1$, $1 \leq i \leq m$. Each $\langle B_i, i\rangle$ may be of the form

- $\langle \varepsilon, i \rangle$, which indicates that the ith nonterminal was deleted in $\bar{G}$;
- $\langle a, i \rangle$, where $a \in T$, which indicates that the ith nonterminal was rewritten to a in $\bar{G}$;
- $\langle A, i \rangle$, where $A \in (\bar{V} - T) - \{\bar{S}\}$.

The application of a production $(A_1, \ldots, A_k) \rightarrow (z_1, \ldots, z_k) \in \bar{P}$, where $k \leq n$, $A_i \in (\bar{V} - T) - \{\bar{S}\}$, for all $1 \leq i \leq k$, can be simulated in G if $B_{j_1} \ldots B_{j_k} = A_1 \ldots A_k$, where $j_i < j_{i+1}$, $1 \leq j_i \leq m$, for all $1 \leq i \leq k$. The productions of G constructed in (2) permute $A_1, \ldots, A_k$ (preserving their order) with symbols from $\left(\bar{V} - \{\bar{S}\}\right) \cup \{\varepsilon\}$ (not preserving their order), and convert them to the corresponding symbols from $(V_1 \cup \cdots \cup V_n) - T$. The same is performed with the right-hand side of the production for the same permutation. As a result, every symbol $\langle B_i, i \rangle$ remains unchanged if $\langle B_i, i \rangle = \langle \varepsilon, i \rangle$, $\langle B_i, i \rangle = \langle a, i \rangle$, where $a \in T$, or the simulated production is not applied to B_i. Otherwise, $\langle B_i, i \rangle$ is rewritten to $x\langle C, i \rangle y$, $x\langle a, i \rangle y$, or $\langle \varepsilon, i \rangle$, where $x, y \in T^*$, $a \in T$, and $C \in (\bar{V} - T) - \{\bar{S}\}$, depending on the right-hand side of the simulated context-free component applied to B_i. Finally, a production from (3) finishes the derivation by rewriting all $\langle a, i \rangle$, where $a \in T$, to a and erasing all $\langle \varepsilon, i \rangle$. ■

The main result of this section follows next.

Theorem 5.28. *For every* $n \geq 1$,

$$\mathscr{L}(SC, LIN, n) = \mathscr{L}(SM, LIN, n),$$
$$\mathscr{L}(SC, LIN) = \mathscr{L}(SM, LIN).$$

Proof. This theorem follows from Lemmas 5.25 and 5.27. ■

A similar result can be proved for right-linear scattered context grammars as well.

Theorem 5.29. *For every* $n \geq 1$,

$$\mathscr{L}(SC, RLIN, n) = \mathscr{L}(SM, RLIN, n),$$
$$\mathscr{L}(SC, RLIN) = \mathscr{L}(SM, RLIN).$$

Proof. The proof is analogous to the proof of Theorem 5.28 and, therefore, left to the reader. ■

Theorems 5.28, 5.29, and Theorems 2.23, 2.24 imply the following two corollaries.

Corollary 5.30. *For every* $n \geq 1$,

$$\mathscr{L}(SC, LIN, n) \subset \mathscr{L}(SC, LIN, n+1),$$
$$\mathscr{L}(SC, RLIN, n) \subset \mathscr{L}(SC, RLIN, n+1),$$
$$\mathscr{L}(SC, RLIN, n) \subset \mathscr{L}(SC, LIN, n).$$

■

Corollary 5.31.

$$\mathscr{L}(CF) - \mathscr{L}(SC, LIN) \neq \emptyset,$$
$$\mathscr{L}(CF) - \mathscr{L}(SC, RLIN) \neq \emptyset,$$

and

$$\mathscr{L}(SC, RLIN) \subset \mathscr{L}(SC, LIN) \subset \mathscr{L}(PSC).$$

■

We have proved that linear scattered context grammars are equivalent to linear simple matrix grammars. The main difference of these grammars consists in the way of applying their productions. While in linear simple matrix grammars every production contains exactly n components, each of which rewrites symbols over its own alphabet, the number of components in the productions of linear scattered context grammars may vary, and all the components share the same alphabet. In addition, we have proved that the generative power of linear scattered context grammars depends on the number of nonterminals appearing in the starting production, but it is independent of the number of components in scattered context productions (see Corollary 5.26). As a result, linear scattered context grammars are more convenient for describing languages than linear simple matrix grammars because the total number of their nonterminals is lower; in addition, their productions can capture only true context dependencies while avoiding unnecessary rewriting of certain symbols.

Interestingly enough, when we restrict scattered context grammars and simple matrix grammars to their linear and right-linear variants, the power of the resulting grammars is identical; as opposed to this identity, ordinary scattered context grammars are more powerful than simple matrix grammars (see Theorem 3.27).

Taking into account the Chomsky hierarchy, we add a concluding note about scattered context grammars with context-sensitive and phrase-structure productions. As obvious, scattered context grammars with context-sensitive productions generate the family of context-sensitive languages while the others characterize the family of phrase-structure languages. Therefore, as these scattered context grammars are as powerful as the grammars underlying them, their use is of little or no interest.

5.6 Extended propagating scattered context grammars

In classical formal language theory, monotone grammars, which generate the family of context-sensitive languages, represent phrase-structure grammars in which every production has its right-hand side at least as long as its left-hand side. In this section, we discuss analogically restricted scattered context grammars. That is, by concatenating all the strings occurring on the right-hand side of any n-component production, we obtain a string of length n or more. Clearly, all propagating scattered context grammars satisfy this requirement, but not all scattered context grammars satisfying this requirement are propagating because they allow the empty string to appear on the right-hand side of their productions. In this sense, they represent an extension of propagating scattered context grammars, so we refer to them as extended propagating scattered context grammars. In [28], it was proved that these grammars generate the family of context-sensitive languages. Before establishing this result, we define these grammars formally.

Definition 5.32. An *extended propagating scattered context grammar* is a scattered context grammar $G = (V, T, P, S)$ in which every

$$(A_1, \ldots, A_n) \to (x_1, \ldots, x_n) \in P$$

satisfies

$$|x_1 \ldots x_n| \geq n.$$

The family of languages generated by extended propagating scattered context grammars is denoted by $\mathscr{L}(PSC, ext)$.

In what follows, we prove that $\mathscr{L}(PSC, ext) = \mathscr{L}(CS)$. We use a slightly modified construction of the proof presented in [28]. First, we prove that $\mathscr{L}(CS) \subseteq \mathscr{L}(PSC, ext)$.

Lemma 5.33. $\mathscr{L}(CS) \subseteq \mathscr{L}(PSC, ext)$.

Proof. Let $G = (V, T, P, S)$ be a context-sensitive grammar in Kuroda normal form (see Definition 2.17). Set

$$\begin{aligned}
\bar{N}_1 &= \{a' : a \in T\}, \\
\bar{N}_2 &= \big\{\hat{a} : a \in (V - T) \cup \bar{N}_1\big\}, \\
\bar{N}_3 &= \big\{\langle a \rangle : a \in (V - T) \cup \bar{N}_1 \cup \bar{N}_2\big\}, \\
\bar{N}_4 &= \{\hat{a} : a \in T\}.
\end{aligned}$$

Define the extended propagating scattered context grammar

$$\bar{G} = \big(V \cup \bar{N}_1 \cup \bar{N}_2 \cup \bar{N}_3 \cup \bar{N}_4 \cup \{\bar{S}\}, T, \bar{P}, \bar{S}\big),$$

where $\bar{P}$ is constructed as follows:

1. For each $S \Rightarrow_G^* w$, where $w \in T^*$ and $|w| \leq 3$, add $(\bar{S}) \to (w)$ to $\bar{P}$.
2. For each $S \Rightarrow_G^* ABCD$, where $A, B, C, D \in V - T$, add $(\bar{S}) \to \big(\langle \hat{A} \rangle BC \langle D \rangle\big)$ to $\bar{P}$.
3. For each $a, b, c \in (V - T) \cup \bar{N}_1$, add
   (a) $\big(\langle a \rangle, b, \langle c \rangle\big) \to \big(\varepsilon, \langle b \rangle, c\langle a \rangle\big)$,
   (b) $\big(\langle \hat{a} \rangle, b, \langle c \rangle\big) \to \big(\varepsilon, \langle b \rangle, c\langle \hat{a} \rangle\big)$,
   (c) $\big(\langle a \rangle, \hat{b}, \langle c \rangle\big) \to \big(\varepsilon, \langle \hat{b} \rangle, c\langle a \rangle\big)$,
   (d) $\big(\langle a \rangle, b, \langle \hat{c} \rangle\big) \to \big(\varepsilon, \langle b \rangle, \hat{c}\langle a \rangle\big)$ to $\bar{P}$.

4. For each $AB \to CD \in P$, where $A, B, C, D \in V - T$, and $a, b \in (V - T) \cup \bar{N}_1$, add
   (a) $(\langle A\rangle, B, a, \langle b\rangle) \to (\varepsilon, \varepsilon, \langle a\rangle, bC\langle D\rangle)$,
   (b) $(\langle \hat{A}\rangle, B, a, \langle b\rangle) \to (\varepsilon, \varepsilon, \langle a\rangle, b\hat{C}\langle D\rangle)$,
   (c) $(\langle A\rangle, B, \hat{a}, \langle b\rangle) \to (\varepsilon, \varepsilon, \langle \hat{a}\rangle, bC\langle D\rangle)$,
   (d) $(\langle A\rangle, B, a, \langle \hat{b}\rangle) \to (\varepsilon, \varepsilon, \langle a\rangle, \hat{b}C\langle D\rangle)$ to $\bar{P}$.
5. For each $A \to BC \in P$, where $A, B, C \in V - T$, and $a, b \in (V - T) \cup \bar{N}_1$, add
   (a) $(\langle A\rangle, a, \langle b\rangle) \to (\varepsilon, \langle a\rangle, bB\langle C\rangle)$,
   (b) $(\langle \hat{A}\rangle, a, \langle b\rangle) \to (\varepsilon, \langle a\rangle, b\hat{B}\langle C\rangle)$,
   (c) $(\langle A\rangle, \hat{a}, \langle b\rangle) \to (\varepsilon, \langle \hat{a}\rangle, bB\langle C\rangle)$,
   (d) $(\langle A\rangle, a, \langle \hat{b}\rangle) \to (\varepsilon, \langle a\rangle, \hat{b}B\langle C\rangle)$ to $\bar{P}$.
6. For each $A \to a \in P$, where $A \in V - T$, $a \in T$, and $b, c \in (V - T) \cup \bar{N}_1$, add
   (a) $(\langle A\rangle, b, \langle c\rangle) \to (\varepsilon, \langle b\rangle, c\langle a\rangle)$,
   (b) $(\langle \hat{A}\rangle, b, \langle c\rangle) \to (\varepsilon, \langle b\rangle, c\langle \hat{a}\rangle)$,
   (c) $(\langle A\rangle, \hat{b}, \langle c\rangle) \to (\varepsilon, \langle \hat{b}\rangle, c\langle a\rangle)$,
   (d) $(\langle A\rangle, b, \langle \hat{c}\rangle) \to (\varepsilon, \langle b\rangle, \hat{c}\langle a\rangle)$ to $\bar{P}$.
7. For each $a, b \in T$, add
   (a) $(\langle \hat{a}'\rangle, \langle b'\rangle) \to (\hat{a}, b')$,
   (b) $(\hat{a}, b') \to (a, \hat{b})$,
   (c) $(\hat{a}) \to (a)$ to $\bar{P}$.

Basic Idea.
The simulation of G is started in $\bar{G}$ by using a production from (2). The simulation is performed by cycling through every sentential form by productions from (3) until the nonterminals to be rewritten appear at the beginning of the current sentential form. Then, depending on the production whose application is being simulated, a production from (4), (5), or (6) is used. After this, another simulation can be performed analogically. The derivation is completed by applying productions from (7).

To be able to cycle through the sentential form, the grammar marks the first and the last nonterminal. During one cycle, the current first symbol is placed to the end of the sentential form and is marked as the last; the previously second symbol is marked as the first. The simulation of an application of a production from G is simulated analogously.

In addition, the grammar records the symbol corresponding to the first symbol of the sentential form of G. The derivation is successful only if this symbol appears at the beginning of the sentential form during the final phase of the derivation.

Formal Proof.
First, we prove Claims 1 through 4 stated below.

Claim 1. Every $w \in L(\bar{G})$, where $|w| \leq 3$, is generated by a production from (1).

Proof. As the constructed grammar is monotone, the only productions that are able to generate sentences consisting of at most 3 terminals are those from (1). □

Claim 2. Every derivation of $w \in L(\bar{G})$, where $|w| \geq 4$, can only be performed in the following way:

$$\begin{aligned}\bar{S} &\Rightarrow_{\bar{G}} x \;\; [p_2] \\ &\Rightarrow_{\bar{G}}^{*} y \;\; [\Xi_1] \\ &\Rightarrow_{\bar{G}} z \;\; [p_{7a}] \\ &\Rightarrow_{\bar{G}}^{*} w \;\; [\Xi_2],\end{aligned}$$

where $x \in \bar{N}_3(V - T)(V - T)\bar{N}_3$, every sentential form y_i in $x \Rightarrow_{\bar{G}}^{*} y$ satisfies

$$y_i \in \big((V - T) \cup \bar{N}_1 \cup \bar{N}_2 \cup \bar{N}_3\big)^+,$$

every sentential form w_i in $z \Rightarrow_{\bar{G}}^{*} w$ satisfies $w_i \in (T \cup \bar{N}_1 \cup \bar{N}_4)^+$, p_2 is a production from (2), p_{7a} is a production from (7a), and Ξ_1 and Ξ_2 are sequences of productions introduced in (3) through (6) and (7), respectively.

Proof. First, observe that the only productions that can start the derivation of $w \in L(\bar{G})$, where $|w| \geq 4$, are those from (2). After the application of a production from (2), we obtain a sentential form $x \in \bar{N}_3(V - T)(V - T)\bar{N}_3$. Productions from (2) cannot be used during the rest of the derivation because $\bar{S}$ does not appear on the right-hand side of any production.

Now, productions from (3) through (6) can be used. Notice that these productions rewrite only symbols from $(V - T) \cup \bar{N}_1 \cup \bar{N}_2 \cup \bar{N}_3$, so after their application, the resulting sentential forms also contain only these symbols. In addition, each of these productions contains precisely two symbols from $\bar{N}_3$ both on its left-hand side and right-hand side. As a result, every sentential form contains exactly two symbols from $\bar{N}_3$. Productions from (7b) and (7c) cannot be used as they require a symbol from $\bar{N}_4$ to be present in the sentential form.

During this phase, a production from (7a) can be used as well. It rewrites the symbols from $\bar{N}_3$ and introduces a symbol from $\bar{N}_4$ to the sentential form. From this moment, only productions from (7b) and (7c) are applicable. As these productions rewrite only symbols from $\bar{N}_1 \cup \bar{N}_4$ and no other productions can be used, every sentential form w_i has to satisfy $w_i \in (T \cup \bar{N}_1 \cup \bar{N}_4)^+$ in order to generate $w \in T^+$. □

Claim 3. In the derivation

$$\begin{aligned}\bar{S} &\Rightarrow_{\bar{G}} x\ [p_2] \\ &\Rightarrow_{\bar{G}}^{*} y\ [\Xi_1] \\ &\Rightarrow_{\bar{G}} z\ [p_{7a}] \\ &\Rightarrow_{\bar{G}}^{*} w\ [\Xi_2]\end{aligned}$$

from Claim 2, every sentential form y_i in $x \Rightarrow_{\bar{G}}^{*} y$ satisfies

$$y_i \in \bar{N}_3\big((V - T) \cup \bar{N}_1 \cup \bar{N}_2\big)^* \bar{N}_3$$

and every sentential form w_i in $z \Rightarrow_{\bar{G}}^{*} w$ satisfies $w_i \in T^* \bar{N}_4 \bar{N}_1^*$.

Proof. To show that

$$y_i \in \bar{N}_3\big((V - T) \cup \bar{N}_1 \cup \bar{N}_2\big)^* \bar{N}_3$$

and $w_i \in T^* \bar{N}_4 \bar{N}_1^*$, first notice that

$$x \in \bar{N}_3\big((V - T) \cup \bar{N}_1 \cup \bar{N}_2\big)^* \bar{N}_3.$$

Furthermore, observe that the form of the productions from (3) through (6) guarantees that a nonterminal from $\bar{N}_3$ remains at the end of y_i. In addition, productions from (3) through (6) move the nonterminal from $\bar{N}_3$ right in the sentential form. Productions from (7) replace this nonterminal with a symbol from $\bar{N}_4$, which can only move right as well. In this way, the grammar guarantees that if any nonterminal appears in front of this symbol, it can never be rewritten during the rest of the derivation, and the derivation is unsuccessful. As a result,

$$y_i \in \bar{N}_3\big((V - T) \cup \bar{N}_1 \cup \bar{N}_2\big)^* \bar{N}_3$$

and $w_i \in T^* \bar{N}_4 \bar{N}_1^*$. □

Claim 4. In the derivation

$$\begin{aligned}\bar{S} &\Rightarrow_{\bar{G}} x\ [p_2] \\ &\Rightarrow_{\bar{G}}^{*} y\ [\Xi_1] \\ &\Rightarrow_{\bar{G}} z\ [p_{7a}] \\ &\Rightarrow_{\bar{G}}^{*} w\ [\Xi_2]\end{aligned}$$

from Claim 2, every sentential form y_i in $x \Rightarrow_{\bar{G}}^{*} y$ contains precisely one symbol from $\bar{N}_2 \cup \{\langle a \rangle : a \in \bar{N}_2\}$.

Proof. Productions from (3) through (6) either do not contain any symbol from $\bar{N}_2 \cup \{\langle a \rangle : a \in \bar{N}_2\}$ or they contain precisely one, occurring both on their left-hand sides and right-hand sides. Because x contains one symbol from $\bar{N}_2 \cup \{\langle a \rangle : a \in \bar{N}_2\}$, this number is preserved after applications of productions from (3) through (6). □

Now, it is easy to see that every production of the form $AB \to CD \in P$ is simulated properly by $\bar{G}$. Indeed, when applying a production from (4), the symbols corresponding to A and B in $\bar{G}$ necessarily occur as two neighbors at the beginning of the sentential form; if some nonterminals occur between them, these nonterminals eventually appear in front of the leading nonterminal from $\bar{N}_3$, and by Claim 3, they can never be rewritten. Symbols corresponding to C and D are placed to the end of the sentential form. Productions from (4b), (4c), and (4d) handle different positions of the nonterminal from $\bar{N}_2 \cup \{\langle a \rangle : a \in \bar{N}_2\}$, and they make sure that its position remains correct after the simulation. In particular, notice that there is no production of the form

$$(\langle A \rangle, \hat{B}, a, \langle b \rangle) \to (\varepsilon, \varepsilon, \langle a \rangle, bC\langle \hat{D} \rangle).$$

This production would check the context between the first and the last nonterminal of the original sentential form of G, which is illegal in context-sensitive grammars. The simulation of $A \to BC \in P$, $A \to a \in P$, and cycling through the sentential form is performed analogously.

In order to enter the final phase by a production from (7a), in which all nonterminals are rewritten to terminals by productions from (7b) and (7c), the symbol from $\{\langle a \rangle : a \in \bar{N}_2\}$ has to appear at the beginning of the sentential form in $\bar{G}$; otherwise, the nonterminals preceding this symbol cannot be rewritten.

From these observations and Claims 1 through 4, we obtain $w \in L(G)$ if and only if $w \in L(\bar{G})$, so the theorem holds. ■

Next, we demonstrate that $\mathscr{L}(PSC, ext) \subseteq \mathscr{L}(CS)$.

Lemma 5.34. $\mathscr{L}(PSC, ext) \subseteq \mathscr{L}(CS)$.

Proof. By definition, the derivations of extended propagating scattered context grammars are monotone. Therefore, their derivations can be simulated by context-sensitive grammars. As a result, $\mathscr{L}(PSC, ext) \subseteq \mathscr{L}(CS)$. ■

Putting Lemmas 5.33 and 5.34 together, we obtain the main result of this section.

Theorem 5.35. $\mathscr{L}(PSC, ext) = \mathscr{L}(CS)$. ■

CHAPTER 6

Reduction and economy

As its central topic, descriptional complexity studies the generative power of grammars in relation to the size of their components. The present chapter discusses this complexity in terms of scattered context grammars. Perhaps most importantly, it studies how to reduce the size of their components without any decrease of their generative power. This reduction obviously makes scattered context rewriting more succinct and economical, which are properties highly appreciated both from a practical and theoretical standpoint.

The present chapter consists of two sections. First, Section 6.1 establishes the crucial results concerning the reduction of scattered context grammars and, therefore, represents the core of this chapter. Then, Section 6.2 adds some closely related results about economical transformations of phrase-structure grammars to scattered context grammars without introducing many new grammatical components.

6.1 Reduction

When studying the descriptional complexity of scattered context grammars in this section, we primarily investigate how to reduce the number of various grammatical components, such as the number of nonterminals or the number of context-sensitive productions, while preserving the generative power of these grammars. For this purpose, we make use of the measures introduced in Definition 2.45 to quantitatively evaluate the achieved reductions. We present several results, which reduce one of these measures while completely ignoring the other measures. Frequently, however, results of this kind are achieved at the cost of an enormous increase of the other measures. Therefore, we also undertake a finer approach to this descriptional complexity by simultaneously reducing several of these measures while keeping the generative power unchanged.

We start by pointing out a corollary of Theorem 4.7.

Theorem 6.1. *One-nonterminal scattered context grammars cannot generate all recursively enumerable languages.*

Proof. Observe that any one-nonterminal scattered context grammar G satisfies $\delta\big(F(G)\big) \subseteq \text{shuffle}\big(\mathit{term}(G)\big)$ (see the terminology introduced by Definitions 4.1 and 4.2), so $L(G) \in \mathscr{L}(SC, \text{term})$, and by Theorem 4.7, $\mathscr{L}(SC, \text{term}) \subset \mathscr{L}(RE)$. ■

For scattered context grammars containing only one context-sensitive production, the following theorem holds.

Theorem 6.2. *There exists a scattered context grammar G such that G defines a non-context-free language, and*

$$\text{dcs}(G) = \text{mcs}(G) = \text{ocs}(G) = 1.$$

Proof. Consider the scattered context grammar

$$G = \big(\{S, A, B, C, D, a, b, c\}, \{a, b, c\}, P, S\big),$$

where the set of productions P is defined as

$$\begin{aligned} P = \big\{&(S) \to (AC), \\ &(A) \to (aAbB), \\ &(A) \to (\varepsilon), \\ &(C) \to (cCD), \\ &(C) \to (\varepsilon), \\ &(B, D) \to (\varepsilon, \varepsilon)\big\}. \end{aligned}$$

It is easy to verify that $L(G) = \{a^n b^n c^n : n \geq 0\}$ and $\text{dcs}(G) = \text{mcs}(G) = \text{ocs}(G) = 1$. ■

Next, we concentrate on reducing the number of nonterminals in scattered context grammars. We demonstrate that the number of nonterminals can be reduced to three or fewer.

Theorem 6.3. *For every recursively enumerable language L, there is a scattered context grammar $G = (V, T, P, S)$ such that $L(G) = L$, and*

$$|V - T| = 3.$$

Proof. Let L be a recursively enumerable language. By Theorem 2.37, there exists a queue grammar $Q = (\bar{V}, T, W, F, R, g)$ such that $L = L(Q)$. Without loss of generality, assume that Q satisfies the properties described in Lemma 2.38. Set $n = |\bar{V} \cup W|$. Introduce a bijective homomorphism β from $\bar{V} \cup W$ to $\{B\}^*\{A\}\{B\}^* \cap \{A, B\}^n$. Without loss of generality, assume that $(\bar{V} \cup W) \cap \{A, B, S\} = \emptyset$. Define the scattered context grammar

$$G = \big(T \cup \{A, B, S\}, T, P, S\big),$$

where P is constructed in the following way:

1. For $g = ab$, where $a \in \bar{V} - T$ and $b \in W - F$, add $(S) \to \big(\beta(b)SS\beta(a)SA\big)$ to P.
2. For each $a \in \{A, B\}$, add $(S, S, a, S) \to (S, \varepsilon, aS, S)$ to P.
3. For each $(a, b, x, c) \in R$, where $a \in \bar{V} - T$, $x \in (\bar{V} - T)^*$, and $b, c \in W - F - \{1\}$, add

$$(b_1, \ldots, b_n, S, a_1, \ldots, a_n, S, S) \\ \to \big(c_1, \ldots, c_n, \varepsilon, e_1, \ldots, e_n, SS, \beta(x)S\big) \text{ to } P,$$

   where $b_1 \ldots b_n = \beta(b)$, $a_1 \ldots a_n = \beta(a)$, $c_1 \ldots c_n = \beta(c)$, and $e_1 \ldots e_n = \varepsilon$.
4. For each $(a, b, x, c) \in R$, where $a \in \bar{V} - T$, $b \in W - F - \{1\}$, $x \in (\bar{V} - T)^*$, and

   (a) $c = 1$, add

$$(b_1, \ldots, b_n, S, a_1, \ldots, a_n, S, S) \\ \to \big(c_1, \ldots, c_n, \varepsilon, e_1, \ldots, e_n, SS, \beta(x)S\big) \text{ to } P;$$

   (b) $c \in F$ and $x = \varepsilon$, add

$$(b_1, \ldots, b_n, S, a_1, \ldots, a_n, S, S, A) \\ \to (e_1, \ldots, e_n, \varepsilon, e_{n+1}, \ldots, e_{2n}, \varepsilon, \varepsilon, \varepsilon) \text{ to } P,$$

   where $b_1 \ldots b_n = \beta(b)$, $a_1 \ldots a_n = \beta(a)$, $c_1 \ldots c_n = \beta(c)$, and $e_1 \ldots e_{2n} = \varepsilon$.
5. For each $(a, 1, x, c) \in R$, where $a \in \bar{V} - T$, $x \in T$, and

   (a) $c = 1$, add

$$(b_1, \ldots, b_n, S, a_1, \ldots, a_n, S, S) \\ \to (c_1, \ldots, c_n, \varepsilon, e_1, \ldots, e_n, SS, xS) \text{ to } P;$$

   (b) $c \in F$, add

$$(b_1, \ldots, b_n, S, a_1, \ldots, a_n, S, S, A) \\ \to (e_1, \ldots, e_n, \varepsilon, e_{n+1}, \ldots, e_{2n}, \varepsilon, \varepsilon, x) \text{ to } P,$$

   where $b_1 \ldots b_n = \beta(1)$, $a_1 \ldots a_n = \beta(a)$, $c_1 \ldots c_n = \beta(c)$, and $e_1 \ldots e_{2n} = \varepsilon$.

Basic Idea.
The constructed scattered context grammar G simulates the queue grammar Q that satisfies the properties described in Lemma 2.38. The production from (1), applied only once, initializes the derivation. One of the productions from (4b) and (5b) terminates the derivation. In greater detail, a production from (4b) is used in the derivation of $\varepsilon \in L(Q)$; in a derivation of every other string, a production from (5b) is used in the last step of the derivation.

Every sentential form of G can be divided into two parts. The first n nonterminals encode the state of Q. The second part represents the queue, where the first symbol S always occurs at the beginning of the queue and the third S always occurs at the end of the queue, followed by the ultimate nonterminal A.

During any successful derivation of G, a production introduced in (2) is always applied after the application of a production introduced in (1), (3), (4a), and (5a). More precisely, to go on performing the successful derivation, after applying productions from (1), (3), (4a), and (5a), G shifts the second occurrence of S right in the current sentential form. G makes this shift by using productions introduced in (2) to obtain a sentential form having precisely n occurrences of $d \in \{A, B\}$ between the first occurrence of S and the second occurrence of S.

Formal Proof.
The following claims demonstrate that the production from (1) can be used only once during a successful derivation.

Claim 1. Let $S \Rightarrow_G^* x$ be a derivation during which G uses the productions introduced in (1) i times, for some $i \geq 1$. Then $|x|_{\{S\}} = 1 + 2i - 3j$, $|x|_{\{B\}} = (n-1)k$, and $|x|_{\{A\}} = k + i - j$, where k is a non-negative integer and j is the number of applications of productions introduced in (4b) and (5b) such that $j \geq 1$ and $1 + 2i \geq 3j$.

Proof. Notice that the productions introduced in (2), (3), (4a), and (5a) preserve the number of A's, B's, and S's present in the sentential form. Next, observe that every application of the production from (1) adds two S's to the sentential form and every application of a production from (4b) or (5b) removes three S's from the sentential form. Finally, notice the last A on the right-hand side of the production from (1) and on the left-hand sides of the productions from (4b) and (5b). Based on these observations, it is easy to see that Claim 1 holds. □

Claim 2. Let $S \Rightarrow_G^* x$ be a derivation in G during which G applies the production introduced in (1) two or more times. Then, $x \notin T^*$.

Proof. Let $S \Rightarrow_G^* x$, where $x \in T^*$. Because $x \in T^*$, $|x|_{\{S\}} = |x|_{\{B\}} = |x|_{\{A\}} = 0$. As a result, we get $k = 0$, and $i = j = 1$ from the equations introduced in Claim 1. Thus, for $i \geq 2$, $x \notin T^*$. □

Next, we demonstrate that productions from (4b) and (5b) can only be used during the last derivation step of a successful derivation.

Claim 3. G generates every $w \in L(G)$ as follows:

$$S \Rightarrow_G u\ [p] \Rightarrow_G^* v \Rightarrow_G w\ [q],$$

where p is the production introduced in (1), q is a production introduced in (4b) or (5b), and during $u \Rightarrow_G^* v$, G makes every derivation step by a production introduced in (2), (3), (4a), or (5a).

Proof. Let $w \in L(G)$. By Claim 2, as $w \in T^*$, G uses the production introduced in (1) only once. Because $S \Rightarrow_G^* w$ begins from S, we can express $S \Rightarrow_G^* w$ as

$$S \Rightarrow_G u\ [p] \Rightarrow_G^* w,$$

where p is the production introduced in (1), and G never uses this production during $u \Rightarrow_G^* w$. Observe that every production r introduced in (2), (3), (4a), and (5a) satisfies $|\text{lhs}(r)|_{\{S\}} = 3$ and $|\text{rhs}(r)|_{\{S\}} = 3$. Furthermore, notice that every production q introduced in (4b) and (5b) satisfies $|\text{lhs}(q)|_{\{S\}} = 3$ and $|\text{rhs}(q)|_{\{S\}} = 0$. These observations imply

$$S \Rightarrow_G u\ [p] \Rightarrow_G^* v \Rightarrow_G w\ [q],$$

where p is the production introduced in (1), q is a production introduced in (4b) or (5b), and during $u \Rightarrow_G^* v$, G makes every step by a production introduced in (2), (3), (4a), or (5a). □

In what follows, we demonstrate that in order to apply a production from (3) through (5), there have to be exactly n nonterminals between the first and the second occurrence of S. This can be accomplished by one or more applications of a production from (2).

Claim 4. If $x \Rightarrow_G y\ [p]$ is a derivation step in a successful derivation of G, where p is a production from (3) through (5), then $x = x_1 S x_2 S x_3 S A$, where $x_1, x_2, x_3 \in (T \cup \{A, B\})^+$, $|x_1|_{\{A,B\}} = k$, $|x_2|_{\{A,B\}} = m$, and $k = m = n$.

Proof. If $k < n$ or $m < n$, no production introduced in (3) through (5) can be used. Therefore, $k \geq n$ and $m \geq n$.

Assume that $k > n$. The only productions that remove the symbols $\{A, B\}$ in front of the first symbol S are those introduced in (4b) and (5b), and these productions remove precisely n nonterminals preceding the first symbol S. For $k > n$, $k - n$ nonterminals remain in the sentential form after the last derivation step so the derivation is unsuccessful. Therefore, $k = n$.

Assume that $m > n$. Then, after the application of a production introduced in (3) through (5), m symbols from $\{A, B\}$ appear in front of the first S. Therefore, the number of nonterminals appearing in front of the first occurrence of S is greater than n, which contradicts the argument given in the previous paragraph. As a result, $m = n$. □

Based on Claims 1 through 4 and the properties of Q, we can express every successful derivation of G as

- either $S \Rightarrow_G \text{rhs}(p_1)\ [p_1] \Rightarrow_G^* u\ [\Xi] \Rightarrow_G v\ [p_{4a}] \Rightarrow_G^* w[\Psi] \Rightarrow_G z[p_{5b}]$, for $z \neq \varepsilon$,
- or $S \Rightarrow_G \text{rhs}(p_1)\ [p_1] \Rightarrow_G^* u\ [\Xi] \Rightarrow_G \varepsilon\ [p_{4b}]$;

p_1, p_{4a}, p_{4b}, and p_{5b}, are productions introduced in (1), (4a), (4b), and (5b), respectively, Ξ is a sequence of productions from (2) and (3), Ψ is a sequence of productions from (2) and (5a), and the derivation satisfies the following properties:

- Every derivation step in $\text{rhs}(p_1) \Rightarrow_G^* u\ [\Xi]$ has one of these forms:

$$\beta(b_1)Sa'_1Sa''_1d_1y'_1SA \Rightarrow_G \beta(b_1)Sa'_1a''_1d_1Sy'_1SA\ [p_2], \text{ or}$$
$$\beta(b_1)S\beta(a_1)S\beta(y_1)SA \Rightarrow_G \beta(c_1)SS\beta(y_1x_1)SA\ [p_3],$$

  where $a'_1, a''_1, y'_1 \in \{A, B\}^*$, $d_1 \in \{A, B\}$, $(a_1, b_1, x_1, c_1) \in R$, $b_1 \neq 1$, $c_1 \neq 1$, $y_1 \in (\bar{V} - T)^*$, and p_2, p_3 are productions introduced in (2), (3), respectively.
- The derivation step $u \Rightarrow_G v\ [p_{4a}]$ has this form:

$$\beta(b_2)S\beta(a_2)S\beta(y_2)SA \Rightarrow_G \beta(1)SS\beta(y_2x_2)SA\ [p_{4a}],$$

  where $(a_2, b_2, x_2, 1) \in R$, $b_2 \neq 1$, and $y_2 \in (\bar{V} - T)^+$. Observe that if $y_2x_2 = \varepsilon$, no production is applicable after this step and the derivation is blocked.
- The derivation step $u \Rightarrow_G \varepsilon\ [p_{4b}]$ has this form:

$$\beta(b_3)S\beta(a_3)S\beta(y_3)SA \Rightarrow_G \varepsilon\ [p_{4b}],$$

  where $(a_3, b_3, \varepsilon, c_3) \in R$, $b_3 \neq 1$, $c_3 \in F$, and $y_3 = \varepsilon$. As no production can be applied after a production from (4b) is used, if $y_3 \neq \varepsilon$, there remain some nonterminals in the sentential form so the derivation is unsuccessful.
- Every derivation step in $v \Rightarrow_G^* w\ [\Psi]$ has one of these forms:

$$\beta(1)Sa'_4Sa''_4d_4y'_4t_4SA \Rightarrow_G \beta(1)Sa'_4a''_4dSy_4t_4SA\ [p_2], \text{ or}$$
$$\beta(1)S\beta(a_4)S\beta(y_4)t_4SA \Rightarrow_G \beta(1)SS\beta(y_4)t_4x_4SA\ [p_{5a}],$$

  where $a'_4, a''_4, y'_4 \in \{A, B\}^*$, $d_4 \in \{A, B\}$, $(a_4, 1, x_4, 1) \in R$, $y_4 \in (\bar{V} - T)^*$, $t_4 \in T^*$, and p_2, p_{5a} are productions introduced in (2), (5a), respectively.
- The derivation step $w \Rightarrow_G z\ [p_{5b}]$ has this form:

$$\beta(1)S\beta(a_5)St_5SA \Rightarrow_G t_5x_5\ [p_{5b}],$$

  where $(a_5, 1, x_5, c_5) \in R$, $c_5 \in F$, and $t_5 \in T^*$.

Observe that

- $S \Rightarrow_G \text{rhs}(p_1)\ [p_1] \Rightarrow_G^* u\ [\Xi] \Rightarrow_G v\ [p_{4a}] \Rightarrow_G^* w\ [\Psi] \Rightarrow_G z\ [p_{5b}]$, for $z \neq \varepsilon$, or
- $S \Rightarrow_G \text{rhs}(p_1)\ [p_1] \Rightarrow_G^* u\ [\Xi] \Rightarrow_G \varepsilon\ [p_{4b}]$,

if and only if

$$\begin{aligned} g \Rightarrow_Q^* a_2y_2b_2 &\Rightarrow_Q y_2x_21\ \big[(a_2, b_2, x_2, 1)\big] \\ \Rightarrow_Q^* a_5t_51 &\Rightarrow_Q zc_5 \quad \big[(a_5, 1, x_5, c_5)\big], \end{aligned}$$

or

$$g \Rightarrow_Q^* a_3y_3b_3 \Rightarrow_Q c_3\ \big[(a_3, b_3, \varepsilon, c_3)\big],$$

respectively. As a result, $L(Q) = L(G)$, so the theorem holds. ■

Up until now, we have reduced only one measure of descriptional complexity regardless of all the other measures. Throughout the rest of this section, we reconsider this topic in a finer way by simultaneously reducing several measures. It turns out that this simultaneous reduction necessitates an increase in all the measures involved. In addition, reducing the number of nonterminals necessarily leads to an increase in the number of context-sensitive productions and vice versa.

Theorem 6.4 (see [29]). *For every recursively enumerable language L, there is a scattered context grammar $G = (V, T, P, S)$ such that $L(G) = L$, and*

$$\begin{aligned} |V - T| &= 5, \\ \mathrm{dcs}(G) &= 2, \\ \mathrm{mcs}(G) &= 3, \\ \mathrm{ocs}(G) &= 6. \end{aligned}$$

Proof. Let

$$G' = \big(\{S', A, B, C, D\} \cup T, T, P' \cup \{AB \to \varepsilon, CD \to \varepsilon\}, S'\big)$$

be a phrase-structure grammar in Geffert normal form, where P' is a set of context-free productions, and $L(G') = L$ (see Lemma 2.19). Define the homomorphism h from $\{A, B, C, D\}^*$ to $\{0, 1\}^*$ so that $h(A) = h(B) = 00$, $h(C) = 10$, and $h(D) = 01$. Define the scattered context grammar

$$G = \big(\{S, \bar{S}, 0, 1, \$\} \cup T, T, P, S\big)$$

with P constructed as follows:

1. For each $S' \to zS'a \in P'$, where $z \in \{A, C\}^*$, $a \in T$, add $(S) \to \big(h(z)Sa\big)$ to P.
2. Add $(S) \to (\bar{S})$ to P.
3. For each $S' \to uS'v \in P'$, where $u \in \{A, C\}^*$, $v \in \{B, D\}^*$, add $(\bar{S}) \to \big(h(u)\bar{S}h(v)\big)$ to P.
4. Add

   (a) $(\bar{S}) \to (\$\$)$,
   (b) $(0, \$, \$, 0) \to (\$, \varepsilon, \varepsilon, \$)$,
   (c) $(1, \$, \$, 1) \to (\$, \varepsilon, \varepsilon, \$)$,
   (d) $(\$) \to (\varepsilon)$ to P.

Observe that G' generates every $a_1 \dots a_k \in L(G')$ in the following way:

$$\begin{aligned} S' &\Rightarrow_{G'} z_{a_k} S' a_k \\ &\Rightarrow_{G'} z_{a_k} z_{a_{k-1}} S' a_{k-1} a_k \\ &\quad \vdots \\ &\Rightarrow_{G'} z_{a_k} \dots z_{a_2} S' a_2 \dots a_k \\ &\Rightarrow_{G'} z_{a_k} \dots z_{a_2} z_{a_1} S' a_1 a_2 \dots a_k \end{aligned}$$

$$
\begin{aligned}
&\Rightarrow_{G'} z_{a_k} \dots z_{a_2} z_{a_1} u_l S' v_l a_1 a_2 \dots a_k \\
&\quad \vdots \\
&\Rightarrow_{G'} z_{a_k} \dots z_{a_1} u_l \dots u_2 S' v_2 \dots v_l a_1 \dots a_k \\
&\Rightarrow_{G'} z_{a_k} \dots z_{a_1} u_l \dots u_2 u_1 v_1 v_2 \dots v_l a_1 \dots a_k \\
&= \quad d_m \dots d_2 d_1 e_1 e_2 \dots e_n a_1 \dots a_k \\
&\Rightarrow_{G'} d_m \dots d_2 e_2 \dots e_n a_1 \dots a_k \\
&\quad \vdots \\
&\Rightarrow_{G'} d_m e_n a_1 \dots a_k \\
&\Rightarrow_{G'} a_1 \dots a_k,
\end{aligned}
$$

where $a_1, \dots, a_k \in T$, $z_{a_1}, \dots, z_{a_k}$, $u_1, \dots, u_l \in \{A, C\}^*$, $v_1, \dots, v_l \in \{B, D\}^*$, $d_1, \dots, d_m \in \{A, C\}$, and $e_1, \dots, e_n \in \{B, D\}$. After erasing S' from the sentential form, G' verifies that the generated strings $z_{a_k} \dots z_{a_1} u_l \dots u_1$ and $v_1 \dots v_l$ are identical. If $m \neq n$, or $d_i e_i \notin \{AB, CD\}$, for some $i \geq 1$, the generated strings do not coincide, and the derivation is blocked, so $a_1 \dots a_k$ does not belong to the generated language.

The above derivation can be straightforwardly simulated by G as follows:

$$
\begin{aligned}
S &\Rightarrow_G h(z_{a_k}) S a_k \\
&\Rightarrow_G h(z_{a_k}) h(z_{a_{k-1}}) S a_{k-1} a_k \\
&\quad \vdots \\
&\Rightarrow_G h(z_{a_k}) \dots h(z_{a_2}) S a_2 \dots a_k \\
&\Rightarrow_G h(z_{a_k}) \dots h(z_{a_2}) h(z_{a_1}) S a_1 a_2 \dots a_k \\
&\Rightarrow_G h(z_{a_k} \dots z_{a_2} z_{a_1}) \bar{S} a_1 a_2 \dots a_k && [p_2] \\
&\Rightarrow_G h(z_{a_k} \dots z_{a_2} z_{a_1}) h(u_l) \bar{S} h(v_l) a_1 a_2 \dots a_k \\
&\quad \vdots \\
&\Rightarrow_G h(z_{a_k} \dots z_{a_1}) h(u_l) \dots h(u_2) \bar{S} h(v_2) \dots h(v_l) a_1 \dots a_k \\
&\Rightarrow_G h(z_{a_k} \dots z_{a_1}) h(u_l) \dots h(u_2) h(u_1) \bar{S} h(v_1) h(v_2) \dots h(v_l) a_1 \dots a_k \\
&\Rightarrow_G h(z_{a_k} \dots z_{a_1}) h(u_l \dots u_2 u_1) \$\$ h(v_1 v_2 \dots v_l) a_1 \dots a_k && [p_{4a}] \\
&= \quad f_r \dots f_2 f_1 \$\$ g_1 g_2 \dots g_s a_1 \dots a_k \\
&\Rightarrow_G f_r \dots f_2 \$\$ g_2 \dots g_s a_1 \dots a_k \\
&\quad \vdots \\
&\Rightarrow_G f_r \$\$ g_s a_1 \dots a_k \\
&\Rightarrow_G \$\$ a_1 \dots a_k \\
&\Rightarrow_G \$ a_1 \dots a_k && [p_{4d}] \\
&\Rightarrow_G a_1 \dots a_k && [p_{4d}],
\end{aligned}
$$

where $f_1, \dots, f_r, g_1, \dots, g_s \in \{0, 1\}$, and p_2, p_{4a}, and p_{4d} are productions introduced in (2), (4a), and (4d), respectively. In this derivation, the context-free productions of G' are simulated by the productions introduced in (1) through (3), and the context-sensitive productions of G' are simulated by the productions introduced in (4b) and (4c). There are several differences between the derivations of G' and G:

- Instead of verifying the identity of $z_{a_k} \dots z_{a_1} u_l \dots u_1$ and $v_1 \dots v_l$, G verifies that $h(z_{a_k} \dots z_{a_1} u_l \dots u_1)$ and $h(v_1 \dots v_l)$ coincide. This means that instead of comparing strings over $\{A, B, C, D\}$, G compares the strings $f_r \dots f_1$ and $g_1 \dots g_s$ over $\{0, 1\}$.
- The production introduced in (2) guarantees that no production from (1) can be used after its application. Similarly, the production introduced in (4a) prevents the productions of (1) through (3) from being applied.
- When applying the productions from (4b) and (4c), some symbols f_i and g_j, where $i, j \geq 1$, can be skipped. However, if some 0's and 1's not directly neighboring with the \$'s are rewritten, the form of these productions guarantees that the skipped nonterminals can never be rewritten later in the derivation, so the derivation is necessarily unsuccessful in this case.
- The production from (4d) can be used anytime the symbol \$ appears in the sentential form. However, when this production is used and some nonterminals from $\{0, 1\}$ occur in the sentential form, these nonterminals can never be removed from the sentential form, so the derivation is blocked. As a result, the production from (4d) has to be applied at the very end of the derivation.

Based on these observations, notice that $L = L(G) = L(G')$, and $|V - T| = 5$, $\text{dcs}(G) = 2$, $\text{mcs}(G) = 3$, $\text{ocs}(G) = 6$, so the theorem holds. ∎

Theorem 6.5. *For every recursively enumerable language L, there is a scattered context grammar $\bar{G} = (V, T, \bar{P}, S)$ such that $L(\bar{G}) = L$, and*

$$\begin{aligned} |V - T| &= 8, \\ \text{dcs}(\bar{G}) &= 6, \\ \text{mcs}(\bar{G}) &= 1, \\ \text{ocs}(\bar{G}) &= 6. \end{aligned}$$

Proof. We slightly modify the construction given in the proof of Theorem 6.4. Define the scattered context grammar

$$\bar{G} = \big(\{S, \bar{S}, 0, 1, \$_L, \$_R, \$_0, \$_1\} \cup T, T, \bar{P}, S\big)$$

and initialize $\bar{P}$ with the set of all productions introduced in steps (1) through (3) of the construction given in the proof of Theorem 6.4. Then, add the following productions to $\bar{P}$:

4. (a) $(\bar{S}) \to (\$_L\$_R)$,
   (b) $(0, \$_L) \to (\$_0, \varepsilon)$, $(\$_R, 0) \to (\varepsilon, \$_0)$, $(\$_0, \$_0) \to (\$_L, \$_R)$,
   (c) $(1, \$_L) \to (\$_1, \varepsilon)$, $(\$_R, 1) \to (\varepsilon, \$_1)$, $(\$_1, \$_1) \to (\$_L, \$_R)$,
   (d) $(\$_L) \to (\varepsilon)$, and $(\$_R) \to (\varepsilon)$.

Observe that a single derivation step made by a production introduced in step (4b) or (4c) of the construction of G is simulated in $\bar{G}$ by the above productions from (4b) or (4c) in three derivation steps. In greater detail, a derivation of the form

$$x0\$\$0yz \Rightarrow_G x\$\$yz \ \big[(0, \$, \$, 0) \to (\$, \varepsilon, \varepsilon, \$)\big]$$

is simulated in $\bar{G}$ as

$$\begin{aligned} x0\$_L\$_R0yz &\Rightarrow_{\bar{G}} x\$_0\$_R0yz \ \big[(0, \$_L) \rightarrow (\$_0, \varepsilon)\big] \\ &\Rightarrow_{\bar{G}} x\$_0\$_0yz \ \big[(\$_R, 0) \rightarrow (\varepsilon, \$_0)\big] \\ &\Rightarrow_{\bar{G}} x\$_L\$_Ryz \ \big[(\$_0, \$_0) \rightarrow (\$_L, \$_R)\big], \end{aligned}$$

where $x, y \in \{0, 1\}^*$, and $z \in T^*$. The rest of the proof resembles the proof of Theorem 6.4 and is, therefore, left to the reader. ■

Theorem 6.6. *For every recursively enumerable language L, there is a scattered context grammar $G = (V, T, P, S)$ such that $L(G) = L$, and*

$$\begin{aligned} |V - T| &= 4, \\ \mathrm{dcs}(G) &= 4, \\ \mathrm{mcs}(G) &= 5, \\ \mathrm{ocs}(G) &= 20. \end{aligned}$$

Proof. Let

$$G' = \big(\{S', A, B, C, D\} \cup T, T, P' \cup \{AB \rightarrow \varepsilon, CD \rightarrow \varepsilon\}, S'\big)$$

be a phrase-structure grammar in Geffert normal form, where P' is a set of context-free productions, and $L(G') = L$. Define the homomorphism h from $\{A, B, C, D\}^*$ to $\{0, 1\}^*$ so that $h(A) = h(B) = 00$, $h(C) = 10$, and $h(D) = 01$. Define the scattered context grammar

$$G = \big(\{S, 0, 1, \$\} \cup T, T, P, S\big)$$

with P constructed as follows:

1. Add $(S) \rightarrow (11S11)$ to P.
2. For each $S' \rightarrow zS'a \in P'$, add
   $(S) \rightarrow \big(h(z)S1a1\big)$ to P.
3. For each $S' \rightarrow uS'v \in P'$, add
   $(S) \rightarrow \big(h(u)Sh(v)\big)$ to P.
4. For each $S' \rightarrow uv \in P'$, add
   $(S) \rightarrow \big(h(u)\$\$h(v)\big)$ to P.
5. Add

   (a) $(0, 0, \$, \$, 0, 0) \rightarrow (\$, \varepsilon, \varepsilon, \varepsilon, \varepsilon, \$)$,
   (b) $(1, 0, \$, \$, 0, 1) \rightarrow (\$, \varepsilon, \varepsilon, \varepsilon, \varepsilon, \$)$,
   (c) $(1, 1, \$, \$, 1, 1) \rightarrow (11\$, \varepsilon, \varepsilon, \varepsilon, \varepsilon, \$)$, and
   (d) $(1, 1, \$, \$, 1, 1) \rightarrow (\varepsilon, \varepsilon, \varepsilon, \varepsilon, \varepsilon, \varepsilon)$ to P.

Basic Idea.
Every successful derivation starts by an application of the production introduced in (1), and this production is not used during the rest of the derivation. Productions

from (2) through (4) simulate the context-free productions of G'. After the production from (4) is used, only productions from (5) are applicable. The productions from (5a) and (5b) verify that the strings over $\{0, 1\}$, generated by the productions from (2) through (4), coincide. The production from (5c) removes the 1's between the terminal symbols and, in addition, makes sure that productions from (2) can never be used in a successful derivation after a production from (3) is applied. Finally, the production from (5d) finishes the derivation.

Formal Proof.
The proof of the theorem is based on several observations, which are stated in the following claims.

Claim 1. Every successful derivation in G can be expressed as

$$\begin{aligned} S &\Rightarrow_G^* v \ [\Xi] \\ &\Rightarrow_G w \ [p_4] \\ &\Rightarrow_G^* y \ [\Psi] \\ &\Rightarrow_G z \ [p_{5d}], \end{aligned}$$

where

$$\begin{aligned} v &\in \{0, 1\}^*\{S\}\big(\{0, 1\} \cup T\big)^*, \\ w &\in \{0, 1\}^+\{\$\}\{\$\}\big(\{0, 1\} \cup T\big)^*, \\ y &\in \{1\}\{1\}\{\$\}T^*\{\$\}T^*\{1\}T^*\{1\}T^*, \end{aligned}$$

$z \in T^*$, p_4 and p_{5d} are productions introduced in (4) and (5d), respectively, and Ξ and Ψ are sequences of productions introduced in (1) through (3) and (5a) through (5c), respectively.

Proof. As S appears on the left-hand side of every production introduced in (1) through (4), all of them are applicable while S occurs in the sentential form. On the other hand, no production from (5) can be used at this point. After p_4 is used, it replaces S with \$\$, so productions from (1) through (4) are not applicable and only productions from (5) can be used. Therefore, the beginning of the derivation can be expressed as

$$\begin{aligned} S &\Rightarrow_G^* v \ [\Xi] \\ &\Rightarrow_G w \ [p_4]. \end{aligned}$$

Because all productions, except for p_{5d}, contain nonterminals on their right-hand sides, p_{5d} has to be applied in the last derivation step and no other production can be applied after its use. Applications of productions from (2) through (4) may introduce some nonterminals 0 and 1 to the sentential form, so in this case, the productions from (5a) and (5b) are applied to remove them. As a result,

$$\begin{aligned} w &\Rightarrow_G^* y \ [\Psi] \\ &\Rightarrow_G z \ [p_{5d}], \end{aligned}$$

and the sentential forms satisfy the conditions given in the claim. □

Claim 2. In $w \Rightarrow_G^+ z$ from Claim 1, every sentential form s satisfies

$$s \in \{0, 1\}^*\{\$\}T^*\{\$\}(\{0, 1\} \cup T)^*.$$

Proof. The form of the productions introduced in (5) implies that whenever a nonterminal appears between the two occurrences of \$, it can never be removed during the rest of the derivation. Therefore, the claim holds. □

Claim 3. In $w \Rightarrow_G^+ z$ from Claim 1, every sentential form s satisfies

$$s \in \{1\}\{1\}(\{1\}\{0\} \cup \{0\}\{0\})^*\{\$\}T^*\{\$\}(\{0, 1\} \cup T)^*.$$

Proof. Claim 2 implies that whenever productions from (5) are used, each of these productions is applied to the nonterminals from {0, 1} immediately preceding the first occurrence of \$ and immediately following the second occurrence of \$; otherwise, the derivation is unsuccessful. As a result, the only production that removes the substring 11 preceding the first occurrence of \$ is (5d). However, by Claim 1, (5d) is used during the very last derivation step, so the substring 11 has to appear at the beginning of the sentential form in order to generate a string over T. □

Claim 4. The derivation

$$S \Rightarrow_G^* v \; [\Xi]$$

from Claim 1 can be expressed in greater detail as

$$\begin{aligned} S &\Rightarrow_G 11S11 \; [p_1] \\ &\Rightarrow_G^* v, \end{aligned}$$

where p_1 is the production introduced in (1), and this production is not used during the rest of the derivation.

Proof. The production introduced in (1) is the only production that introduces the substring 11 in front of the first occurrence of \$. By Claim 3, in front of the first \$, this substring appears only at the beginning of every sentential form in $w \Rightarrow_G^+ z$, so p_1 has to be applied at the beginning of the derivation and cannot be used later in the derivation. □

Claim 5. The derivation

$$\begin{aligned} w &\Rightarrow_G^* y \; [\Psi] \\ &\Rightarrow_G z \; [p_{5d}] \end{aligned}$$

from Claim 1 can be expressed in greater detail as

$$\begin{aligned} w &\Rightarrow_G^* x \; [\Psi_1] \\ &\Rightarrow_G^* y \; [\Psi_2] \\ &\Rightarrow_G z \; [p_{5d}], \end{aligned}$$

where

$$x \in \{1\}\{1\}(\{1\}\{0\} \cup \{0\}\{0\})^*\{\$\}T^*\{\$\}(\{0, 1\} \cup T)^*,$$

Ψ_1 is a sequence of productions introduced in (5a) and (5b), and Ψ_2 is a sequence of productions introduced in (5c).

Proof. The proof of this claim follows immediately from Claims 2 and 3. □

Claim 6. The derivation

$$11S11 \Rightarrow_G^* v$$

from Claims 1 and 4 can be expressed in greater detail as

$$\begin{aligned} 11S11 &\Rightarrow_G^* u\ [\Xi_1] \\ &\Rightarrow_G^* v\ [\Xi_2], \end{aligned}$$

where

$$u \in \{1\}\{1\}(\{1\}\{0\} \cup \{0\}\{0\})^* S(\{0\}\{1\} \cup \{0\}\{0\})^* (\{1\}T\{1\})^* \{1\}\{1\},$$

and Ξ_1, Ξ_2 are sequences of productions introduced in (2), (3), respectively.

Proof. By Claim 4, every derivation starts by an application of the production from (1). Therefore, u ends by the substring 11. Next, notice that the two nonterminals 1 surrounding a, where $a \in T$, introduced by every application of a production from (2) can only be removed by the production from (5c). Indeed, by Claim 2, any other production leaves a nonterminal between the two symbols \$, so the derivation is unsuccessful. By Claim 5, productions from (5a) and (5b) cannot be applied after the production from (5c) is used. As a result, the generation of the strings over $\{0, 1\}$ by productions from (2) and (3) has to correspond to their removal by (5a), (5b), and (5c). This implies that productions from (2) have to be applied before productions from (3). □

Putting Claims 1 through 6 together, we obtain the following form of every successful derivation:

$$\begin{aligned} S &\Rightarrow_G 11S11\ [p_1] \\ &\Rightarrow_G^* u \quad [\Xi_1] \\ &\Rightarrow_G^* v \quad [\Xi_2] \\ &\Rightarrow_G w \quad [p_4] \\ &\Rightarrow_G^* x \quad [\Psi_1] \\ &\Rightarrow_G^* y \quad [\Psi_2] \\ &\Rightarrow_G z \quad [p_{5d}]. \end{aligned}$$

As the rest of this proof can be made by analogy with the proof of Theorem 6.4, we leave this task to the reader. ■

In conclusion of this section, we point out several open problems. Recall that one-nonterminal scattered context grammars are incapable of generating all recursively enumerable languages; in fact, they cannot even generate some context-sensitive languages (see Theorem 6.1). By Theorem 6.3, three-nonterminal scattered context grammars characterize $\mathscr{L}(RE)$.

Open Problem 6.7. What is the generative power of two-nonterminal scattered context grammars?

By Theorem 6.4, scattered context grammars with two context-sensitive productions characterize $\mathscr{L}(RE)$.

Open Problem 6.8. What is the generative power of scattered context grammars with one context-sensitive production?

We suggest these open problems as further investigation topics.

6.2 Economical transformations

The generation of languages is frequently performed in a specifically required way and based upon a prescribed set of grammatical components, such as a certain collection of nonterminals or productions. On the other hand, if these requirements are met, the generation can be based upon grammars of various types. For this purpose, we make use of transformations that convert grammars of some type to equivalent grammars of another type so the transformed grammars strongly resemble the original grammars regarding the way they work as well as the components they consist of. In other words, we want the output grammars resulting from these transformations to work similarly to the way the given original grammars work and, perhaps even more importantly, to contain the same set of grammatical components possibly extended by very few additional components. Transformations that produce scattered context grammars in this economical way are discussed in the present section. Because phrase-structure grammars represent one of the very basic grammatical models in formal language theory, this section pays a special attention to the economical transformations that convert these fundamental grammars to equivalent scattered context grammars.

To compare the measures of scattered context and phrase-structure grammars, we first define the degree of context sensitivity of phrase-structure grammars analogously to the degree of context sensitivity of scattered context grammars (see Definition 2.45).

Definition 6.9. Let $G = (V, T, P, S)$ be a phrase-structure grammar. Its *degree of context sensitivity*, symbolically written as $\mathrm{dcs}(G)$, is defined as

$$\mathrm{dcs}(G) = \left|\{x \to y : x \to y \in P, |x| \geq 2\}\right|.$$

Next, we present the main result of this section.

Theorem 6.10. *For every phrase-structure grammar $G = (V, T, P, S)$ in Kuroda normal form, there is a scattered context grammar $\bar{G} = (\bar{V}, T, \bar{P}, \bar{S})$ such that*

$L(\bar{G}) = L(G)$, and

$$|\bar{V}| = |V| + 5,$$
$$|\bar{P}| = |P| + 4,$$
$$\text{dcs}(\bar{G}) = \text{dcs}(G) + 2.$$

Proof. Let $G = (V, T, P, S)$ be a phrase-structure grammar in Kuroda normal form. Without loss of generality, assume that $V \cap \{\bar{S}, F, 0, 1, \$\} = \emptyset$. Set $\bar{V} = V \cup \{\bar{S}, F, 0, 1, \$\}$. Define the scattered context grammar $\bar{G} = (\bar{V}, T, \bar{P}, \bar{S})$, where $\bar{P}$ is constructed as follows:

1. Add $(\bar{S}) \to (FFFS)$ to $\bar{P}$.
2. For each $AB \to CD \in P$, add
   $(A, B) \to (C0, 1D)$ to $\bar{P}$.
3. For each $A \to BC \in P$, add
   $(A) \to (BC)$ to $\bar{P}$.
4. For each $A \to a \in P$, where $a \in T \cup \{\varepsilon\}$, add
   $(A) \to (\$a)$ to $\bar{P}$.
5. Add
   (a) $(F, 0, 1, F, F) \to (\varepsilon, F, F, \varepsilon, F)$,
   (b) $(F, F, F, \$) \to (\varepsilon, \varepsilon, F, FF)$,
   (c) $(F) \to (\varepsilon)$ to $\bar{P}$.

Basic Idea.
The production from (1) starts a derivation and introduces three occurrences of the nonterminal F, which are present in every sentential form until three applications of the production from (5c) complete the derivation. Productions from (2), (3), and (4) simulate the corresponding productions of Kuroda normal form behind the last occurrence of F. The productions from (5a) and (5b) guarantee that before (5c) is applied for the first time, every sentential form in a successful derivation belongs to

$$T^*\{F\}\big(T \cup \{\varepsilon\}\big)\{0^i 1^i : i \geq 0\}\{F\}\{F\}\big(V \cup \{0, 1, \$\}\big)^*,$$

and, thereby, the simulation of every derivation of G is performed properly. Notice that there are only terminals in front of the first nonterminal F. Moreover, the only nonterminals appearing between the first occurrence and the second occurrence of F are from $\{0, 1\}$, and there is no symbol between the second and the third occurrence of F in a successful derivation.

Formal Proof.
Next, we establish several claims to demonstrate that $L(G) = L(\bar{G})$ in a rigorous way.

Claim 1. Every successful derivation of $\bar{G}$ can be expressed as

$$\begin{aligned}
\bar{S} &\Rightarrow_{\bar{G}} FFFS && [p_1] \\
&\Rightarrow_{\bar{G}}^* uFvFxFy && [\Psi] \\
&\Rightarrow_{\bar{G}}^* w && \\
&\Rightarrow_{\bar{G}}^3 z && [p_{5c}p_{5c}p_{5c}],
\end{aligned}$$

where $u, z \in T^*$, $v, x, y \in \left(\bar{V} - \{\bar{S}, F\}\right)^*$, $w \in \left(\bar{V} - \{\bar{S}\}\right)^*$, p_1 and p_{5c} are productions introduced in (1) and (5c), respectively, and Ψ is a sequence of productions introduced in (2) through (5b).

Proof. The only production with $\bar{S}$ on its left-hand side is the production introduced in (1), and because no production contains $\bar{S}$ on its right-hand side, this production is not used during the rest of the derivation process. As a result,

$$\bar{S} \Rightarrow_{\bar{G}} FFFS\,[p_1].$$

Observe that no production from (2) through (4) contains the nonterminal F and productions from (5a) and (5b) contain three nonterminals F on their left-hand sides as well as their right-hand sides. The production from (5c), which is the only production with its right-hand side over T, removes F from the sentential form, so no production from (5a) and (5b) can be used once it is applied. Notice that productions from (4) simulate $A \to a$, where $A \in V - T$, $a \in T \cup \{\varepsilon\}$, and these productions introduce \$ to the sentential form. In addition, observe that only the production from (5b) rewrites \$. Consequently, to generate a string over T, productions from (2) through (4) cannot be used after the production from (5c) is applied. Therefore,

$$w \Rightarrow_{\bar{G}}^{3} z\,[p_{5c}p_{5c}p_{5c}].$$

Notice that productions from (5a) and (5b) cannot rewrite any symbol in u. If $\mathrm{alph}(u) \cap (\bar{V} - T) \neq \emptyset$, then a nonterminal from $\{0, 1, \$\}$ remains in front of the first F because productions from (2) through (4) cannot rewrite u to a string over T, so the derivation would be unsuccessful in this case. Therefore, $u \in T^*$, and the claim holds. □

Claim 2. Every derivation

$$\bar{S} \Rightarrow_{\bar{G}}^{+} uFvFxFy \Rightarrow_{\bar{G}}^{*} w \Rightarrow_{\bar{G}}^{3} z,$$

where $u, z \in T^*$, $v, x, y \in \left(\bar{V} - \{\bar{S}, F\}\right)^*$, and $w \in \left(\bar{V} - \{\bar{S}\}\right)^*$, satisfies $x \in T^*$.

Proof. First, notice that if $(\bar{V} - T) \cap \mathrm{alph}(x) \neq \emptyset$, x cannot be rewritten to a string over T by using only productions from (2) through (4). Next, examine the productions from (5a) and (5b) to see that these productions cannot rewrite any symbol from x, and the production from (5b) moves x in front of the first occurrence of F. However, by Claim 1, no nonterminal can appear in front of the first F. As a result, $(\bar{V} - T) \cap \mathrm{alph}(x) = \emptyset$, so $x \in T^*$. □

Claim 3. Every derivation

$$\bar{S} \Rightarrow_{\bar{G}}^{+} uFvFxFy \Rightarrow_{\bar{G}}^{*} w \Rightarrow_{\bar{G}}^{3} z,$$

where $u, z \in T^*$, $v, x, y \in \left(\bar{V} - \{\bar{S}, F\}\right)^*$, and $w \in \left(\bar{V} - \{\bar{S}\}\right)^*$, satisfies $v = v'v''$, where $v' \in \left(\{0\} \cup T\right)^*$, $v'' \in \left(\{1\} \cup T\right)^*$, and $|v'|_{\{0\}} = |v''|_{\{1\}}$.

Proof. First, notice that if $(\bar{V} - T) \cap \mathrm{alph}(v) \neq \emptyset$, v cannot be rewritten to a string over T by using only productions from (2) through (4). Next, examine the productions from (5a) and (5b).

First, observe that the production from (5b) can only be applied if $v \in T^*$. Indeed, (5b) moves v in front of the first F and if $(\bar{V} - T) \cap \mathrm{alph}(v) \neq \emptyset$, by Claim 1, the derivation is unsuccessful. Therefore, $(\bar{V} - T) \cap \mathrm{alph}(v) = \emptyset$ before the production from (5b) is applied. Second, observe that because the production from (5a) rewrites only nonterminals over $\{0, 1\}$ in v, $\big((V - T) \cup \{\$\}\big) \cap \mathrm{alph}(v) = \emptyset$. Finally, observe that the production from (5a) has to be applied so that the first 0 following the first F and the first 1 preceding the second F is rewritten by (5a). If this property is not satisfied, the form of (5a) implies that 0 appears in front of the first F or 1 appears in between the second F and the third F. However, by Claims 1 and 2, this leads to an unsuccessful derivation.

Based on these observations, we see that in order to generate $z \in T^*$, v has to satisfy $v = v'v''$, where $v' \in \big(\{0\} \cup T\big)^*$, $v'' \in \big(\{1\} \cup T\big)^*$, and $|v'|_{\{0\}} = |v''|_{\{1\}}$.

□

Claim 4. Every derivation

$$\bar{S} \Rightarrow_{\bar{G}}^{+} uFvFxFy \Rightarrow_{\bar{G}}^{*} w \Rightarrow_{\bar{G}}^{3} z,$$

where $u, z \in T^*$, $v, x, y \in \big(\bar{V} - \{\bar{S}, F\}\big)^*$, and $w \in \big(\bar{V} - \{\bar{S}\}\big)^*$, satisfies

$$y \in \big(T \cup \{\varepsilon\}\big)\big(\{0^i 1^i : i \geq 0\}K\big)^*$$

with $K = (V - T) \cup \{\$\}\big(T \cup \{\varepsilon\}\big)$,

$$v \in \big(T \cup \{\varepsilon\}\big)\{0^i 1^i : i \geq 0\},$$

and $x = \varepsilon$.

Proof. First, consider the production introduced in (5b). This production rewrites \$ to FF in its last component. Because the nonterminal \$ is introduced by productions from (4), \$ may be followed by $a \in T$. Therefore, after (5b) is applied, the last nonterminal F may be followed by a. As a result, the prefix of y is always over $T \cup \{\varepsilon\}$.

Second, notice that when the production (5b) is used, the first nonterminal \$ following the third nonterminal F has to be rewritten. In addition, the substring appearing between these symbols has to be in $\{0^i 1^i : i \geq 0\}$. The form of the production introduced in (5b) implies that after its application, this substring is moved in between the first occurrence of F and the second occurrence of F, so the conditions given by Claim 3 are satisfied. Therefore,

$$v \in \big(T \cup \{\varepsilon\}\big)\{0^i 1^i : i \geq 0\},$$

and because no terminal appears in the suffix of v, the proof of Claim 3 implies $x = \varepsilon$. By induction, prove that

$$y \in \big(T \cup \{\varepsilon\}\big)\big(\{0^i 1^i : i \geq 0\}K\big)^*.$$

The induction part is left to the reader. □

Next, we define the homomorphism α from $\bar{V}^*$ to V^* as $\alpha(\bar{A}) = \varepsilon$, for all $\bar{A} \in \bar{V} - V$, and $\alpha(A) = A$, for all $A \in V$, and use this homomorphism in the following claims.

Claim 5. Let $\bar{S} \Rightarrow_{\bar{G}}^{m} w \Rightarrow_{\bar{G}}^{*} z$, where $m \geq 1$, $z \in T^*$, and $w \in \bar{V}^*$. Then, $S \Rightarrow_{G}^{*} \alpha(w)$.

Proof. This claim is established by induction on m.

Basis. Let $m = 1$. Then, $\bar{S} \Rightarrow_{\bar{G}} FFFS$. Because $\alpha(FFFS) = S$, $S \Rightarrow_{G}^{0} S$, so the basis holds.

Induction Hypothesis. Suppose that the claim holds for every $m \leq j$, where $j \geq 1$.

Induction Step. Let $\bar{S} \Rightarrow_{\bar{G}}^{j+1} w \Rightarrow_{\bar{G}}^{*} z$, where $z \in T^*$ and $w \in \bar{V}^*$. Based on Claims 1 and 4, express this derivation as

$$\begin{aligned} \bar{S} &\Rightarrow_{\bar{G}}^{j} uFvFxFy \\ &\Rightarrow_{\bar{G}} w\ [p] \\ &\Rightarrow_{\bar{G}}^{*} z, \end{aligned}$$

where $u \in T^*$, $x = \varepsilon$,

$$y \in \big(T \cup \{\varepsilon\}\big)\big(\{0^i 1^i : i \geq 0\}K\big)^*$$

with $K = (V - T) \cup \{\$\}\big(T \cup \{\varepsilon\}\big)$, and

$$v \in \big(T \cup \{\varepsilon\}\big)\{0^i 1^i : i \geq 0\}.$$

By the induction hypothesis, $S \Rightarrow_{G}^{*} \alpha(uFvFxFy)$. Next, this proof considers all possible forms of p:

- Assume that $p = (A, B) \rightarrow (C0, 1D) \in \bar{P}$, where $A, B, C, D \in V - T$. Claim 4 and its proof imply $y = y'Ay''By'''$, where $y'' \in \{0^i 1^i : i \geq 0\}$, and

  $$w = uFvFxFy'C0y''1Dy'''.$$

  As $(A, B) \rightarrow (C0, 1D) \in \bar{P}$, $AB \rightarrow CD \in P$ holds true. Because $\alpha(y'') = \varepsilon$,

  $$\alpha(uFvFxFy'Ay''By''') \Rightarrow_{G} \alpha(uFvFxFy'C0y''1Dy''').$$

  Therefore, $S \Rightarrow_{G}^{*} \alpha(w)$.

- Assume that $p = (A) \rightarrow (BC) \in \bar{P}$, where $A, B, C \in V - T$. Claim 4 implies $y = y'Ay''$, and
$$w = uFvFxFy'BCy''.$$
As $(A) \rightarrow (BC) \in \bar{P}$, $A \rightarrow BC \in P$ holds true. Notice that
$$\alpha(uFvFxFy'Ay'') \Rightarrow_G \alpha(uFvFxFy'BCy'').$$
Therefore, $S \Rightarrow_G^* \alpha(w)$.
- Assume that $p = (A) \rightarrow (\$a) \in \bar{P}$, where $A \in V - T$ and $a \in T \cup \{\varepsilon\}$. Claim 4 implies $y = y'Ay''$, and
$$w = uFvFxFy'\$ay''.$$
As $(A) \rightarrow (\$a) \in \bar{P}$, $A \rightarrow a \in P$ holds true. Notice that
$$\alpha(uFvFxFy'Ay'') \Rightarrow_G \alpha(uFvFxFy'\$ay'').$$
Therefore, $S \Rightarrow_G^* \alpha(w)$.
- Assume that p is a production from (5). Notice that these productions rewrite only nonterminals over $\{0, 1, F, \$\}$. Therefore, $\alpha(w) = \alpha(uFvFxFy)$, so $S \Rightarrow_G^* \alpha(w)$.

Based on the arguments above, $\bar{S} \Rightarrow_{\bar{G}}^j uFvFxFy \Rightarrow_{\bar{G}} w\ [p]$, for any $p \in \bar{P}$, implies $S \Rightarrow_G^* \alpha(w)$. Thus, the claim holds. □

Claim 6. $L(\bar{G}) \subseteq L(G)$.

Proof. By Claim 5, if $\bar{S} \Rightarrow_{\bar{G}}^+ z$ with $z \in T^*$, then $S \Rightarrow_G^* z$. Therefore, the claim holds. □

Claim 7. Let $S \Rightarrow_G^m w \Rightarrow_G^* z$, where $m \geq 0$, $w \in V^*$, and $z \in T^*$. Then, $\bar{S} \Rightarrow_{\bar{G}}^+ uFvFxFy$, where $u \in T^*$,
$$y \in \big(T \cup \{\varepsilon\}\big)\big(\{0^i 1^i : i \geq 0\}K\big)^*$$
with $K = (V - T) \cup \{\$\}\big(T \cup \{\varepsilon\}\big)$,
$$v \in \big(T \cup \{\varepsilon\}\big)\{0^i 1^i : i \geq 0\},$$
and $x = \varepsilon$, so that $w = \alpha(uFvFxFy)$.

Proof. This claim is established by induction on m.

Basis. Let $m = 0$. Then, $S \Rightarrow_G^0 S \Rightarrow_G^* z$. Notice that $\bar{S} \Rightarrow_{\bar{G}} FFFS$ by using the production introduced in (1), and $S = \alpha(FFFS)$. Thus, the basis holds.

Induction Hypothesis. Suppose that the claim holds for every $m \leq j$, where $j \geq 1$.

Induction Step. Let $S \Rightarrow_G^{j+1} w \Rightarrow_G^* z$, where $w \in V^*$, and $z \in T^*$. Express this derivation as

$$\begin{aligned} S &\Rightarrow_G^j t \\ &\Rightarrow_G w\ [p] \\ &\Rightarrow_G^* z, \end{aligned}$$

where $w \in V^*$ and $p \in P$. By the induction hypothesis, $\bar{S} \Rightarrow_{\bar{G}}^+ uFvFxFy$, where $u \in T^*$,

$$y \in \big(T \cup \{\varepsilon\}\big)\big(\{0^i 1^i : i \geq 0\}K\big)^*$$

with $K = (V - T) \cup \{\$\}\big(T \cup \{\varepsilon\}\big)$,

$$v \in \big(T \cup \{\varepsilon\}\big)\{0^i 1^i : i \geq 0\},$$

and $x = \varepsilon$, so that $t = \alpha(uFvFxFy)$. Next, this proof considers all possible forms of p:

- Assume that $p = AB \to CD \in P$, where $A, B, C, D \in V - T$. Express $t \Rightarrow_G w$ as $t'ABt'' \Rightarrow_G t'CDt''$, where $t'ABt'' = t$ and $t'CDt'' = w$. Claim 4 implies that $y = y'A0^k 1^k By''$, where $k \geq 0$, $\alpha(uFvFxFy') = t'$, and $\alpha(y'') = t''$. As $AB \to CD \in P$, $(A, B) \to (C0, 1D) \in \bar{P}$ holds true. Then,

  $$uFvFxFy'A0^k 1^k By'' \Rightarrow_{\bar{G}} uFvFxFy'C0^{k+1}1^{k+1}Dy''.$$

  Therefore,

  $$\bar{S} \Rightarrow_{\bar{G}}^+ uFvFxFy'C0^{k+1}1^{k+1}Dy'',$$

  and $w = \alpha(uFvFxFy'C0^{k+1}1^{k+1}Dy'')$.
- Assume that $p = A \to BC \in P$, where $A, B, C \in V - T$. Express $t \Rightarrow_G w$ as $t'At'' \Rightarrow_G t'BCt''$, where $t'At'' = t$ and $t'BCt'' = w$. Claim 4 implies that $y = y'Ay''$, where $\alpha(uFvFxFy') = t'$ and $\alpha(y'') = t''$. As $A \to BC \in P$, $(A) \to (BC) \in \bar{P}$ holds true. Then,

  $$uFvFxFy'Ay'' \Rightarrow_{\bar{G}} uFvFxFy'BCy''.$$

  Therefore,

  $$\bar{S} \Rightarrow_{\bar{G}}^+ uFvFxFy'BCy'',$$

  and $w = \alpha(uFvFxFy'BCy'')$.
- Assume that $p = A \to a \in P$, where $A \in V - T$ and $a \in T \cup \{\varepsilon\}$. Express $t \Rightarrow_G w$ as $t'At'' \Rightarrow_G t'at''$, where $t'At'' = t$ and $t'at'' = w$. Claim 4 implies that $y = y'Ay''$, where $\alpha(uFvFxFy') = t'$ and $\alpha(y'') = t''$. As $A \to a \in P$, $(A) \to (\$a) \in \bar{P}$ holds true. Then,

  $$uFvFxFy'Ay'' \Rightarrow_{\bar{G}} uFvFxFy'\$ay''.$$

  Therefore,

  $$\bar{S} \Rightarrow_{\bar{G}}^+ uFvFxFy'\$ay'',$$

  and $w = \alpha(uFvFxFy'\$ay'')$.

Based on the arguments above, $S \Rightarrow_G^j t \Rightarrow_G w\ [p]$, for any $p \in P$, implies $\bar{S} \Rightarrow_{\bar{G}}^+ s$, where $w = \alpha(s)$. Thus, the claim holds. □

Claim 8. $L(G) \subseteq L(\bar{G})$.

Proof. By Claims 1, 4, and 7, if $S \Rightarrow_G^* z$, where $z \in T^*$, then $\bar{S} \Rightarrow_{\bar{G}}^+ z$. Therefore, Claim 8 holds. □

By Claims 6 and 8, $L(\bar{G}) = L(G)$. Observe that $|\bar{V}| = |V| + 5$, $|\bar{P}| = |P| + 4$, and $\text{dcs}(\bar{G}) = \text{dcs}(G) + 2$. Thus, the theorem holds. ■

In the conclusion, we recommend two further areas related to the investigation of this section:

- Revert the transformation under discussion and study economical transformations of scattered context grammars to phrase-structure grammars.
- From a much broader perspective, apart from the transformations between scattered context grammars and phrase-structure grammars, study economical transformations between other types of grammars.

CHAPTER 7

Parses and their generators

In this chapter, we discuss parsing, which is important to all scientific areas that grammatically analyze and process languages, ranging from compiler design through linguistics to molecular biology. *Parses*—that is, the sequences of productions according to which sentences are generated—usually represent the goal information we want to achieve by parsing. (Let us note that the notion of a *parse* represents a synonym of several other notions, including a *derivation word*, a *Szilard word*, and a *control word*—see page 18 in [30].) It thus comes as no surprise that we concentrate our attention on obtaining parses by using scattered context grammars. As a crucial result, we demonstrate that for every recursively enumerable language L, there exists a propagating scattered context grammar whose language consists of sentences in L followed by their parses. In this way, we actually simultaneously obtain two valuable pieces of parsing-related information. First, by eliminating all the suffixes representing the parses, we obtain precisely the recursively enumerable language L. Second, we also have the parses according to which the corresponding sentences are derived, so by using them, we can construct the grammatical derivation of sentences whenever needed.

This characterization of recursively enumerable languages is of some interest because it is based on propagating scattered context grammars whose languages are included in the family of context-sensitive languages, which is properly contained in the family of recursively enumerable languages. Similar characterization was achieved in [31]. It demonstrated that any recursively enumerable language can be characterized by a propagating scattered context grammar so that every string x of this language is represented by $\{\$\}^*x$ in the propagating scattered context grammar, where \$ is a symbol not occurring in the language. This result was later improved by Meduna [32], which used only leftmost and rightmost derivations, and by Meduna [20], which reduced the number of nonterminals needed for the generation. In this chapter, we present a more general way of characterizing recursively enumerable languages by propagating scattered context grammars. Instead of appending a sequence of meaningless symbols to the beginning or to the end of every sentence as in the above results, we add a useful piece of information about the generating process—the parse.

Noteworthy, languages consisting of sentences followed by their parses were discussed in terms of matrix grammars in Section 7.2 of [19], which refers to these languages as *extended Szilard languages*. Apart from using different grammars, however, this section dealt with areas different from the topics of this chapter.

The present chapter consists of four sections. In Section 7.1, we introduce basic terminology concerning parses and their generators based upon scattered context grammars. In Section 7.2, we describe scattered context generators that produce their sentences followed by the corresponding parses. As canonical leftmost and rightmost derivations fulfill a crucial role in parsing, in Section 7.3, we modify these generators to their canonical versions that do the same job so they only perform either leftmost or rightmost derivations. Finally, in Section 7.4, we reduce the grammatical size of these generators.

7.1 Terminology

In this section, we define and illustrate basic notions used later in this chapter. We begin by introducing production labels, by which we refer to productions recorded in parses.

Definition 7.1. Assume that for every scattered context grammar $G = (V, T, P, S)$, there is a set of *production labels*, denoted by $\text{lab}(G)$, such that $|\text{lab}(G)| = |P|$; as usual, $\text{lab}(G)^*$ denotes the set of all strings over $\text{lab}(G)$. Furthermore, there is a bijection from P to $\text{lab}(G)$ such that if this bijection maps a production $(A_1, \ldots, A_n) \rightarrow (x_1, \ldots, x_n) \in P$ to a label $l \in \text{lab}(G)$, we say that $(A_1, \ldots, A_n) \rightarrow (x_1, \ldots, x_n)$ *is labeled with* l, symbolically written as

$$l : (A_1, \ldots, A_n) \rightarrow (x_1, \ldots, x_n).$$

To make the following text more readable, we use $\text{lhs}(l)$ and $\text{rhs}(l)$ instead of $\text{lhs}((A_1, \ldots, A_n) \rightarrow (x_1, \ldots, x_n))$ and $\text{rhs}((A_1, \ldots, A_n) \rightarrow (x_1, \ldots, x_n))$, respectively. By analogy with labeling every production in every scattered context grammar, we label every production (a, b, x, c) in every queue grammar as $l : (a, b, x, c)$. To express that $x \Rightarrow_G^* y$, where $x, y \in V^*$, by using a sequence of productions labeled with $p_1, \ldots, p_n$, we write $x \Rightarrow_G^* y\ [\rho]$, where $\rho = p_1 \ldots p_n \in \text{lab}(G)^*$.

As we also use canonical generators, we define the derivations performed in a leftmost and a rightmost way.

Definition 7.2. If every derivation step in every successful derivation in a scattered context grammar G is leftmost, *G generates $L(G)$ in a leftmost way*. If every derivation step in every successful derivation in G is rightmost, *G generates $L(G)$ in a rightmost way*.

Finally, we introduce the most important definition of this chapter—a proper generator of its sentences with their parses.

Definition 7.3. Let $G = (V, T, P, S)$ be a scattered context grammar, and let $S \Rightarrow_G^* x\ [\rho]$, where $x \in T^*$ and $\rho \in \text{lab}(G)^*$; then, x is a *sentence generated by G according to parse* ρ. Let $\text{lab}(G) \subseteq T$. G is a *proper generator of its sentences with their parses* if and only if

$$L(G) = \left\{x : x = y\rho,\ y \in \left(T - \text{lab}(G)\right)^*,\ \rho \in \text{lab}(G)^*,\ S \Rightarrow_G^* x\ [\rho]\right\};$$

in addition, if G generates $L(G)$ in a leftmost or a rightmost way, G is a *proper leftmost* or a *proper rightmost generator of its sentences with their parses*. Similarly, G is a *proper generator of its sentences preceded by their parses* if and only if

$$L(G) = \left\{x : x = \rho y,\ y \in \left(T - \text{lab}(G)\right)^*,\ \rho \in \text{lab}(G)^*,\ S \Rightarrow_G^* x\ [\rho]\right\};$$

in addition, if G generates $L(G)$ in a leftmost way, G is a *proper leftmost generator of its sentences preceded by their parses.*

Notice that these definitions impose no restrictions on derivations in a proper leftmost generator. However, every proper leftmost generator G satisfies the property that if G makes a non-leftmost step during a derivation, then this derivation cannot generate a member of $L(G)$. The same property applies to proper rightmost generators as well.

Example 7.4. We illustrate these definitions by four scattered context grammars, each of which has its set of production labels equal to $\{1, 2, 3, 4\}$.

1. Consider the scattered context grammar

$$G_1 = \left(\{S, A, B, C, a, b, c\}, \{a, b, c\}, P_1, S\right)$$

with P_1 containing

$$\begin{aligned} &1 : (S) \to (\varepsilon), \\ &2 : (S) \to (ABC), \\ &3 : (A, B, C) \to (aA, bB, cC), \\ &4 : (A, B, C) \to (a, b, c). \end{aligned}$$

As $\{1, 2, 3, 4\} \nsubseteq \{a, b, c\}$, G_1 is not a proper generator of its sentences with their parses.

2. Consider the scattered context grammar

$$G_2 = \left(\{S, A, B, C, a, b, c, 1, 2, 3, 4\}, \{a, b, c, 1, 2, 3, 4\}, P_2, S\right)$$

with P_2 containing

$$\begin{aligned} &1 : (S) \to (1), \\ &2 : (S) \to (ABC2), \\ &3 : (A, B, C) \to (aA, bB, cC3), \\ &4 : (A, B, C) \to (a, b, c4). \end{aligned}$$

Notice that $\{1, 2, 3, 4\} \subseteq \{a, b, c, 1, 2, 3, 4\}$. However,

$$\begin{aligned} L(G_2) &= \{a^n b^n c^n \operatorname{rev}(\rho) : n \geq 0, S \Rightarrow^*_{G_2} a^n b^n c^n \operatorname{rev}(\rho)\ [\rho]\} \\ &\neq \{a^n b^n c^n \rho : n \geq 0, S \Rightarrow^*_{G_2} a^n b^n c^n \rho\ [\rho]\}, \end{aligned}$$

so G_2 is not a proper generator of its sentences with their parses either.

3. Consider the scattered context grammar

$$G_3 = (\{S, A, B, C, \$, a, b, c, 1, 2, 3, 4\}, \{a, b, c, 1, 2, 3, 4\}, P_3, S)$$

with P_3 containing

$$\begin{aligned} &1 : (S) \rightarrow (1), \\ &2 : (S) \rightarrow (ABC2\$), \\ &3 : (A, B, C, \$) \rightarrow (AA, BB, CC, 3\$), \\ &4 : (A, B, C, \$) \rightarrow (a, b, c, 4). \end{aligned}$$

Observe that

$$L(G_3) = \{a^n b^n c^n \rho : n \geq 0, S \Rightarrow^*_{G_3} a^n b^n c^n \rho\ [\rho]\},$$

so G_3 is a proper generator of its sentences with their parses. However, as G_3 does not have to generate every sentence in a leftmost or a rightmost way, G_3 is neither a proper leftmost nor a proper rightmost generator of its sentences with their parses.

4. Consider the scattered context grammar

$$G_4 = (\{S, A, B, C, \$, a, b, c, 1, 2, 3, 4\}, \{a, b, c, 1, 2, 3, 4\}, P_4, S)$$

with P_4 containing

$$\begin{aligned} &1 : (S) \rightarrow (1), \\ &2 : (S) \rightarrow (ABC2\$), \\ &3 : (A, B, C, \$) \rightarrow (aA, bB, cC, 3\$), \\ &4 : (A, B, C, \$) \rightarrow (a, b, c, 4). \end{aligned}$$

Observe that

$$L(G_4) = \{a^n b^n c^n \rho : n \geq 0, S \Rightarrow^*_{G_4} a^n b^n c^n \rho\ [\rho]\},$$

and every derivation step in G_4 is both leftmost and rightmost, so G_4 is both a proper leftmost and a proper rightmost generator of its sentences with their parses.

7.2 General generators

In this section, we demonstrate that for every recursively enumerable language L, there is a propagating scattered context grammar G that represents a proper generator of its sentences with their parses such that L results from $L(G)$ by eliminating all production labels in $L(G)$.

Theorem 7.5. *For every recursively enumerable language L, there is a propagating scattered context grammar G such that G is a proper generator of its sentences with their parses, and* $L = L(G) // \operatorname{lab}(G)^+$.

Proof. Let L be a recursively enumerable language. Then, there is a scattered context grammar $\bar{G} = (\bar{V}, T, \bar{P}, \bar{S})$ such that $L = L(\bar{G})$ (see Theorem 3.20). Set $\Phi = \{\bar{a} : a \in T\}$. Define the homomorphism $\bar{\gamma}$ from $\bar{V}^*$ to $\big(\Phi \cup (\bar{V} - T) \cup \{Y\}\big)^*$ as $\bar{\gamma}(a) = \bar{a}$, for all $a \in T$, and $\bar{\gamma}(A) = A$, for all $A \in \bar{V} - T$. Define the function γ such that $\gamma(x) = \bar{\gamma}(x)$, for all $x \neq \varepsilon$, and $\gamma(\varepsilon) = Y$. Set $\Gamma = \{\$_1, \$_2, \$_3\}$ and

$$V = \bar{V} \cup \operatorname{lab}(G) \cup \Phi \cup \Gamma \cup \{S, X, Y, Z\}.$$

Define the propagating scattered context grammar

$$G = \big(\bar{V} \cup \operatorname{lab}(G) \cup \Phi \cup \Gamma \cup \{S, X, Y, Z\}, T \cup \operatorname{lab}(G), P, S\big)$$

with

$$\operatorname{lab}(G) = \big\{(\!|1|\!), (\!|1_\varepsilon|\!), (\!|2|\!), (\!|2_\varepsilon|\!), (\!|3|\!), (\!|4|\!)\big\} \cup \Xi_1 \cup \Xi_2 \cup \Xi_3,$$

where $\Xi_1 = \big\{(\!|1p|\!) : p \in \operatorname{lab}(\bar{G})\big\}$, $\Xi_2 = \{(\!|2a|\!) : a \in T\}$, $\Xi_3 = \{(\!|3a|\!) : a \in T\}$; without loss of generality, assume that $\operatorname{lab}(G) \cap \operatorname{alph}(L) = \emptyset$. Construct P as follows:

1. Add
   (a) $(\!|1|\!) : (S) \to \big(X(\!|1|\!)\$_1 Z\bar{S}\big)$, and
   (b) $(\!|1_\varepsilon|\!) : (S) \to \big((\!|1_\varepsilon|\!)\$_1\bar{S}\big)$ to P.
2. (a) For each $p : (A_1, \dots, A_n) \to (x_1, \dots, x_n) \in \bar{P}$, add
   $(\!|1p|\!) : (\$_1, A_1, \dots, A_n) \to \big((\!|1p|\!)\$_1, \gamma(x_1), \dots, \gamma(x_n)\big)$ to P.
   (b) Add
      (i) $(\!|2|\!) : (\$_1) \to \big((\!|2|\!)\$_2\big)$, and
      (ii) $(\!|2_\varepsilon|\!) : (\$_1) \to \big((\!|2_\varepsilon|\!)\$_3\big)$ to P.
3. For each $a \in T$, add
   (a) $(\!|2a|\!) : (X, \$_2, Z, \bar{a}) \to \big(aX, (\!|2a|\!)\$_2, Y, Z\big)$ and
   (b) $(\!|3a|\!) : (X, \$_2, Z, \bar{a}) \to \big(a, (\!|3a|\!)\$_3, Y, Y\big)$ to P.
4. Add $(\!|3|\!) : (\$_3, Y) \to \big((\!|3|\!), \$_3\big)$ to P.
5. Add $(\!|4|\!) : (\$_3) \to \big((\!|4|\!)\big)$ to P.

Basic Idea.
First, we explain how G derives a non-empty sentence followed by its parse; then, we explain the derivation of the empty sentence followed by its parse.

G makes the derivation of $a_1 \dots a_n \rho$, where $n \geq 1$, each $a_i \in T$, and ρ is the corresponding parse, by productions introduced in (1) through (5) in this order. After starting this derivation by using the production from (1a), it applies productions introduced in (2a), which simulate the applications of productions from $\bar{P}$. More precisely, it simulates the application of

$$p : (A_1, \dots, A_n) \to (x_1, \dots, x_n) \in \bar{P}$$

by using

$$⦇1p⦈ : (\$_1, A_1, \dots, A_n) \to \big(⦇1p⦈\$_1, \gamma(x_1), \dots, \gamma(x_n)\big) \in P$$

so that it places its own label, $⦇1p⦈$, right behind the previously generated production labels; this substring of labels occurs between the leftmost symbol, X, and $\$_1$ in the sentential form. Otherwise,

$$⦇1p⦈ : (\$_1, A_1, \dots, A_n) \to \big(⦇1p⦈\$_1, \gamma(x_1), \dots, \gamma(x_n)\big)$$

is analogical to $p : (A_1, \dots, A_n) \to (x_1, \dots, x_n)$ except that (1) the former has the fill-in symbol Y where the latter has ε, and (2) the former has $\bar{a}$ where the latter has a. After using productions introduced in (2), the sentential form of G has the form

$$X\tau\$_2 Z u_0 \bar{a}_1 u_1 \dots u_{n-1} \bar{a}_n u_n,$$

where τ is a prefix of ρ and $u_i \in \{Y\}^*$. By using productions from (3), it places $a_1 \dots a_n$ to the beginning of the sentential form while replacing each $\bar{a}_i$ with Y and generating the production labels. By using productions labeled with $⦇3⦈$, G replaces each Y with $⦇3⦈$ while shifting $\$_3$ to the right. The application of the production labeled with $⦇4⦈$ completes the derivation of $a_1 \dots a_n \rho$.

Finally, let us explain how G makes the derivation of the empty sentence ε followed by its parse. By using productions labeled with $⦇1_\varepsilon⦈$ and $⦇2_\varepsilon⦈$ instead of $⦇1⦈$ and $⦇2⦈$, respectively, the process of placing terminal symbols to the beginning of the sentential form by productions from (3) is skipped; otherwise, the derivation proceeds as above.

Formal Proof.
We establish the theorem by Claims 1 through 5 stated below.

Claim 1. G generates every $w \in L(G) - \text{lab}(G)^+$ in the following way:

$$\begin{aligned} S &\Rightarrow_G X⦇1⦈\$_1 Z\bar{S} && [⦇1⦈] \\ &\Rightarrow_G^+ x && [\rho] \\ &\Rightarrow_G y && [⦇2⦈] \\ &\Rightarrow_G^* z && [\sigma] \\ &\Rightarrow_G u && [⦇3a⦈] \\ &\Rightarrow_G^+ v && [\tau] \\ &\Rightarrow_G w && [⦇4⦈], \end{aligned}$$

where $x, y, z, u, v, w \in V^*$, $⦇3a⦈ \in \Xi_3$, $\tau \in \{⦇3⦈\}^+$, $\rho \in \Xi_1^+$, and $\sigma \in \Xi_2^*$.

Proof. First, let us make these four observations:

- Since the only productions with S on their left-hand sides are the productions introduced in (1), $S \Rightarrow_G^+ w$ surely starts with a derivation step made by one of these productions. Furthermore, $S \notin \text{alph}(\text{rhs}(p))$, for any $p \in P$. Therefore, these productions are not used during the rest of the derivation. This derivation ends by applying the production labeled with $⦇4⦈$ because it is the only production with its right-hand side over $(T \cup \text{lab}(G))^*$. Thus, $S \Rightarrow_G^+ w$ can be expressed as
$$\begin{aligned} S &\Rightarrow_G X⦇1⦈\$_1 Z\bar{S} && [⦇1⦈] \\ &\Rightarrow_G^+ v \\ &\Rightarrow_G w && [⦇4⦈]. \end{aligned}$$
- Let p be a label of any production introduced in (2) through (4); then, $|\text{lhs}(p)|_\Gamma = |\text{rhs}(p)|_\Gamma = 1$. In greater detail, for each $⦇1p⦈ \in \Xi_1$, $⦇2a⦈ \in \Xi_2$, and $⦇3a⦈ \in \Xi_3$, the constructed productions satisfy
$$\begin{aligned} 1 &= \left|\text{lhs}(⦇1p⦈)\right|_{\{\$_1\}} = \left|\text{rhs}(⦇1p⦈)\right|_{\{\$_1\}} \\ &= \left|\text{lhs}(⦇2⦈)\right|_{\{\$_1\}} = \left|\text{rhs}(⦇2⦈)\right|_{\{\$_2\}} \\ &= \left|\text{lhs}(⦇2_\varepsilon⦈)\right|_{\{\$_1\}} = \left|\text{rhs}(⦇2_\varepsilon⦈)\right|_{\{\$_3\}} \\ &= \left|\text{lhs}(⦇2a⦈)\right|_{\{\$_2\}} = \left|\text{rhs}(⦇2a⦈)\right|_{\{\$_2\}} \\ &= \left|\text{lhs}(⦇3a⦈)\right|_{\{\$_2\}} = \left|\text{rhs}(⦇3a⦈)\right|_{\{\$_3\}} \\ &= \left|\text{lhs}(⦇3⦈)\right|_{\{\$_3\}} = \left|\text{rhs}(⦇3⦈)\right|_{\{\$_3\}}. \end{aligned}$$
- Because $X \in \text{alph}(x)$ and only productions labeled with $p \in \Xi_3$ satisfy $X \in \text{alph}(\text{lhs}(p))$ and $X \notin \text{alph}(\text{rhs}(p))$, the production labeled with $⦇2_\varepsilon⦈$ cannot be used.
- Let p be the label of any production introduced in (1) through (5); then, $|\text{rhs}(p)|_{\{p\}} = 1$.

Based on these observations, notice that G generates every $w \in L(G) - \text{lab}(G)^+$ in the way described in the formulation of Claim 1. □

Claim 2. Consider the derivation from Claim 1. In its beginning,

$$\begin{aligned} S &\Rightarrow_G X\llparenthesis 1\rrparenthesis\$_1 Z\bar{S} && [\llparenthesis 1\rrparenthesis] \\ &\Rightarrow_G^+ x && [\rho] \\ &\Rightarrow_G y && [\llparenthesis 2\rrparenthesis], \end{aligned}$$

every sentential form s in $X\llparenthesis 1\rrparenthesis\$_1 Z\bar{S} \Rightarrow_G^+ x$ satisfies

$$s \in \{X\}\,\mathrm{lab}(G)^+\{\$_1\}\{Z\}\big(\Phi \cup (\bar{V} - T) \cup \{Y\}\big)^+,$$
$$y \in \{X\}\,\mathrm{lab}(G)^+\{\$_2\}\{Z\}\big(\Phi \cup \{Y\}\big)^+.$$

Proof. By the definition of γ, productions labeled with $\llparenthesis 1p\rrparenthesis$, where $p \in \mathrm{lab}(\bar{G})$, rewrite symbols over $\Phi \cup (\bar{V} - T) \cup \{Y\}$ and change $\$_1$ to $\llparenthesis 1p\rrparenthesis\$_1$. Since $\bar{V} \cap \{X, \$_1, Z\} = \emptyset$, every sentential form s in $X\llparenthesis 1\rrparenthesis\$_1 Z\bar{S} \Rightarrow_G^+ x$ satisfies

$$s \in \{X\}\,\mathrm{lab}(G)^+\{\$_1\}\{Z\}\big(\Phi \cup (\bar{V} - T) \cup \{Y\}\big)^+.$$

Only productions labeled with $\llparenthesis 1p\rrparenthesis \in \Xi_1$ satisfy

$$\mathrm{alph}\Big(\mathrm{lhs}\big(\llparenthesis 1p\rrparenthesis\big)\Big) \cap (\bar{V} - T) \neq \emptyset.$$

Therefore, to generate $w \in \big(T \cup \mathrm{lab}(G)\big)^*$, productions labeled with $\llparenthesis 1p\rrparenthesis$ have to be applied until

$$s \in \{X\}\,\mathrm{lab}(G)^+\{\$_1\}\{Z\}\big(\Phi \cup \{Y\}\big)^+.$$

Finally, the production labeled with $\llparenthesis 2\rrparenthesis$ is used, so

$$y \in \{X\}\,\mathrm{lab}(G)^+\{\$_2\}\{Z\}\big(\Phi \cup \{Y\}\big)^+,$$

and the claim holds. □

Claim 3. In

$$\begin{aligned} y &\Rightarrow_G^* z && [\llparenthesis\sigma\rrparenthesis] \\ &\Rightarrow_G u && [\llparenthesis 3a\rrparenthesis] \end{aligned}$$

of the derivation from Claim 1, every sentential form o in $y \Rightarrow_G^* z$ can be expressed as

$$o \in T^*\{X\}\,\mathrm{lab}(G)^+\{\$_2\}\{Y\}^*\{Z\}\big(\Phi \cup \{Y\}\big)^+,$$

and $u \in T^+\,\mathrm{lab}(G)^+\{\$_3\}\{Y\}^+$. In greater detail,

$$\begin{aligned} & X\llparenthesis p_1\rrparenthesis\ldots\llparenthesis p_n\rrparenthesis\$_2 Z Y^{i_0}\bar{b}_1 Y^{i_1}\bar{b}_2 Y^{i_2}\ldots\bar{b}_m Y^{i_m} = y \\ \Rightarrow_G\ & b_1 X\llparenthesis p_1\rrparenthesis\ldots\llparenthesis p_n\rrparenthesis\llparenthesis 2b_1\rrparenthesis\$_2 Y^{i_0+1} Z Y^{i_1}\bar{b}_2 Y^{i_2}\ldots\bar{b}_m Y^{i_m} && [\llparenthesis 2b_1\rrparenthesis] \\ \Rightarrow_G\ & b_1 b_2 X\llparenthesis p_1\rrparenthesis\ldots\llparenthesis p_n\rrparenthesis\llparenthesis 2b_1\rrparenthesis\llparenthesis 2b_2\rrparenthesis\$_2 Y^{i_0+1}Y^{i_1+1} Z Y^{i_2}\ldots\bar{b}_m Y^{i_m} && [\llparenthesis 2b_2\rrparenthesis] \\ \Rightarrow_G^{m-3}\ & b_1\ldots b_{m-1} X\llparenthesis p_1\rrparenthesis\ldots\llparenthesis p_n\rrparenthesis\llparenthesis 2b_1\rrparenthesis\ldots\llparenthesis 2b_{m-1}\rrparenthesis\$_2 Y^{i_0+1}\ldots \\ & \ldots Y^{i_{m-2}+1} Z Y^{i_{m-1}}\bar{b}_m Y^{i_m} && [\bar{\sigma}] \\ \Rightarrow_G\ & b_1\ldots b_m\llparenthesis p_1\rrparenthesis\ldots\llparenthesis p_n\rrparenthesis\llparenthesis 2b_1\rrparenthesis\ldots\llparenthesis 2b_{m-1}\rrparenthesis\llparenthesis 3b_m\rrparenthesis\$_3 Y^{i_0+1}\ldots \\ & \ldots Y^{i_m+1} = u && [\llparenthesis 3b_m\rrparenthesis], \end{aligned}$$

where $(\!|p_1|\!), \ldots, (\!|p_n|\!) \in \mathrm{lab}(G)$ are labels that denote productions introduced in (1) and (2), $b_1, \ldots, b_m \in T$, $\bar{\sigma} = (\!|2b_3|\!) \ldots (\!|2b_{m-1}|\!)$, $i_0, \ldots, i_m \geq 0$, and $m = |s|$, where $s \in L(\bar{G})$ is the corresponding sentence of the scattered context grammar $\bar{G}$.

Proof. Notice that

$$\begin{aligned} 1 &= \left|\mathrm{lhs}\big((\!|2a|\!)\big)\right|_{\{X\}} = \left|\mathrm{rhs}\big((\!|2a|\!)\big)\right|_{\{X\}} \\ &= \left|\mathrm{lhs}\big((\!|2a|\!)\big)\right|_{\{Y\}} = \left|\mathrm{rhs}\big((\!|2a|\!)\big)\right|_{\{Y\}}, \end{aligned}$$

where $(\!|2a|\!) \in \Xi_2$. In every derivation step of $y \Rightarrow_G^* z$, the first symbol $\bar{b} \in \Phi$ following Z is replaced with Z, X is changed to bX, and $\$_2$ is changed to $(\!|2a|\!)\$_2$, where $(\!|2a|\!) \in \Xi_2$. As only productions from (3), labeled with p, satisfy $\mathrm{alph}\big(\mathrm{lhs}(p)\big) \cap \Phi \neq \emptyset$, $\mathrm{alph}\big(\mathrm{rhs}(p)\big) \cap \Phi = \emptyset$, Z can replace only the first occurrence of $\bar{b} \in \Phi$ behind Z to generate $w \in \big(T \cup \mathrm{lab}(G)\big)^*$. Productions labeled with $(\!|2a|\!)$ are used $m - 1$ times. Thus, $y \Rightarrow_G^* z$ has the form

$$\begin{aligned} & X(\!|p_1|\!) \ldots (\!|p_n|\!)\$_2 Z Y^{i_0} \bar{b}_1 Y^{i_1} \bar{b}_2 Y^{i_2} \ldots \bar{b}_m Y^{i_m} \\ \Rightarrow_G\ & b_1 X (\!|p_1|\!) \ldots (\!|p_n|\!)(\!|2b_1|\!)\$_2 Y^{i_0+1} Z Y^{i_1} \bar{b}_2 Y^{i_2} \ldots \bar{b}_m Y^{i_m} \quad \big[(\!|2b_1|\!)\big] \\ \Rightarrow_G\ & b_1 b_2 X (\!|p_1|\!) \ldots (\!|p_n|\!)(\!|2b_1|\!)(\!|2b_2|\!)\$_2 Y^{i_0+1} Y^{i_1+1} Z Y^{i_2} \ldots \bar{b}_m Y^{i_m} \quad \big[(\!|2b_2|\!)\big] \\ \Rightarrow_G^{m-3}\ & b_1 \ldots b_{m-1} X (\!|p_1|\!) \ldots (\!|p_n|\!)(\!|2b_1|\!)(\!|2b_{m-1}|\!)\$_2 Y^{i_0+1} \ldots \\ & \ldots Y^{i_{m-2}+1} Z Y^{i_{m-1}} \bar{b}_m Y^{i_m} \quad [\bar{\sigma}], \end{aligned}$$

where every sentential form satisfies

$$T^*\{X\}\,\mathrm{lab}(G)^+\{\$_2\}\{Y\}^*\{Z\}\big(\Phi \cup \{Y\}\big)^+.$$

Finally, a production labeled with $(\!|3a|\!)$ is applied; therefore, $z \Rightarrow_G u$ can be expressed as

$$\begin{aligned} & b_1 \ldots b_{m-1} X (\!|p_1|\!) \ldots (\!|p_n|\!)(\!|2b_1|\!) \ldots (\!|2b_{m-1}|\!)\$_2 Y^{i_0+1} \ldots \\ & \ldots Y^{i_{m-2}+1} Z Y^{i_{m-1}} \bar{b}_m Y^{i_m} \\ \Rightarrow_G\ & b_1 \ldots b_m (\!|p_1|\!) \ldots (\!|p_n|\!)(\!|2b_1|\!) \ldots (\!|2b_{m-1}|\!)(\!|3b_m|\!)\$_3 Y^{i_0+1} \ldots Y^{i_m+1} \quad \big[(\!|3b_m|\!)\big] \end{aligned}$$

with $u \in T^+\,\mathrm{lab}(G)^+\{\$_3\}\{Y\}^+$.

Putting together the previous parts of the derivation, we obtain the formulation of Claim 3. □

Claim 4. In

$$\begin{aligned} u &\Rightarrow_G^+ v \ [\tau] \\ &\Rightarrow_G w \ \big[(\!|4|\!)\big] \end{aligned}$$

of the derivation from Claim 1, every sentential form s of $u \Rightarrow_G^+ v$ satisfies $s \in T^+\,\mathrm{lab}(G)^+\{\$_3\}\{Y\}^*$, and $w \in T^+\,\mathrm{lab}(G)^+$. In greater detail, this derivation can be expressed as

$$
\begin{aligned}
& b_1 \dots b_m \llparenthesis p_1 \rrparenthesis \dots \llparenthesis p_n \rrparenthesis \{\$_3\} Y^i \\
\Rightarrow_G \;& b_1 \dots b_m \llparenthesis p_1 \rrparenthesis \dots \llparenthesis p_n \rrparenthesis \llparenthesis 3 \rrparenthesis \{\$_3\} Y^{i-1} \; [\llparenthesis 3 \rrparenthesis] \\
\Rightarrow_G^{i-2} \;& b_1 \dots b_m \llparenthesis p_1 \rrparenthesis \dots \llparenthesis p_n \rrparenthesis \llparenthesis 3 \rrparenthesis^{i-1} \{\$_3\} Y \; [\bar{\tau}] \\
\Rightarrow_G \;& b_1 \dots b_m \llparenthesis p_1 \rrparenthesis \dots \llparenthesis p_n \rrparenthesis \llparenthesis 3 \rrparenthesis^{i} \{\$_3\} \quad [\llparenthesis 3 \rrparenthesis] \\
\Rightarrow_G \;& b_1 \dots b_m \llparenthesis p_1 \rrparenthesis \dots \llparenthesis p_n \rrparenthesis \llparenthesis 3 \rrparenthesis^{i} \llparenthesis 4 \rrparenthesis \quad [\llparenthesis 4 \rrparenthesis],
\end{aligned}
$$

where each $b_j \in T$, for all $1 \leq j \leq m$, $\llparenthesis p_k \rrparenthesis \in \mathrm{lab}(G)$, for all $1 \leq k \leq n$, are labels that denote productions introduced in (1) through (3), and $\bar{\tau} \in \{\llparenthesis 3 \rrparenthesis\}^*$.

Proof. Observe that in order to generate $w \in (T \cup \mathrm{lab}(G))^*$, the first occurrence of Y following $\$_3$ has to be rewritten by the production labeled with $\llparenthesis 3 \rrparenthesis$ in every derivation step. Finally, the production labeled with $\llparenthesis 4 \rrparenthesis$ is applied. At this point, w satisfies $w \in T^+ \mathrm{lab}(G)^+$. □

The following claim formally demonstrates how G generates the empty sentence ε followed by its parse.

Claim 5. G generates every $w \in \mathrm{lab}(G)^+$ in the following way:

$$
\begin{aligned}
S \Rightarrow_G \;& \llparenthesis 1_\varepsilon \rrparenthesis \$_1 \bar{S} \; [\llparenthesis 1_\varepsilon \rrparenthesis] \\
\Rightarrow_G^+ \;& x \quad [\rho] \\
\Rightarrow_G \;& y \quad [\llparenthesis 2_\varepsilon \rrparenthesis] \\
\Rightarrow_G^+ \;& v \quad [\tau] \\
\Rightarrow_G \;& w \quad [\llparenthesis 4 \rrparenthesis],
\end{aligned}
$$

where $\rho \in \Xi_1^+$ and $\tau \in \{\llparenthesis 3 \rrparenthesis\}^+$.

Proof. Notice that $\mathrm{alph}(w) \cap T = \emptyset$, and only productions labeled with $p \in \Xi_3$ satisfy $X \in \mathrm{alph}(\mathrm{lhs}(p))$, $X \notin \mathrm{alph}(\mathrm{rhs}(p))$, and $a \in \mathrm{alph}(\mathrm{rhs}(p))$, where $a \in T$. Therefore, X cannot appear in any sentential form of $S \Rightarrow_G^* w$, so the derivation starts with a step made by the production labeled with $\llparenthesis 1_\varepsilon \rrparenthesis$. As $X \notin \mathrm{alph}(x)$, and for $p \in \Xi_2 \cup \Xi_3$, $X \in \mathrm{alph}(\mathrm{lhs}(p))$, the production labeled with $\llparenthesis 2_\varepsilon \rrparenthesis$ has to be used. Observe that other derivation steps are made in the way described in Claims 2 and 4. □

From Claims 1 through 5, it follows that for every recursively enumerable language L, there is a propagating scattered context grammar G such that G is a proper generator of its sentences with their parses, and $L = L(G) // \mathrm{lab}(G)^+$. ■

In addition, Theorem 7.5 immediately implies Corollary 3.17. Clearly, by constructing a proper generator of its sentences with their parses G whose language satisfies $L = L(G) // \mathrm{lab}(G)^+$ and defining h so that it erases every symbol from lab(G) and preserves all other symbols, we get a constructive proof of Corollary 3.17.

By a straightforward modification of the construction, we can also prove an analogous result for sentences that are preceded by their parses.

Theorem 7.6. *For every recursively enumerable language L, there is a propagating scattered context grammar G such that G is a proper generator of its sentences preceded by their parses, and* $L = \mathrm{lab}(G)^{+}\backslash\backslash L(G)$. ■

Compare this theorem with the result presented in [31]:

Theorem 7.7. *For every recursively enumerable language L, there is a propagating scattered context grammar G such that* $L = \{\$\}^{+}\backslash\backslash L(G)$.

Clearly, Theorem 7.7 is an immediate corollary of Theorem 7.6 because instead of generating a production label in every derivation step, we can generate the fill-in symbol \$ so the resulting sentence is preceded by a sequence of \$'s.

7.3 Canonical generators

In this section, we characterize the family of recursively enumerable languages based upon leftmost and rightmost generators. We demonstrate that for every recursively enumerable language L, there exists a propagating scattered context grammar G that represents a proper leftmost generator of its sentences with their parses so that L results from $L(G)$ by eliminating all production labels in $L(G)$; in addition, we achieve an analogical result in terms of rightmost generators as well. Notice that there exists a significant advantage of canonical generators over general generators: because only leftmost derivations are used, a sentence generated by leftmost generators contains information that is sufficient to reproduce its derivation. On the contrary, this is not true for ordinary generators because the provided parse does not specify how the productions should be applied during the derivation.

Theorem 7.8. *For every recursively enumerable language L, there is a propagating scattered context grammar* $G = (\bar{V}, \bar{T}, P, S)$ *such that G is a proper leftmost generator of its sentences with their parses,* $|\bar{V} - \bar{T}| \leq 6$, *and* $L = L(G)// \mathrm{lab}(G)^{+}$.

Proof. Let L be a recursively enumerable language. Let $Q = (V, T, W, F, R, g)$ be a queue grammar such that $L(Q) = L - \{\varepsilon\}$, and Q satisfies the properties described in Lemma 2.38 and Corollary 2.39. Recall that lab(Q) is the set of production labels of Q. Define an injective homomorphism α from $\mathrm{lab}(Q)^*$ to $\{0\}^*\{1\}$. Further, define the substitution f on V^* so that $f(\varepsilon) = \{\varepsilon\}$ and

$$f(a) = \{\alpha(r) : r : (a, b, x, d) \in R\},$$

for all $a \in V$. Similarly, define the substitution g on W^* so that

$$g(b) = \{\alpha(r) : r : (a, b, x, d) \in R\},$$

for all $b \in W$. Set

$$\begin{aligned}
\Xi_1 &= \{⦇1\bar{a}_0\bar{q}_0⦈ : g = a_0q_0, \bar{a}_0 \in f(a_0), \bar{q}_0 \in g(q_0)\},\\
\Xi_2 &= \{⦇2r\bar{x}\bar{d}⦈ : r : (a, b, x, d) \in R, x \in (V - T)^*, d \in W - F,\\
&\qquad \bar{x} \in f(x), \bar{d} \in g(d)\},\\
\Xi_4 &= \{⦇4r\bar{d}⦈ : r : (a, b, c, d) \in R, c \in T, d \in W - F, \bar{d} \in g(d)\},\\
\Xi_5 &= \{⦇5r⦈ : r : (a, b, c, d) \in R, c \in T, d \in F\}.
\end{aligned}$$

Define the propagating scattered context grammar G as

$$G = (\{S, A, B, \#, 0, 1\} \cup T \cup \mathrm{lab}(G), T \cup \mathrm{lab}(G), P, S),$$

where

$$\mathrm{lab}(G) = \Xi_1 \cup \Xi_2 \cup \Xi_4 \cup \Xi_5 \cup \{⦇3⦈, ⦇6⦈, ⦇7⦈, ⦇8⦈, ⦇9⦈, ⦇10⦈\},$$

and P is constructed as follows:

1. For each $\bar{a}_0 \in f(a_0), \bar{q}_0 \in g(q_0)$ such that $g = a_0q_0$, add $⦇1\bar{a}_0\bar{q}_0⦈ : (S) \to (A⦇1\bar{a}_0\bar{q}_0⦈AA\bar{q}_0A\bar{a}_0AB)$ to P.
2. For each $r : (a, b, x, d) \in R$, $x \in (V - T)^*$, $d \in W - F$, and $\bar{x} \in f(x)$, $\bar{d} \in g(d)$, add $⦇2r\bar{x}\bar{d}⦈ : (A, A, A, A, A, B) \to (A, ⦇2r\bar{x}\bar{d}⦈A, \alpha(r)A, \bar{d}A, \bar{x}A, B)$ to P.
3. Add $⦇3⦈ : (A, A, A, A, A, B) \to (A, ⦇3⦈A, A, A, B, A)$ to P.
4. For each $r : (a, b, c, d) \in R$, $c \in T$, $d \in (W - F)$, and $\bar{d} \in g(d)$, add $⦇4r\bar{d}⦈ : (A, A, A, A, B, A) \to (cA, ⦇4r\bar{d}⦈A, \alpha(r)A, \bar{d}A, B, A)$ to P.
5. For each $r : (a, b, c, d) \in R$, $c \in T$, and $d \in F$, add $⦇5r⦈ : (A, A, A, A, B, A) \to (c, ⦇5r⦈A, \alpha(r)A, A, B, AA)$ to P.
6. Add
   (a) $⦇6⦈ : (A, 0, A, 0, A, 0, B, A, A) \to (⦇6⦈, A, \#, A, \#, A, B, A, A)$ and
   (b) $⦇7⦈ : (A, 1, A, 1, A, 1, B, A, A) \to (⦇7⦈, A, \#, A, \#, A, B, A, A)$ to P.
7. Add
   (a) $⦇8⦈ : (A, A, A, B, A, A) \to (⦇8⦈B, \#, \#, \#, \#, \#)$,
   (b) $⦇9⦈ : (B, \#) \to (⦇9⦈, B)$, and
   (c) $⦇10⦈ : (B) \to (⦇10⦈)$ to P.

Basic Idea.
G simulates every successful derivation of a sentence $x \in L(Q)$ and, simultaneously, records the productions it applies. At the end of the simulation, G moves the generated sentence x to the left so it occurs in front of the recorded labels. G makes

all this derivation so that it represents a proper leftmost generator of its sentences with their parses, and $L(Q) = L(G) // \mathrm{lab}(G)^+$.

To describe the way G works in greater detail, observe that G generates every sentence so that it applies its productions in the order corresponding to steps (1) through (7) in the construction above. First, G applies a production introduced in (1) and, thereby, starts the simulation of a derivation of x by Q. That is, for $g = a_0q_0$, G inserts the binary representation of q_0 and a_0 in front of the fourth and the fifth nonterminal A, respectively. Every production introduced in (2) simulates a production of the form $r : (a, b, x, d)$ in Q, where $x \in (V - T)^*$ and $d \in W - F$. This production places the binary representation of r in front of the third occurrence of A and inserts the binary representation of d and x in front of the fourth and the fifth occurrence of A, respectively. After the application of the production labeled with $(\!|3|\!)$, G simulates only productions of the form (a, b, c, d) with $c \in T$ and $d \in W - F$ by productions introduced in (4). This simulation places c so that it precedes the first occurrence of A; otherwise, it works similarly to the simulation by productions introduced in (2). By a production constructed in (5), G completes the simulation of the derivation of x in Q. To successfully complete the derivation, all the three binary substrings that follow each of the first three occurrences of A have to coincide. By the productions constructed in (6), G verifies this coincidence so that it replaces the first coinciding binary symbol with the applied production label, and it changes the other two symbols to #'s. If G successfully completes this verification process, the production labeled with $(\!|8|\!)$ replaces all A's with #'s, and moves B to the very end of the sequence of the recorded labels. Then, G uses the production labeled with $(\!|9|\!)$ to replace all #'s with $(\!|9|\!)$'s. Finally, it completes the derivation by using the production labeled with $(\!|10|\!)$ to replace B with $(\!|10|\!)$.

Formal Proof.
We establish the theorem by Claims 1 through 5 stated below.

Claim 1. Every sentence $w \in L(G)$ is generated in this way:

$$\begin{aligned}
S &\Rightarrow_G A(\!|1\bar{a}_0\bar{q}_0|\!)AA\bar{q}_0A\bar{a}_0AB && [(\!|1\bar{a}_0\bar{q}_0|\!)] \\
&\Rightarrow_G^* x && [\rho] \\
&\Rightarrow_G y && [(\!|3|\!)] \\
&\Rightarrow_G^* z && [\sigma] \\
&\Rightarrow_G u && [(\!|5r|\!)] \\
&\Rightarrow_G^* v && [\tau] \\
&\Rightarrow_G w_1 && [(\!|8|\!)] \\
&\Rightarrow_G^* w_2 && [\omega] \\
&\Rightarrow_G w && [(\!|10|\!)],
\end{aligned}$$

where

$$x, y, z, u, v, w_1, w_2, w \in \left(\{S, A, B, \#, 0, 1\} \cup T \cup \mathrm{lab}(G)\right)^*,$$

$(\!|1\bar{a}_0\bar{q}_0|\!) \in \Xi_1$, $(\!|5r|\!) \in \Xi_5$, $\rho \in \Xi_2^*$, $\sigma \in \Xi_4^*$, $\tau \in \{(\!|6|\!), (\!|7|\!)\}^*$, and $\omega \in \{(\!|9|\!)\}^*$.

Proof. Since the only productions with S on their left-hand sides are the productions introduced in (1), $S \Rightarrow_G^* w$ necessarily starts with a derivation step made by one of these productions. As S does not occur on the right-hand side of any production, no production constructed in (1) is applied later in the derivation.

All derivations end by applying the production labeled with $(\!|10|\!)$ because it is the only production with its right-hand side over $(T \cup \mathrm{lab}(G))^*$. Thus, $S \Rightarrow_G^* w$ can be expressed as

$$\begin{aligned} S &\Rightarrow_G A(\!|1\bar{a}_0\bar{q}_0|\!)AA\bar{q}_0A\bar{a}_0AB && [(\!|1\bar{a}_0\bar{q}_0|\!)] \\ &\Rightarrow_G^* w_2 \\ &\Rightarrow_G w && [(\!|10|\!)]. \end{aligned}$$

Furthermore, notice that every production introduced in (2) through (6) contains exactly five A's and one B on both its left-hand side and right-hand side. As all five A's and one B are rewritten during every derivation step made by productions from (2) through (6), the position of B implies that

$$\begin{aligned} S &\Rightarrow_G A(\!|1\bar{a}_0\bar{q}_0|\!)AA\bar{q}_0A\bar{a}_0AB && [(\!|1\bar{a}_0\bar{q}_0|\!)] \\ &\Rightarrow_G^* w_2 \end{aligned}$$

can be expressed as

$$\begin{aligned} S &\Rightarrow_G A(\!|1\bar{a}_0\bar{q}_0|\!)AA\bar{q}_0A\bar{a}_0AB && [(\!|1\bar{a}_0\bar{q}_0|\!)] \\ &\Rightarrow_G^* x && [\rho] \\ &\Rightarrow_G y && [(\!|3|\!)] \\ &\Rightarrow_G^* z && [\sigma] \\ &\Rightarrow_G u && [(\!|5r|\!)] \\ &\Rightarrow_G^* v && [\tau] \\ &\Rightarrow_G w_1 && [(\!|8|\!)] \\ &\Rightarrow_G^* w_2. \end{aligned}$$

The production labeled with $(\!|8|\!)$ replaces all A's with #'s. After this replacement, only productions labeled with $(\!|9|\!)$ and $(\!|10|\!)$ can be used. The production labeled with $(\!|9|\!)$ requires that #'s are present behind B; this requirement is satisfied by the production labeled with $(\!|8|\!)$. The production labeled with $(\!|10|\!)$ is used during the very last derivation step because it removes B from the sentential form and B occurs on the left-hand sides of all other productions. Based on these observations, notice that G generates every $w \in L(G)$ in the way described in Claim 1. □

Claim 2. Consider the derivation from Claim 1. In its beginning,

$$\begin{aligned} S &\Rightarrow_G A(\!|1\bar{a}_0\bar{q}_0|\!)AA\bar{q}_0A\bar{a}_0AB && [(\!|1\bar{a}_0\bar{q}_0|\!)] \\ &\Rightarrow_G^* x && [\rho] \\ &\Rightarrow_G y && [(\!|3|\!)], \end{aligned}$$

where $(\!|1\bar{a}_0\bar{q}_0|\!) \in \Xi_1$, $\rho \in \Xi_2^*$, and every sentential form s in

$$A(\!|1\bar{a}_0\bar{q}_0|\!)AA\bar{q}_0A\bar{a}_0AB \Rightarrow_G^* x$$

satisfies

$$s \in \{A\}\,\mathrm{lab}(G)^+\{A\}\{0,1\}^*\{A\}\{0,1\}^*\{A\}\{0,1\}^*\{A\}\{B\},$$
$$y \in \{A\}\,\mathrm{lab}(G)^+\{A\}\{0,1\}^*\{A\}\{0,1\}^*\{A\}\{0,1\}^*\{B\}\{A\}.$$

Proof. Productions introduced in (2) simulate the productions of Q of the form $r : (a, b, z, d)$, where $z \in (V - T)^*$ and $d \in W - F$. Every production inserts its label in front of the second occurrence of A, $\alpha(r)$ in front of the third occurrence of A, $\bar{d} \in g(d)$ in front of the fourth occurrence of A, and finally, $\bar{z}$, where $\bar{z} \in f(z)$, in front of the fifth occurrence of A. Intuitively, $\alpha(r)$ is the binary representation of currently simulated production, $\bar{d}$ is the binary representation of the production $r' : (a', b', z', d')$, where $b' = d$, that is simulated in the following derivation step, and $\bar{z}$ is the binary representation of productions that are eventually simulated as soon as the first symbol of the sentential form of Q becomes $c_1, \ldots, c_n$, where $c_1, \ldots, c_n = z$. As for all $l \in \mathrm{lab}(Q)$, $\alpha(l) \in \{0\}^*\{1\}$ holds true, and for each $u \in f(a)$, $v \in g(b)$ with $a \in V$, $b \in W$, $u, v \in \{0\}^*\{1\}$, every sentential form s in

$$A(\!|1\bar{a}_0\bar{q}_0|\!)AA\bar{q}_0A\bar{a}_0AB \Rightarrow_G^* x$$

satisfies

$$s \in \{A\}\,\mathrm{lab}(G)^+\{A\}\{0,1\}^*\{A\}\{0,1\}^*\{A\}\{0,1\}^*\{A\}\{B\}.$$

Finally, after the production labeled with $(\!|3|\!)$ is used,

$$y \in \{A\}\,\mathrm{lab}(G)^+\{A\}\{0,1\}^*\{A\}\{0,1\}^*\{A\}\{0,1\}^*\{B\}\{A\}.$$

Therefore, the claim holds. □

Claim 3. In

$$\begin{aligned} y &\Rightarrow_G^* z\ [\sigma] \\ &\Rightarrow_G u\ [(\!|5r|\!)] \end{aligned}$$

of the derivation from Claim 1, where $\sigma \in \Xi_4^*$ and $(\!|5r|\!) \in \Xi_5$, every sentential form s in $y \Rightarrow_G^* z$ satisfies

$$s \in T^*\{A\}\,\mathrm{lab}(G)^+\{A\}\{0,1\}^*\{A\}\{0,1\}^*\{A\}\{0,1\}^*\{B\}\{A\},$$
$$u \in T^+\,\mathrm{lab}(G)^+\{A\}\{0,1\}^*\{A\}\{0,1\}^*\{A\}\{0,1\}^*\{B\}\{A\}\{A\}.$$

Proof. The productions introduced in (4) simulate the productions of Q of the form $r : (a, b, c, d)$, where $c \in T$ and $d \in W - F$, by analogy with the productions introduced in (2) except that c is placed in front of the first occurrence of A because

$c \in T$ is not further rewritten in Q during the rest of the derivation. Therefore, every sentential form s in $y \Rightarrow_G^* z$ satisfies

$$s \in T^*\{A\}\,\mathrm{lab}(G)^+\{A\}\{0,1\}^*\{A\}\{0,1\}^*\{A\}\{0,1\}^*\{B\}\{A\}.$$

The final step in Q is made by a production satisfying $d \in F$ that is simulated by productions introduced in (5). After its application,

$$u \in T^+\,\mathrm{lab}(G)^+\{A\}\{0,1\}^*\{A\}\{0,1\}^*\{A\}\{0,1\}^*\{B\}\{A\}\{A\},$$

so the claim holds. □

Claim 4. In

$$\begin{aligned} u &\Rightarrow_G^* v \;\; [\tau] \\ &\Rightarrow_G w_1 \; [(\!|8|\!)] \end{aligned}$$

of the derivation from Claim 1, where $\tau \in \{(\!|6|\!), (\!|7|\!)\}^*$, every sentential form s in $u \Rightarrow_G^* v$ satisfies

$$s \in T^+\,\mathrm{lab}(G)^+\{A\}\{0,1\}^*\{\#\}^*\{A\}\{0,1\}^*\{\#\}^*\{A\}\{0,1\}^*\{B\}\{A\}\{A\},$$

and $w_1 \in T^+\,\mathrm{lab}(G)^+\{B\}\{\#\}^*$.

Proof. Observe that G properly simulates Q if and only if the substrings over $\{0,1\}$ that follow each of the first three nonterminals A in the sentential form u are identical. The productions introduced in (6) check whether this property holds. As no production labeled with $(\!|8|\!)$, $(\!|9|\!)$, $(\!|10|\!)$ rewrites symbols over $\{0,1\}$, and $w \in (T \cup \mathrm{lab}(G))^*$, all symbols from $\{0,1\}$ have to be rewritten with $(\!|6|\!)$ and $(\!|7|\!)$. While the first three nonterminals A are moving right in the sentential form, the symbols following the first nonterminal A are replaced with production labels and the symbols following the second and third nonterminal A with #'s. Observe that every step in this derivation is necessarily leftmost. Therefore, every sentential form s in $u \Rightarrow_G^* v$ satisfies

$$s \in T^+\,\mathrm{lab}(G)^+\{A\}\{0,1\}^*\{\#\}^*\{A\}\{0,1\}^*\{\#\}^*\{A\}\{0,1\}^*\{B\}\{A\}\{A\}.$$

Finally, the production labeled with $(\!|8|\!)$ rewrites each A to # and, thereby, produces $w_1 \in T^+\,\mathrm{lab}(G)^+\{B\}\{\#\}^*$. The claim thus holds. □

Claim 5. In

$$\begin{aligned} w_1 &\Rightarrow_G^* w_2 \; [\omega] \\ &\Rightarrow_G w \;\; [(\!|10|\!)] \end{aligned}$$

of the derivation from Claim 1, where $\omega \in \{(\!|9|\!)\}^*$, every sentential form s in $w_1 \Rightarrow_G^* w_2$ satisfies $s \in T^+\,\mathrm{lab}(G)^+\{B\}\{\#\}^*$, and $w \in T^+\,\mathrm{lab}(G)^+$.

Proof. Observe that in order to generate $w \in (T \cup \text{lab}(G))^*$, the first occurrence of # following B is changed to $⦇9⦈$ in every derivation step. After each # is changed in this way, the production labeled with $⦇10⦈$ is applied to obtain $w \in T^+ \text{lab}(G)^+$. □

By Claims 1 through 5, $L(Q) = L(G)// \text{lab}(G)^+$ and G is a proper leftmost generator of its sentences with their parses. If $\varepsilon \in L$, include $⦇0⦈$ into lab(G) and a production of the form $⦇0⦈ : (S) \rightarrow (⦇0⦈)$ into P. At this point, $L = L(Q) \cup \{\varepsilon\} = L(G)// \text{lab}(G)^+$. Finally, notice that G contains only six nonterminals. Therefore, Theorem 7.8 holds. ■

Next, we establish a result that parallels Theorem 7.8 in terms of proper rightmost generators.

Theorem 7.9. *For every recursively enumerable language L, there is a propagating scattered context grammar* $G = (\bar{V}, \bar{T}, P, S)$ *such that G is a proper rightmost generator of its sentences with their parses,* $|\bar{V} - \bar{T}| \leq 6$, *and* $L = L(G)// \text{lab}(G)^+$.

Proof. The proper rightmost generator of its sentences with their parses can be constructed analogically to the construction described in the proof of Theorem 7.8. The constructed grammar contains exactly the same set of nonterminal and terminal symbols with a slightly modified set of productions. Specifically, the productions introduced in steps (1) through (5) of the construction given in the proof of Theorem 7.8 rewrite the sentential form in both the leftmost and the rightmost way, so they can be used without any modification. However, to construct the rightmost generator, one more nonterminal A is needed in the sentential form, so an additional symbol A has to appear in each of these productions in front of the nonterminal B.

The productions introduced in steps (6) and (7) of the construction given in the proof of Theorem 7.8 are changed in the following way:

6. Add

   (a) $⦇6⦈ : (A,0,A,0,A,0,A,B,A,A) \rightarrow (⦇6⦈A,A,\#,A,\#,A,\#,B,A,A)$,
   (b) $⦇7⦈ : (A,1,A,1,A,1,A,B,A,A) \rightarrow (⦇7⦈A,A,\#,A,\#,A,\#,B,A,A)$ to P.

7. Add

   (a) $⦇8⦈ : (A,A,A,A,B,A,A) \rightarrow (\#,\#,\#,\#,\#,\#,BB)$,
   (b) $⦇9⦈ : (\#,B,B) \rightarrow (B,⦇9⦈,B)$, and
   (c) $⦇10⦈ : (B,B) \rightarrow (⦇8⦈,⦇10⦈)$ to P.

The productions introduced in (6) verify whether the substrings over $\{0, 1\}$ in front of the second, third, and fourth occurrence of A are identical. Observe that the productions introduced in this construction make this verification in the rightmost way. Indeed, the productions introduced in (7) replace the #'s with the rest of the parse; the rightmost generator, however, takes always the rightmost #. The production labeled with (|8|) replaces each A with # and places BB to the end of the sentential form. Noteworthy, this production does not insert its label in the sentential form (this insertion takes place later on as explained shortly). The production labeled with (|9|) moves the first nonterminal B to the left and replaces # with its label, leaving the second nonterminal B at the end of the sentential form. Finally, when there is no # in the sentential form, the first occurrence of B and the second occurrence of B are replaced with (|8|) and (|10|), respectively. Observe that this grammar is a proper rightmost generator of its sentences with their parses. ■

Concluding this section, let us compare the present result with the result published in [32] that states the following theorem.

Theorem 7.10. *For every recursively enumerable language L, there is a propagating scattered context grammar G that generates its language in a rightmost way, and* $L = L(G)//\{\$\}^*$.

Clearly, if we generate the fill-in symbol \$ instead of every production's label in the proof of Theorem 7.9, we obtain the same result.

Finally, taking a closer look at another aspect of the presented result, we see that if we use scattered context grammars with erasing productions and substitute every label for ε on the right-hand side of every production, we characterize the family of recursively enumerable languages. Thus, the proofs of Theorems 7.8 and 7.9 also give us constructive proofs that establish this important result. In addition, every derivation step is leftmost so this result also implies the result of [15]. As a matter of fact, the presented result is stronger in the sense that every derivation step is leftmost in a successful derivation of the constructed grammar although this leftmost restriction is not explicitly placed on derivations at all.

Theorem 7.11. *For every recursively enumerable language L, there is a scattered context grammar G that generates its language in a leftmost way and* $L = L(G)$. ■

7.4 Reduced generators

Naturally, we want to construct the generators discussed in this chapter as economically and succinctly as possible. Therefore, in this closing section of Chapter 7, we explain how to reduce them in two ways. First, we want to reduce the number of their nonterminals as much as possible. Second, we want to keep the left-hand sides of their productions as short as possible because this reduction means fewer context-dependency checks during their application. In fact, we achieve both of these reductions simultaneously. We demonstrate that for every recursively enumerable language L, there is a propagating scattered context grammar G such that G is reduced in the two-fold way sketched above, and at the same time, it represents a proper leftmost generator of its sentences preceded by their parses so that L results from $L(G)$ by eliminating all production labels in $L(G)$. As a matter of fact, regarding the two-fold reduction, we achieve this result in two different ways.

Theorem 7.12. *For every recursively enumerable language L, there is a propagating scattered context grammar* $G = (\bar{V}, \bar{T}, P, S)$ *such that G is a proper leftmost generator of its sentences preceded by their parses,* $|\bar{V} - \bar{T}| \leq 6$, $\text{mcs}(G) = 3$, *and* $L = \text{lab}(G)^+ \backslash\backslash L(G)$.

Proof. Let $L \subseteq T^*$ be any recursively enumerable language over an alphabet $T = \{a_1, \ldots, a_n\}$. Then, by Theorem 2.35, there is an Extended Post Correspondence $E = \big(D, (z_{a_1}, \ldots, z_{a_n})\big)$, where $D = \big\{(u_1, v_1), \ldots, (u_r, v_r)\big\}$, $u_i, v_i, z_{a_j} \in \{0,1\}^*$, for every $1 \leq i \leq r, 1 \leq j \leq n$, such that $L(E) = L$. Define the propagating scattered context grammar

$$G = \big(\{S, A, B, 0, 1, \#\} \cup T \cup \text{lab}(G), T \cup \text{lab}(G), P, S\big),$$

where

$$\begin{aligned}\text{lab}(G) = {} & \big\{\llparenthesis 1 \rrparenthesis, \llparenthesis 3 \rrparenthesis, \llparenthesis 3_0 \rrparenthesis, \llparenthesis 3_1 \rrparenthesis, \llparenthesis 4 \rrparenthesis, \llparenthesis 4_0 \rrparenthesis, \llparenthesis 4_1 \rrparenthesis, \llparenthesis 4_2 \rrparenthesis\big\} \\ & \cup \big\{\llparenthesis 1_a \rrparenthesis : a \in T\big\} \cup \big\{\llparenthesis 2_{u_i v_i} \rrparenthesis, \llparenthesis 2_{0 u_i v_i} \rrparenthesis : (u_i, v_i) \in D\big\},\end{aligned}$$

and P is constructed as follows:

1. For each $a \in T$, add

   (a) $\llparenthesis 1 \rrparenthesis : (S) \to \big(\llparenthesis 1 \rrparenthesis AA\big)$,
   (b) $\llparenthesis 1_a \rrparenthesis : (A, A) \to \big(\llparenthesis 1_a \rrparenthesis A z_a, Aa\big)$ to P.

2. For each $(u_i, v_i) \in D$, $1 \leq i \leq r$, add

   (a) $\llparenthesis 2_{u_i v_i} \rrparenthesis : (A, A) \to \big(\llparenthesis 2_{u_i v_i} \rrparenthesis B u_i, B v_i\big)$,
   (b) $\llparenthesis 2_{0 u_i v_i} \rrparenthesis : (B, B) \to \big(\llparenthesis 2_{0 u_i v_i} \rrparenthesis B u_i, B v_i\big)$ to P.

3. Add

   (a) $\llparenthesis 3 \rrparenthesis : (B, B) \to \big(\llparenthesis 3 \rrparenthesis A, B\big)$,
   (b) $\llparenthesis 3_0 \rrparenthesis : (A, 0, B, 0) \to \big(\llparenthesis 3_0 \rrparenthesis, A, \#, B\big)$,
   (c) $\llparenthesis 3_1 \rrparenthesis : (A, 1, B, 1) \to \big(\llparenthesis 3_1 \rrparenthesis, A, \#, B\big)$ to P.

4. Add

   (a) $\llparenthesis 4 \rrparenthesis : (A, B) \to \big(\llparenthesis 4 \rrparenthesis B, A\big)$,
   (b) $\llparenthesis 4_0 \rrparenthesis : (B, \#) \to \big(\llparenthesis 4_0 \rrparenthesis, B\big)$,
   (c) $\llparenthesis 4_1 \rrparenthesis : (B, A) \to \big(\llparenthesis 4_1 \rrparenthesis, B\big)$,
   (d) $\llparenthesis 4_2 \rrparenthesis : (B) \to \big(\llparenthesis 4_2 \rrparenthesis\big)$ to P.

First, observe that every production introduced in (1b) through (4a) contains exactly two nonterminals from the set $\{A, B\}$ on its left-hand side as well as its right-hand side. Therefore, there are always exactly two nonterminals from this set in every single sentential form during the application of these productions.

Every successful derivation starts by using the production labeled with $(\!|1|\!)$ because it is the only production with S on its left-hand side. As no other production contains S on its right-hand side, it is not applied during the rest of the derivation process. Therefore, every derivation starts by

$$S \Rightarrow_G (\!|1|\!)AA\ \left[(\!|1|\!)\right].$$

At this point, only productions from (1b) and (2a) are applicable. Productions from (1b) non-deterministically generate a sentence so that each of them adds $a \in T$ behind the second occurrence of A and simultaneously adds the binary representation of a behind the first occurrence of A in the sentential form. Finally, a production from (2a) replaces both occurrences of A with B, so after its application, no production from (1) can be applied. This part of the derivation can be formally expressed as

$$\begin{aligned}(\!|1|\!)AA &\Rightarrow_G^* u\ [\Xi_1]\\ &\Rightarrow_G v\ [p_2],\end{aligned}$$

where $u \in \text{lab}(G)^+\{A\}\{0,1\}^*\{A\}T^*$,

$$v \in \text{lab}(G)^+\{B\}\{0,1\}^+\{B\}\{0,1\}^+T^*,$$

Ξ_1 is a sequence of labels of productions introduced in (1b), and p_2 is a label of a production introduced in (2a).

Every production from (2) non-deterministically selects some $(u_i, v_i) \in D$, where $1 \le i \le r$, and adds u_i and v_i behind the first and the second occurrence of B, respectively. Observe that only productions introduced in (2b) and the productions labeled with $(\!|3|\!)$ and $(\!|4_2|\!)$ are applicable at this point. However, as the production labeled with $(\!|4_2|\!)$ removes B from the sentential form, its use leads to an unsuccessful derivation. The production labeled with $(\!|3|\!)$ is applied to complete this part of the derivation by rewriting the first occurrence of B with A. The corresponding part of the derivation is of the form

$$\begin{aligned}v &\Rightarrow_G^* w\ [\Xi_2]\\ &\Rightarrow_G x\ \left[(\!|3|\!)\right],\end{aligned}$$

where

$$\begin{aligned}w &\in \text{lab}(G)^+\{B\}\{0,1\}^+\{B\}\{0,1\}^+T^*,\\ x &\in \text{lab}(G)^+\{A\}\{0,1\}^+\{B\}\{0,1\}^+T^*,\end{aligned}$$

and Ξ_2 is a sequence of labels of productions introduced in (2b).

In greater detail, the sentential form x can be expressed as $x_1Ax_2x_3Bx_4x_5$, where $x_1 \in \text{lab}(G)^+$, $x_2 = u_{s_1} \dots u_{s_l}$, for some $s_1, \dots, s_l \in \{1, \dots, r\}$, $l \ge 1$, $x_3 = z_{b_1} \dots z_{b_k}$, for some $b_1, \dots, b_k \in T$, $k \ge 0$, $x_4 = v_{s_1} \dots v_{s_l}$, and $x_5 = b_1 \dots b_k$. From the definition of the language represented by an Extended Post Correspondence, for $b_1 \dots b_k \in L(E)$,

$$u_{s_1} \dots u_{s_l} z_{b_1} \dots z_{b_k} = v_{s_1} \dots v_{s_l},$$

therefore, in the sentential form x, $x_2x_3 = x_4$. This equivalence is verified by the productions labeled with $\llparenthesis 3_0 \rrparenthesis$ and $\llparenthesis 3_1 \rrparenthesis$. The production labeled with $\llparenthesis 3_0 \rrparenthesis$ replaces the 0's following A and B with A and B. Furthermore, it replaces A and B with $\llparenthesis 3_0 \rrparenthesis$ and #, respectively. Analogously, the production labeled with $\llparenthesis 3_1 \rrparenthesis$ replaces the 1's following A and B with A and B. Furthermore, it replaces A and B with $\llparenthesis 3_1 \rrparenthesis$ and #, respectively. While these productions are applicable, every sentential form y can be expressed as $y_1Ay_20y_3y_4By_50y_6y_7$, or $y_1Ay_21y_3y_4By_51y_6y_7$, where $y_1 \in \text{lab}(G)^+$, y_2, y_3, y_5, $y_6 \in \{0, 1\}^*$, $y_4 \in \{\#\}^*$, and $y_7 \in T^*$. Then, the production labeled with $\llparenthesis 3_0 \rrparenthesis$ or $\llparenthesis 3_1 \rrparenthesis$ can be applied, so

$$
\begin{aligned}
&y_1Ay_20y_3y_4By_50y_6y_7 \Rightarrow_G y_1\llparenthesis 3_0 \rrparenthesis y_2Ay_3y_4\#y_5By_6y_7 \left[\llparenthesis 3_0 \rrparenthesis\right], \text{ or}\\
&y_1Ay_21y_3y_4By_51y_6y_7 \Rightarrow_G y_1\llparenthesis 3_1 \rrparenthesis y_2Ay_3y_4\#y_5By_6y_7 \left[\llparenthesis 3_1 \rrparenthesis\right].
\end{aligned}
$$

We demonstrate that $y_2 = y_5 = \varepsilon$ by contradiction.

- Suppose that $y_2 \neq \varepsilon$. As the non-empty string y_2 cannot be removed by any production, y_2 satisfies $y_2 = \varepsilon$.
- Suppose that $y_5 \neq \varepsilon$. Then, y_5 can be removed only by the production labeled with $\llparenthesis 3_0 \rrparenthesis$ or $\llparenthesis 3_1 \rrparenthesis$. After its application (in the case when $y_2 = \varepsilon$), we get a sentential form of the form $y_1'y_3y_4\#Ay_5'\#By_6'y_7$, where $y_1' \in \text{lab}(G)^+$ and y_5', $y_6' \in \{0, 1\}^*$. Then, the substring $y_3y_4\#$ cannot be removed by any production, so y_5 satisfies $y_5 = \varepsilon$.

As a result, the occurrences of 0 and 1 immediately following A and B have to be rewritten during every derivation step performed by productions labeled with $\llparenthesis 3_0 \rrparenthesis$ and $\llparenthesis 3_1 \rrparenthesis$. A complete removal of 0's and 1's from the sentential form implies that $x_2x_3 = x_4$ holds.

While the productions labeled with $\llparenthesis 3_0 \rrparenthesis$ and $\llparenthesis 3_1 \rrparenthesis$ are applicable, other productions cannot be used. Specifically, the use of the productions labeled with $\llparenthesis 4 \rrparenthesis$, $\llparenthesis 4_2 \rrparenthesis$ before all 0's and 1's are removed from the sentential form results in an unsuccessful derivation. After all 0's and 1's are removed, the production labeled with $\llparenthesis 4 \rrparenthesis$ is used, and this application completes this part of the derivation. Therefore, this part of the derivation can be performed only as follows:

$$
\begin{aligned}
x &\Rightarrow_G^+ y \left[\Xi_3\right]\\
&\Rightarrow_G z \left[\llparenthesis 4 \rrparenthesis\right],
\end{aligned}
$$

where

$$
\begin{aligned}
y &\in \text{lab}(G)^+\{A\}\{\#\}^+\{B\}T^*,\\
z &\in \text{lab}(G)^+\{B\}\{\#\}^+\{A\}T^*,
\end{aligned}
$$

and $\Xi_3 \in \left\{\llparenthesis 3_0 \rrparenthesis, \llparenthesis 3_1 \rrparenthesis\right\}^+$.

The remaining part of a successful derivation can be expressed as

$$
\begin{aligned}
z &\Rightarrow_G^+ q_1 \left[\Xi_4\right]\\
&\Rightarrow_G q_2 \left[\llparenthesis 4_1 \rrparenthesis\right]\\
&\Rightarrow_G q \;\left[\llparenthesis 4_2 \rrparenthesis\right],
\end{aligned}
$$

where $q_1 \in \mathrm{lab}(G)^+\{B\}\{A\}T^*$, $q_2 \in \mathrm{lab}(G)^+\{B\}T^*$, $q \in \mathrm{lab}(G)^+T^*$, and $\Xi_4 \in \{\llparenthesis 4_0 \rrparenthesis\}^+$. The production labeled with $\llparenthesis 4_2 \rrparenthesis$ is applied in the last derivation step as it removes B from the sentential form. The production labeled with $\llparenthesis 4_1 \rrparenthesis$ replaces A, which occurs as the last nonterminal in the sentential form, with B, so it can be used only if all #'s are removed by previous applications of the production labeled with $\llparenthesis 4_0 \rrparenthesis$.

Putting the previous observations together, we obtain the derivation of any string $q \in L(E)$ preceded by its parses in the following form:

$$
\begin{aligned}
S &\Rightarrow_G \llparenthesis 1 \rrparenthesis AA \; [\llparenthesis 1 \rrparenthesis] \Rightarrow_G^* u \; [\Xi_1] \\
&\Rightarrow_G v \qquad [p_2] \;\; \Rightarrow_G^* w \; [\Xi_2] \\
&\Rightarrow_G x \qquad [\llparenthesis 3 \rrparenthesis] \Rightarrow_G^+ y \; [\Xi_3] \\
&\Rightarrow_G z \qquad [\llparenthesis 4 \rrparenthesis] \Rightarrow_G^+ q_1 \; [\Xi_4] \Rightarrow_G q_2 \; [\llparenthesis 4_1 \rrparenthesis] \Rightarrow_G q \; [\llparenthesis 4_2 \rrparenthesis].
\end{aligned}
$$

By examining the derivation and the applied productions, observe that (1) each of the productions adds its label to the end of the sequence of labels in every sentential form, and (2) every derivation step is leftmost. Therefore, G is a proper leftmost generator of its sentences preceded by their parses, so Theorem 7.12 holds. ■

Theorem 7.13. *For every recursively enumerable language L, there is a propagating scattered context grammar $G' = (\bar{V}', \bar{T}', P', S)$ such that G is a proper leftmost generator of its sentences preceded by their parses, $|\bar{V}' - \bar{T}'| \leq 9$, $\mathrm{mcs}(G) = 1$, and $L = \mathrm{lab}(G)^+\backslash\backslash L(G)$.*

Proof. Consider the grammar G introduced in the proof of Theorem 7.12. Define the propagating scattered context grammar

$$G' = \left(\{S, A, B, C, 0, 1, \$_0, \$_1, \#\} \cup T \cup \mathrm{lab}(G'), T \cup \mathrm{lab}(G'), P', S\right),$$

where

$$
\begin{aligned}
\mathrm{lab}(G') = &\left(\mathrm{lab}(G) - \{\llparenthesis 3_0 \rrparenthesis, \llparenthesis 3_1 \rrparenthesis\}\right) \\
&\cup \{\llparenthesis 3_{01} \rrparenthesis, \llparenthesis 3_{02} \rrparenthesis, \llparenthesis 3_{03} \rrparenthesis, \llparenthesis 3_{04} \rrparenthesis, \llparenthesis 3_{11} \rrparenthesis, \llparenthesis 3_{12} \rrparenthesis, \llparenthesis 3_{13} \rrparenthesis, \llparenthesis 3_{14} \rrparenthesis\},
\end{aligned}
$$

and P' contains all productions of P except for the productions introduced in (3). Furthermore, it contains the productions from the following construction:

3. Add

(a) $\llparenthesis 3 \rrparenthesis : (B, B) \to (\llparenthesis 3 \rrparenthesis A, B)$,

(b) $\llparenthesis 3_{01} \rrparenthesis : (B, 0) \to (\#, \$_0)$,
$\llparenthesis 3_{02} \rrparenthesis : (A, \$_0) \to (C, \$_0)$,
$\llparenthesis 3_{03} \rrparenthesis : (C, 0) \to (\llparenthesis 3_{01} \rrparenthesis \llparenthesis 3_{02} \rrparenthesis \llparenthesis 3_{03} \rrparenthesis, \$_0)$,
$\llparenthesis 3_{04} \rrparenthesis : (\$_0, \$_0) \to (\llparenthesis 3_{04} \rrparenthesis A, B)$,

(c) $\llparenthesis 3_{11} \rrparenthesis : (B, 1) \to (\#, \$_1)$,
$\llparenthesis 3_{12} \rrparenthesis : (A, \$_1) \to (C, \$_1)$,
$\llparenthesis 3_{13} \rrparenthesis : (C, 1) \to (\llparenthesis 3_{11} \rrparenthesis \llparenthesis 3_{12} \rrparenthesis \llparenthesis 3_{13} \rrparenthesis, \$_1)$,
$\llparenthesis 3_{14} \rrparenthesis : (\$_1, \$_1) \to (\llparenthesis 3_{14} \rrparenthesis A, B)$ to P'.

Every successful derivation is performed analogically to the derivation of G except that the productions labeled with $\llparenthesis 3_0 \rrparenthesis$ and $\llparenthesis 3_1 \rrparenthesis$ are simulated by the productions labeled with $\llparenthesis 3_{01} \rrparenthesis$, $\llparenthesis 3_{02} \rrparenthesis$, $\llparenthesis 3_{03} \rrparenthesis$, $\llparenthesis 3_{04} \rrparenthesis$ and $\llparenthesis 3_{11} \rrparenthesis$, $\llparenthesis 3_{12} \rrparenthesis$, $\llparenthesis 3_{13} \rrparenthesis$, $\llparenthesis 3_{14} \rrparenthesis$, respectively. Consider a sentential form of the form $u_1 A0 u_2 u_3 B0 u_4 u_5$, where $u_1 \in \text{lab}(G')^+$, $u_2, u_4 \in \{0, 1\}^*$, $u_3 \in \{\#\}^*$, and $u_5 \in T^*$. Then,

$$u_1 A0 u_2 u_3 B0 u_4 u_5 \Rightarrow_G u_1 \llparenthesis 3_0 \rrparenthesis A u_2 u_3 \# B u_4 u_5 \ [\llparenthesis 3_0 \rrparenthesis]$$

in a successful derivation of G. This derivation step is simulated by G' as follows:

$$\begin{aligned} u_1' A0 u_2 u_3 B0 u_4 u_5 &\Rightarrow_{G'} u_1' A0 u_2 u_3 \# \$_0 u_4 u_5 && [\llparenthesis 3_{01} \rrparenthesis] \\ &\Rightarrow_{G'} u_1' C0 u_2 u_3 \# \$_0 u_4 u_5 && [\llparenthesis 3_{02} \rrparenthesis] \\ &\Rightarrow_{G'} u_1' \llparenthesis 3_{01} \rrparenthesis \llparenthesis 3_{02} \rrparenthesis \llparenthesis 3_{03} \rrparenthesis \$_0 u_2 u_3 \# \$_0 u_4 u_5 && [\llparenthesis 3_{03} \rrparenthesis] \\ &\Rightarrow_{G'} u_1' \llparenthesis 3_{01} \rrparenthesis \llparenthesis 3_{02} \rrparenthesis \llparenthesis 3_{03} \rrparenthesis \llparenthesis 3_{04} \rrparenthesis A u_2 u_3 \# B u_4 u_5 && [\llparenthesis 3_{04} \rrparenthesis], \end{aligned}$$

where $u_1' \in \text{lab}(G)^+$. The production of G labeled with $\llparenthesis 4_1 \rrparenthesis$ is simulated by G' analogously.

Next, we demonstrate that the productions introduced in (3) cannot be used during the rest of the derivation. We consider two special cases of the derivation. First, consider a sentential form $v_1 B0 v_2 B0 v_3 v_4$, where $v_1 \in \text{lab}(G)^+$, $v_2, v_3 \in \{0, 1\}^*$, and $v_4 \in T^*$, which is obtained after the application of a production from (2a). Then,

$$\begin{aligned} v_1 B0 v_2 B0 v_3 v_4 &\Rightarrow_{G'} v_1 \# \$_0 v_2 B0 v_3 v_4 && [\llparenthesis 3_{01} \rrparenthesis] \\ &\Rightarrow_{G'} v_1 \# \$_0 v_2 \# \$_0 v_3 v_4 && [\llparenthesis 3_{01} \rrparenthesis] \\ &\Rightarrow_{G'} v_1 \# \llparenthesis 3_{04} \rrparenthesis A v_2 \# B v_3 v_4 && [\llparenthesis 3_{04} \rrparenthesis]. \end{aligned}$$

However, in this sentential form, the first occurrence of # cannot be removed by any production, so the derivation is not successful.

Second, consider a sentential form $z_1 A z_2 B00 z_3$, where $z_1 \in \text{lab}(G)^+$, $z_2 \in \{\#\}^+$, and $z_3 \in T^*$, which is obtained when some 0's behind B are not removed by productions labeled with $\llparenthesis 3_0 \rrparenthesis$. Then,

$$\begin{aligned} z_1 A z_2 B00 z_3 &\Rightarrow_{G'} z_1 \llparenthesis 4 \rrparenthesis B z_2 A00 z_3 && [\llparenthesis 4 \rrparenthesis] \\ &\Rightarrow_{G'}^{+} z_1' BA00 z_3 && [\Xi_4] \\ &\Rightarrow_{G'} z_1' \# A \$_0 0 z_3 && [\llparenthesis 3_{01} \rrparenthesis] \\ &\Rightarrow_{G'} z_1' \# C \$_0 0 z_3 && [\llparenthesis 3_{02} \rrparenthesis] \\ &\Rightarrow_{G'} z_1' \# \llparenthesis 3_{01} \rrparenthesis \llparenthesis 3_{02} \rrparenthesis \llparenthesis 3_{03} \rrparenthesis \$_0 \$_0 z_3 && [\llparenthesis 3_{03} \rrparenthesis] \\ &\Rightarrow_{G'} z_1' \# \llparenthesis 3_{01} \rrparenthesis \llparenthesis 3_{02} \rrparenthesis \llparenthesis 3_{03} \rrparenthesis \llparenthesis 3_{04} \rrparenthesis AB z_3 && [\llparenthesis 3_{04} \rrparenthesis], \end{aligned}$$

where $z_1' \in \text{lab}(G)^+$ and $\Xi_4 \in \{\llparenthesis 4_0 \rrparenthesis\}^+$. Again, the symbol # cannot be removed by any production, so the derivation is not successful. Other special cases and more detailed proof of this theorem are left to the reader. ■

In the conclusion of this chapter, let us recall that we have demonstrated that for every recursively enumerable language, there exists a propagating scattered context grammar that generates its sentences followed by their parses. In addition, we have proved analogical results in terms of canonical and reduced versions of these generators. Apart from parses, there exist other pieces of information that can be stored during the derivation of a string, such as positions of nonterminals rewritten during the derivation or one-dimensional representation of derivation trees. We suggest this as a topic of future investigation.

PART III

Applications and conclusion

CHAPTER 8

Applications in linguistics

So far, we have focused our attention on the discussion of scattered context grammars from a rather theoretical viewpoint in this book. As opposed to this theoretical approach, in the present chapter, we describe some of their applications in order to demonstrate their quite realistic use in practice. As a matter of fact, these grammars are useful to every scientific field that formalizes its results by strings in which there exist some scattered context dependencies spread over the strings. Since numerous scientific areas, ranging from cellular biology through neurology up to logic, formalize and study their results by using strings involving dependencies of this kind, describing applications of scattered context grammars in all these areas would be unbearably sketchy and, therefore, didactically inappropriate. Instead of an encyclopedic approach like this, we focus on *linguistics*, which represents a classical application area of formal grammars. We primarily narrow our attention to the investigation of *English syntax*, which describes the rules concerning how words relate to each other in order to form well-formed grammatical English sentences. We have selected syntax of this language because the reader is surely familiar with English very well. Nevertheless, analogical ideas can be applied to members of other language families, including Indo-European, Sino-Tibetan, Niger-Congo, Afro-Asiatic, Altaic, and Japonic families of languages. We explore several common linguistic phenomena involving scattered context in English syntax and explain how to express these phenomena by scattered context grammars.

By no means is this chapter intended to be exhaustive in any way. Rather, we consider only selected topics concerning English syntax and demonstrate how scattered context grammars allow us to explore them clearly, elegantly, and precisely. Compared to the previous parts of this book, which are written in a strictly mathematical way, we discuss and describe scattered context grammars less formally here because we are interested in demonstrating real applications rather than theoretical properties. Specifically, we primarily use scattered context grammars to transform and, simultaneously, verify that the English sentences under discussion are grammatical.

Apart from linguistic applications, discussed in this chapter, the next chapter, which concludes this book, sketches further application areas of these grammars.

8.1 Syntax and related linguistic terminology

In the linguistic study concerning English syntax, we discuss and describe the principles and rules according to which we correctly construct and transform grammatical English sentences. To give an insight into the discussion of English syntax, we open this section by some simple examples that illustrate how we connect the theoretically oriented discussion of scattered context grammars in the previous chapters with the application-oriented discussion of English syntax in the present chapter. Then, we introduce the basic terminology used in syntax-oriented linguistics.

Introduction through examples

Observe that many common English sentences contain expressions and words that mutually depend on each other although they are not adjacent to each other in the sentences. For example, consider this sentence:

He usually goes to work early.

The subject (*he*) and the predicator (*goes*) are related; sentences

**He usually go to work early.*

and

**I usually goes to work early.*

are ungrammatical because the form of the predicator depends on the form of the subject, according to which the combinations **he... go* and **I... goes* are illegal (throughout this chapter, * denotes ungrammatical sentences or their parts). Clearly, any change of the subject implies the corresponding change of the predicator as well. Linguistic dependencies of this kind can be easily and elegantly captured by scattered context grammars. Let us construct a scattered context grammar that contains this production:

$$(\text{He}, \text{goes}) \rightarrow (\text{We}, \text{go}).$$

This production checks whether the subject is the pronoun *he* and whether the verb *go* is in third person singular. If the sentence satisfies this property, it can be transformed to the grammatically correct sentence

We usually go to work early.

Observe that the related words may occur far away from each other in the sentence in question. In the above example, the word *usually* occurs between the subject and the predicator. While it is fairly easy to use context-sensitive grammars to model context dependencies where only one word occurs between the related words, note that the number of the words appearing between the subject and the predicator can be virtually unlimited. We can say

He almost regularly goes to work early.

but also

He usually, but not always, goes to work early.

and many more grammatical sentences like this. To model these context dependencies by ordinary context-sensitive grammars, many auxiliary productions have to be introduced to send the information concerning the form of a word to another word, which may occur at the opposite end of the sentence. As opposed to this awkward and tedious description, the single scattered context production above is needed to perform the same job regardless of the number of the words appearing between the subject and the predicator.

We next give another example that illustrates the advantage of scattered context grammars over classical context-sensitive grammars under some circumstances. Consider these two sentences:

John recommended it.

and

Did John recommend it?

There exists a relation between the basic clause and its interrogative counterpart. Indeed, we obtain the second, interrogative clause by adding *did* in front of *John* and by changing *recommended* to *recommend* while keeping the rest of the sentence unchanged. In terms of scattered context grammars, this transformation can be described by the scattered context production

$$(\text{John}, \text{recommended}) \rightarrow (\text{Did John}, \text{recommend});$$

clearly, when applied to the first sentence, this production performs exactly the same transformation as we have just described. Although this transformation is possible by using an ordinary context production, the inverse transformation is much more difficult to achieve. The inverse transformation can be performed by a scattered context production

$$(\text{Did}, \text{recommend}) \rightarrow (\varepsilon, \text{recommended});$$

obviously, by erasing *did* and changing *recommend* to *recommended*, we obtain the first sentence from the second one. Again, instead of *John* the subject may consist of a noun phrase containing several words, which makes it difficult to capture this context dependency by ordinary context-sensitive grammars.

Considering the examples above, the advantage of scattered context grammars is more than obvious: scattered context grammars allow us to change only some words during the transformation while keeping the others unchanged. On the other hand, context-sensitive grammars are inconvenient to perform transformations of this kind. A typical context-sensitive grammar that performs this job usually needs many more context-sensitive productions by which it repeatedly traverses the transformed sentence in question just to change very few context-dependent words broadly spread across the sentence.

Terminology

Taking into account the intuitive insight given above, we see that there are structural rules and regularities underlying syntactically well-formed English sentences and their transformations. Although we have already used some common linguistic notions, such as subject or predicator, we now introduce this elementary linguistic terminology more systematically so we can express these English sentences in terms of their syntactic structure in a more exact and general way. However, we restrict this introduction only to the very basic linguistic notions, most of which are taken from [33, 34]. In the next chapter, which closes this book, we recommend several further excellent linguistic treatments closely related to the discussion of this chapter.

Throughout the rest of this section, we narrow our discussion primarily to verbs and personal pronouns, whose proper use depends on the context in which they occur. For instance, *is, are, was*, and *been* are different forms of the same verb *be*, and their proper use depends on the context in which they appear. We say that words in these categories *inflect* and call this property *inflection*. Verbs and personal pronouns often represent the key elements of a clause—the *subject* and the *predicate*. In simple clauses like

She loves him.

we can understand the notion of the subject and the predicate so that some information is "predicated of" the subject (*she*) by the predicate (*loves him*). In more complicated clauses, the best way to determine the subject and the predicate is the examination of their syntactic properties (see [33] for more details). The predicate is formed by a *verb phrase*—the most important word of this phrase is the verb, also known as the *predicator*. In some verb phrases, there occur several verbs. For example, in the sentence

He has been working for hours.

the verb phrase contains three verbs—*has, been*, and *working*. The predicator is, however, always the first verb of a verb phrase (*has* in the above example). In this study, we focus on the most elementary clauses—*canonical clauses*. In these clauses, the subject always precedes the predicate, and these clauses are positive, declarative, and without subordinate or coordinate clauses.

Next, we describe the basic categorization of verbs and personal pronouns, and further characterize their inflectional forms in greater detail.

Verbs

We distinguish several kinds of verbs based upon their grammatical properties. The set of all verbs is divided into two subsets—the set of *auxiliary verbs*, and the set of *lexical verbs*. Further, the set of auxiliary verbs consists of *modal verbs* and *non-modal verbs*. The set of modal verbs includes the following verbs—*can, may, must, will, shall, ought, need, dare*; the verbs *be, have*, and *do* are non-modal. All the remaining verbs are lexical. In reality, the above defined classes overlap in certain situations; for example, there are sentences, where *do* appears as an auxiliary verb, and in different situations, *do* behaves as a lexical verb. For simplicity, we do not take into account these special cases in what follows.

Inflectional forms of verbs are called *paradigms*. In English, every verb, except for the verb *be*, may appear in each of the six paradigms described in Table 8.1 (see [33]). Verbs in *primary form* may occur as the only verb in a clause and form the head of its verb phrase (predicator); on the other hand, verbs in *secondary form* have to be accompanied by a verb in primary form.

Table 8.1: Paradigms of English verbs.

Form	Paradigm	Person	Example
Primary	Present	3rd sg	*She* walks *home.*
		Other	*They* walk *home.*
	Preterite		*She* walked *home.*
Secondary	Plain form		*They should* walk *home.*
	Gerund-participle		*She is* walking *home.*
	Past participle		*She has* walked *home.*

The verb *be* has nine paradigms in its neutral form. All primary forms have, in addition, their negative contracted counterparts. Compared to other verbs, there is one more verb paradigm called *irrealis*. The irrealis form *were* (and *weren't*) is used in sentences of an unrealistic nature, such as

I wish I were rich.

All these paradigms are presented in Table 8.2.

Personal pronouns

Personal pronouns exhibit a great amount of inflectional variation as well. Table 8.3 summarizes all their inflectional forms. The most important for us is the class of pronouns in *nominative* because these pronouns often appear as the subject of a clause.

8.2 Transformational scattered context grammars

As we have already mentioned, in this chapter, we primarily apply scattered context grammars to transform grammatical English sentences to other grammatical English

Table 8.2: Paradigms of the verb *be*.

Form	Paradigm	Person	Neutral	Negative
Primary	Present	1st sg	*am*	*aren't*
		3rd sg	*is*	*isn't*
		Other	*are*	*aren't*
	Preterite	1st sg, 3rd sg	*was*	*wasn't*
		Other	*were*	*weren't*
	Irrealis	1st sg, 3rd sg	*were*	*weren't*
Secondary	Plain form		*be*	—
	Gerund-participle		*being*	—
	Past participle		*been*	—

Table 8.3: Personal pronouns.

Non-reflexive				Reflexive
Nominative	Accusative	Genitive		
Plain		Dependent	Independent	
I	*me*	*my*	*mine*	*myself*
you	*you*	*your*	*yours*	*yourself*
he	*him*	*his*	*his*	*himself*
she	*her*	*her*	*hers*	*herself*
it	*it*	*its*	*its*	*itself*
we	*us*	*our*	*ours*	*ourselves*
you	*you*	*your*	*yours*	*yourselves*
they	*them*	*their*	*theirs*	*themselves*

sentences. To do so, we next slightly modify scattered context grammars so they start their derivations from a language rather than a single start symbol. Even more importantly, these grammars define transformations of languages, not just their generation.

Definition 8.1. A *transformational scattered context grammar* is a quadruple

$$G = (V, T, P, I),$$

where

- V is the *total vocabulary*;
- $T \subset V$ is the set of terminals (or the *output vocabulary*);

- P is a finite set of scattered context productions;
- $I \subset V$ is the *input vocabulary*.

The derivation step is defined as in scattered context grammars (see Definition 2.40). The *transformation T that G defines from $K \subseteq I^*$* is denoted by $T(G, K)$ and defined as

$$T(G, K) = \{(x, y) : x \Rightarrow_G^* y, x \in K, y \in T^*\}.$$

If $(x, y) \in T(G, K)$, we say that *x is transformed to y* by G; x and y are called the *input* and the *output sentence*, respectively.

As already pointed out, while scattered context grammars generate strings, transformational scattered context grammars translate them. In a sense, however, the language generated by any scattered context grammar $G = (V, T, P, S)$ can be expressed by using a transformational scattered context grammar $H = (V, T, P, \{S\})$ as well. Observe that

$$L(G) = \Big\{y : (S, y) \in T\big(H, \{S\}\big)\Big\}.$$

Before we make use of transformational scattered context grammars in terms of English syntax in the next section, we give two examples to demonstrate a close relation of these grammars to the theoretically oriented studies given previously in this book. To link the theoretical discussions given in the previous chapters of this book to the present chapter, the first example presents a transformational scattered context grammar that works with purely abstract languages. In the second example, we discuss a transformational scattered context grammar that is somewhat more linguistically oriented.

Example 8.2. Define the transformational scattered context grammar

$$G = (V, T, P, I),$$

where $V = \{A, B, C, a, b, c\}$, $T = \{a, b, c\}$, $I = \{A, B, C\}$, and

$$P = \{(A, B, C) \rightarrow (a, bb, c)\}.$$

For example, for the input sentence $AABBCC$,

$$AABBCC \Rightarrow_G aABbbcC \Rightarrow_G aabbbbcc.$$

Therefore, the input sentence $AABBCC \in I^*$ is transformed to the output sentence $aabbbbcc \in T^*$, and

$$(AABBCC, aabbbbcc) \in T(G, I^*).$$

If we restrict the input sentences to the language $L = \{A^n B^n C^n : n \geq 1\}$, we get

$$T(G, L) = \{(A^n B^n C^n, a^n b^{2n} c^n) : n \geq 1\},$$

so every $A^n B^n C^n$, where $n \geq 1$, is transformed to $a^n b^{2n} c^n$.

In the following example, we modify strings consisting of English letters by a transformational scattered context grammar, and in this way, we relate these grammars to lexically oriented linguistics—that is, the area of linguistics that concentrates its study on vocabulary analysis and dictionary design.

Example 8.3. We demonstrate how to lexicographically order alphabetic strings and, simultaneously, convert them from their uppercase versions to lowercase versions. More specifically, we describe a transformational scattered context grammar G that takes any alphabetic strings that consist of English uppercase letters enclosed in angle brackets, lexicographically orders the letters, and converts them to the corresponding lowercases. For instance, G transforms $\langle XXUY \rangle$ to $uxxy$.

More precisely, let J and T be alphabets of English uppercases and English lowercases, respectively. Let $\prec$ denote *lexical order* over J; that is, $A \prec B \prec \cdots \prec Z$. Furthermore, let h be the function that maps the uppercases to the corresponding lowercases; that is, $h(A) = a$, $h(B) = b, \dots, h(Z) = z$. Let i denote the inverse of h, so $i(a) = A$, $i(b) = B, \dots, i(z) = Z$. Let $N = \{\hat{a} : a \in T\}$. We define the transformational scattered context grammar $G = (V, T, P, I)$, where T is defined as above, $I = J \cup \{\langle, \rangle\}$, $V = I \cup N \cup T$, and P is constructed as follows:

1. For each $A, B \in I$, where $A \prec B$, add
   $(B, A) \to (A, B)$ to P.
2. For each $a \in T$, add
   $(\langle) \to (\hat{a})$ to P.
3. For each $a \in T$ and $A \in J$, where $i(a) = A$, add
   $(\hat{a}, A) \to (a, \hat{a})$ to P.
4. For each $a, b \in T$, where $i(a) \prec i(b)$, add
   $(\hat{a}) \to (\hat{b})$ to P.
5. For each $a \in T$, add
   $(\hat{a}, \rangle) \to (\varepsilon, \varepsilon)$ to P.

Set $K = \{\langle\}J^*\{\rangle\}$. For instance, G transforms $\langle ORDER \rangle \in K$ to $deorr \in T^*$ as

$$
\begin{aligned}
\langle ORDER \rangle \Rightarrow_G \langle OEDRR \rangle &\Rightarrow_G \langle DEORR \rangle \\
&\Rightarrow_G \hat{d}DEORR\rangle \Rightarrow_G d\hat{d}EORR\rangle \Rightarrow_G d\hat{e}EORR\rangle \Rightarrow_G de\hat{e}ORR\rangle \\
&\Rightarrow_G de\hat{o}ORR\rangle \Rightarrow_G deo\hat{o}RR\rangle \Rightarrow_G deo\hat{r}RR\rangle \Rightarrow_G deor\hat{r}R\rangle \\
&\Rightarrow_G deorr\hat{r}\rangle \Rightarrow_G deorr,
\end{aligned}
$$

so $(\langle ORDER \rangle, deorr) \in T(G, K)$. Clearly, G can make the same transformation in many more ways; on the other hand, notice that the set of all transformations of $\langle ORDER \rangle$ to $deorr$ is finite.

More formally, we claim that G transforms every $\langle A_1 \dots A_n \rangle \in K$ to $b_1 \dots b_n \in T^*$, for some $n \geq 0$, so that $i(b_1) \dots i(b_n)$ represents a permutation of $A_1 \dots A_n$, and for all $1 \leq j \leq n-1$, $i(b_j) \prec i(b_{j+1})$ (the case when $n = 0$ means that $A_1 \dots A_n = b_1 \dots b_n = \varepsilon$). To see why this claim holds, notice that $T \cap I = \emptyset$, so every successful transformation of a string from K to a string from T^* is performed so that all symbols are rewritten during the computation. By productions introduced in (1), G lexicographically orders the input uppercases. By a production of the form $(\langle) \rightarrow (\hat{a})$ introduced in (2), G changes the leftmost symbol $\langle$ to $\hat{a}$. By productions introduced in (3) and (4), G verifies that the alphabetic string is properly ordered and, simultaneously, converts its uppercase symbols into the corresponding lowercases in a strictly left-to-right one-by-one way. Observe that a production introduced in (2) is applied precisely once during every successful transformation because the left-to-right conversion necessities its application, and on the other hand, no production can produce $\langle$. By a production from (5), G completes the transformation; notice that if this completion is performed prematurely with some uppercases left, the transformation is necessary unsuccessful because the uppercases cannot be turned to the corresponding lowercases. Based upon these observations, it should be obvious that G performs the desired transformation.

Having illustrated the lexically oriented application, we devote the next section solely to the applications of transformational scattered context grammars in English syntax.

8.3 Scattered context in English syntax

In this section, we apply transformational scattered context grammars to English syntax. Before opening this topic, let us make an assumption regarding the set of all English words. We assume that this set, denoted by T, is finite and fixed. From a practical point of view, this is obviously a reasonable assumption because we all commonly use a finite and fixed vocabulary of words in everyday English (purely hypothetically, however, this may not be the case as illustrated by the study that closes this section). Next, we subdivide this set into subsets with respect to the classification of verbs and pronouns described in Section 8.1:

- T is the set of all words including all their inflectional forms;
- $T_V \subset T$ is the set of all verbs including all their inflectional forms;
- $T_{VA} \subset T_V$ is the set of all auxiliary verbs including all their inflectional forms;
- $T_{Vpl} \subset T_V$ is the set of all verbs in plain form;
- $T_{PPn} \subset T$ is the set of all personal pronouns in nominative.

To describe all possible paradigms of a verb $v \in T_{Vpl}$, we use the following notation:

- $\pi_{3rd}(v)$ is the verb v in third person singular present;
- $\pi_{pres}(v)$ is the verb v in present (other than third person singular);
- $\pi_{pret}(v)$ is the verb v in preterite.

There are several conventions we use throughout this section in order to simplify the presented case studies:

- We do not take into account capitalization and punctuation. Therefore, according to this convention,

He is your best friend.

and

he is your best friend

are equivalent.

- To make the following studies as simple and readable as possible, we expect every input sentence to be a canonical clause. In some examples, however, we make slight exceptions to this rule; for instance, sometimes we permit the input sentence to be negative. The first example and the last example also demonstrate a simple type of coordinated canonical clauses.
- The input vocabulary is the set $I = \{\langle x \rangle : x \in T\}$, where T is the set of all English words as stated above. As a result, every transformational scattered context grammar in this section takes an input sentence over I and transforms it to an output sentence over T. For instance, in the case of the declarative-to-interrogative transformation,

  $$\langle \text{he} \rangle \langle \text{is} \rangle \langle \text{your} \rangle \langle \text{best} \rangle \langle \text{friend} \rangle$$

  is transformed to

  is he your best friend

  As we have already mentioned, we omit punctuation and capitalization, so the above sentence corresponds to

  Is he your best friend?

Next, we give several studies that describe how to transform various kinds of grammatical sentences to other grammatical sentences by using transformational scattered context grammars.

Clauses with *neither* and *nor*

The first example shows how to use transformational scattered context grammars to negate clauses that contain the pair of the words *neither* and *nor*, such as

Neither Thomas nor his wife went to the party.

Clearly, the words *neither* and *nor* are related, but there is no explicit limit of the number of the words appearing between them. The following transformational scattered context grammar G converts the above sentence to

Both Thomas and his wife went to the party.

In fact, the constructed grammar G is general enough to negate every grammatical clause that contains the pair of the words *neither* and *nor*.

Set $G = (V, T, P, I)$, where $V = T \cup I$, and P is defined as follows:

$$\begin{aligned} P = & \left\{ (\langle \text{neither} \rangle, \langle \text{nor} \rangle) \rightarrow (\text{both}, \text{and}) \right\} \\ \cup & \left\{ (\langle x \rangle) \rightarrow (x) : x \in T - \{\text{neither}, \text{nor}\} \right\}. \end{aligned}$$

For example, for the above sentence, the transformation can proceed in this way:

$$\begin{aligned} &\langle\text{neither}\rangle\langle\text{thomas}\rangle\langle\text{nor}\rangle\langle\text{his}\rangle\langle\text{wife}\rangle\langle\text{went}\rangle\langle\text{to}\rangle\langle\text{the}\rangle\langle\text{party}\rangle \\ \Rightarrow_G\ &\text{both } \langle\text{thomas}\rangle \text{ and } \langle\text{his}\rangle\langle\text{wife}\rangle\langle\text{went}\rangle\langle\text{to}\rangle\langle\text{the}\rangle\langle\text{party}\rangle \\ \Rightarrow_G\ &\text{both thomas and } \langle\text{his}\rangle\langle\text{wife}\rangle\langle\text{went}\rangle\langle\text{to}\rangle\langle\text{the}\rangle\langle\text{party}\rangle \\ \Rightarrow_G\ &\text{both thomas and his } \langle\text{wife}\rangle\langle\text{went}\rangle\langle\text{to}\rangle\langle\text{the}\rangle\langle\text{party}\rangle \\ \Rightarrow_G^5\ &\text{both thomas and his wife went to the party.} \end{aligned}$$

The production

$$\big(\langle\text{neither}\rangle, \langle\text{nor}\rangle\big) \rightarrow (\text{both}, \text{and})$$

replaces *neither* and *nor* with *both* and *and*, respectively. Every other word $\langle w\rangle \in I$ is changed to $w \in T$. Therefore, if we denote all possible input sentences, described in the introduction of this example, by K, $T(G, K)$ represents the set of all negated sentences from K, and

$$\begin{aligned} \big(&\langle\text{neither}\rangle\langle\text{thomas}\rangle\langle\text{nor}\rangle\langle\text{his}\rangle\langle\text{wife}\rangle\langle\text{went}\rangle\langle\text{to}\rangle\langle\text{the}\rangle\langle\text{party}\rangle, \\ &\text{both thomas and his wife went to the party}\big) \in T(G, K). \end{aligned}$$

Existential clauses

In English, clauses that indicate an existence are called *existential*. These clauses are usually formed by the dummy subject *there*; for example,

There was a nurse present.

However, this dummy subject is not mandatory in all situations. For instance, the above example can be rephrased as

A nurse was present.

We construct a transformational scattered context grammar G that converts any canonical existential clause without the dummy subject *there* to an equivalent existential clause with *there*.

Set $G = (V, T, P, I)$, where $V = T \cup I \cup \{X\}$ (X is a new symbol such that $X \notin T \cup I$), and P is defined as follows:

$$\begin{aligned} P = \Big\{ &\big(\langle x\rangle, \langle\text{is}\rangle\big) \rightarrow (\text{there is } xX, \varepsilon), \\ &\big(\langle x\rangle, \langle\text{are}\rangle\big) \rightarrow (\text{there are } xX, \varepsilon), \\ &\big(\langle x\rangle, \langle\text{was}\rangle\big) \rightarrow (\text{there was } xX, \varepsilon), \\ &\big(\langle x\rangle, \langle\text{were}\rangle\big) \rightarrow (\text{there were } xX, \varepsilon) : x \in T \Big\} \\ \cup \Big\{ &\big(X, \langle x\rangle\big) \rightarrow (X, x) : x \in T \Big\} \\ \cup \Big\{ &(X) \rightarrow (\varepsilon) \Big\}. \end{aligned}$$

For the above sample sentence, we get the following derivation:

$$\begin{aligned} & \langle \text{a}\rangle\langle \text{nurse}\rangle\langle \text{was}\rangle\langle \text{present}\rangle \\ \Rightarrow_G\ & \text{there was a } X\langle \text{nurse}\rangle\langle \text{present}\rangle \\ \Rightarrow_G\ & \text{there was a } X \text{ nurse } \langle \text{present}\rangle \\ \Rightarrow_G\ & \text{there was a } X \text{ nurse present} \\ \Rightarrow_G\ & \text{there was a nurse present.} \end{aligned}$$

A production from the first set has to be applied first because initially there is no symbol X in the sentential form and all other productions require X to be present in the sentential form. In our case, the production

$$\big(\langle \text{a}\rangle, \langle \text{was}\rangle\big) \rightarrow (\text{there was a } X, \varepsilon)$$

is applied; the use of other productions from this set depends on what tense is used in the input sentence and whether the subject is in singular or plural. The production non-deterministically selects the first word of the sentence, puts *there was* in front of it, and the symbol X behind it; in addition, it erases *was* in the middle of the sentence. Next, all words $\langle w\rangle \in I$ are replaced with $w \in T$ by productions from the second set. These productions also verify that the previous non-deterministic selection was made at the beginning of the sentence; if not, there remains a word $\langle w\rangle \in I$ in front of X that cannot be rewritten. Finally, the derivation ends by erasing X from the sentential form.

This form of the derivation implies that if we denote the input existential clauses described in the introduction of this example by K, $T(G, K)$ represents the set of these clauses with the dummy subject *there*. As a result,

$$\big(\langle \text{a}\rangle\langle \text{nurse}\rangle\langle \text{was}\rangle\langle \text{present}\rangle, \text{there was a nurse present}\big) \in T(G, K).$$

Interrogative clauses

In English, there are two ways of transforming declarative clauses into interrogative clauses depending on the predicator. If the predicator is an auxiliary verb, the interrogative clause is formed simply by swapping the subject and the predicator. For example, we get the interrogative clause

Is he mowing the lawn?

by swapping *he*, which is the subject, and *is*, which is the predicator, in

He is mowing the lawn.

On the other hand, if the predicator is a lexical verb, the interrogative clause is formed by adding the dummy *do* to the beginning of the declarative clause. The dummy *do* has to be of the same paradigm as the predicator in the declarative clause and the predicator itself is converted to its plain form. For instance,

She usually gets up early.

is a declarative clause with the predicator *gets*, which is in third person singular, and the subject *she*. By inserting *do* in third person singular to the beginning of the sentence and converting *gets* to its plain form, we obtain

Does she usually get up early?

To simplify the following transformational scattered context grammar G, which performs this conversion, we assume that the subject is a personal pronoun in nominative.

Set $G = (V, T, P, I)$, where $V = T \cup I \cup \{X\}$ (X is a new symbol such that $X \notin T \cup I$), and P is defined as follows:

$$\begin{aligned} P = &\Big\{\big(\langle p\rangle, \langle v\rangle\big) \to (vp, X) : v \in T_{VA}, p \in T_{PPn}\Big\} \\ \cup &\Big\{\big(\langle p\rangle, \langle \pi_{pret}(v)\rangle\big) \to (\text{did } p, vX), \\ &\big(\langle p\rangle, \langle \pi_{3rd}(v)\rangle\big) \to (\text{does } p, vX), \\ &\big(\langle p\rangle, \langle \pi_{pres}(v)\rangle\big) \to (\text{do } p, vX) : v \in T_{Vpl} - T_{VA}, p \in T_{PPn}\Big\} \\ \cup &\Big\{\big(\langle x\rangle, X\big) \to (x, X), \\ &\big(X, \langle y\rangle\big) \to (X, y) : x \in T - T_V, y \in T\Big\} \\ \cup &\big\{(X) \to (\varepsilon)\big\}. \end{aligned}$$

For sentences whose predicator is an auxiliary verb, the transformation made by G proceeds as follows:

$$\begin{aligned} &\langle\text{he}\rangle\langle\text{is}\rangle\langle\text{mowing}\rangle\langle\text{the}\rangle\langle\text{lawn}\rangle \\ \Rightarrow_G\ &\text{is he } X\langle\text{mowing}\rangle\langle\text{the}\rangle\langle\text{lawn}\rangle \\ \Rightarrow_G\ &\text{is he } X \text{ mowing } \langle\text{the}\rangle\langle\text{lawn}\rangle \\ \Rightarrow_G\ &\text{is he } X \text{ mowing the } \langle\text{lawn}\rangle \\ \Rightarrow_G\ &\text{is he } X \text{ mowing the lawn} \\ \Rightarrow_G\ &\text{is he mowing the lawn.} \end{aligned}$$

The derivation starts by the application of a production from the first set, which swaps the subject and the predicator, and puts X behind them. Next, productions from the third set rewrite every word $\langle w\rangle \in I$ to $w \in T$. Finally, X is removed from the sentential form.

The transformation of the sentences in which the predicator is a lexical verb is more complicated:

$$\begin{aligned} &\langle\text{she}\rangle\langle\text{usually}\rangle\langle\text{gets}\rangle\langle\text{up}\rangle\langle\text{early}\rangle \\ \Rightarrow_G\ &\text{does she } \langle\text{usually}\rangle \text{ get } X\langle\text{up}\rangle\langle\text{early}\rangle \\ \Rightarrow_G\ &\text{does she usually get } X\langle\text{up}\rangle\langle\text{early}\rangle \\ \Rightarrow_G\ &\text{does she usually get } X \text{ up } \langle\text{early}\rangle \\ \Rightarrow_G\ &\text{does she usually get } X \text{ up early} \\ \Rightarrow_G\ &\text{does she usually get up early.} \end{aligned}$$

As the predicator is in third person singular, a production from

$$\Big\{\big(\langle p\rangle, \langle\pi_{3rd}(v)\rangle\big) \rightarrow (\text{does } p, vX) : v \in T_{Vpl} - T_{VA}, p \in T_{PPn}\Big\}$$

is applied at the beginning of the derivation. It inserts *does* to the beginning of the sentence, converts the predicator *gets* to its plain form *get*, and puts X behind it. Next, productions from

$$\Big\{\big(\langle x\rangle, X\big) \rightarrow (x, X) : x \in T - T_V\Big\}$$

rewrite every word $\langle w\rangle \in I$ appearing in front of the predicator to $w \in T$. Notice that they do not rewrite verbs—in this way, the grammar verifies that the first verb in the sentence was previously selected as the predicator. For instance, in the sentence

He has been working for hours.

has must be selected as the predicator; otherwise, the derivation is unsuccessful. Finally, the grammar rewrites all words behind X, and erases X in the last step as in the previous case.

Based on this intuitive explanation, we can see that the set of all input sentences K described in the introduction of this example is transformed by G to $T(G, K)$, which is the set of all interrogative sentences constructed from K. Therefore,

$$\big(\langle\text{he}\rangle\langle\text{is}\rangle\langle\text{mowing}\rangle\langle\text{the}\rangle\langle\text{lawn}\rangle, \text{is he mowing the lawn}\big) \in T(G, K),$$
$$\big(\langle\text{she}\rangle\langle\text{usually}\rangle\langle\text{gets}\rangle\langle\text{up}\rangle\langle\text{early}\rangle, \text{does she usually get up early}\big) \in T(G, K).$$

Question tags

Question tags are special constructs that are primarily used in spoken language. They are used at the end of declarative clauses, and we customarily use them to ask for agreement or confirmation. For instance, in

Your sister is married, isn't she?

isn't she is a question tag, and we expect an answer stating that she is married. The polarity of question tags is always opposite to the polarity of the main clause—if the main clause is positive, the question tag is negative, and vice versa. If the predicator is an auxiliary verb, the question tag is formed by the same auxiliary verb. For lexical verbs, the question tag is made by using *do* as

He plays the violin, doesn't he?

There are some special cases that have to be taken into account. First, the verb *be* has to be treated separately because it has more paradigms than other verbs and the question tag for first person singular is irregular:

I am always right, aren't I?

Second, for the verb *have*, the question tag depends on whether it is used as an auxiliary verb, or a lexical verb. In the first case, *have* is used in the question tag as

He has been working hard, hasn't he?

in the latter case, the auxiliary *do* is used as

They have a dog, don't they?

To explain the basic concepts as simply as possible, we omit the special cases of the verb *have* in the following transformational scattered context grammar G, which supplements a canonical clause with a question tag. For the same reason, we only sketch its construction and do not mention all the created productions explicitly. In addition, we suppose that the subject is represented by a personal pronoun.

Set $G = (V, T, P, I)$, where $V = T \cup I \cup \{X, Y\}$ (X, Y are new symbols such that $X, Y \notin T \cup I$), and P is defined as follows:

$$\begin{aligned}
P = &\Big\{\big(\langle p\rangle, \langle \text{will}\rangle, \langle x\rangle\big) \rightarrow (p, \text{will } X, Yx \text{ won't } p),\\
&\big(\langle p\rangle, \langle \text{won't}\rangle, \langle x\rangle\big) \rightarrow (p, \text{won't } X, Yx \text{ will } p),\\
&\ldots : p \in T_{PPn}, x \in T\Big\}\\
\cup &\Big\{\big(\langle \text{I}\rangle, \langle \text{am}\rangle, \langle x\rangle\big) \rightarrow (\text{I}, \text{am } X, Yx \text{ aren't I}),\\
&\big(\langle \text{you}\rangle, \langle \text{are}\rangle, \langle x\rangle\big) \rightarrow (\text{you}, \text{are } X, Yx \text{ aren't you}),\\
&\ldots : x \in T\Big\}\\
\cup &\Big\{\big(\langle p\rangle, \langle v\rangle, \langle x\rangle\big) \rightarrow (p, vX, Yx \text{ doesn't } p),\\
&\big(\langle q\rangle, \langle v\rangle, \langle x\rangle\big) \rightarrow (q, vX, Yx \text{ don't } q) :\\
&p \in \{\text{he, she, it}\}, q \in T_{PPn} - \{\text{he, she, it}\}, v \in T_V - T_{VA}, x \in T\Big\}\\
&\vdots\\
\cup &\Big\{\big(\langle x\rangle, X\big) \rightarrow (x, X),\\
&\big(X, \langle y\rangle, Y\big) \rightarrow (X, y, Y) : x \in T - T_V, y \in T\Big\}\\
\cup &\Big\{(X, Y) \rightarrow (\varepsilon, \varepsilon)\Big\}.
\end{aligned}$$

First, we describe the generation of question tags for clauses whose predicator is an auxiliary verb:

$$\begin{aligned}
&\langle \text{I}\rangle\langle \text{am}\rangle\langle \text{always}\rangle\langle \text{right}\rangle\\
\Rightarrow_G\ &\text{I am } X\langle \text{always}\rangle Y \text{ right aren't I}\\
\Rightarrow_G\ &\text{I am } X \text{ always } Y \text{ right aren't I}\\
\Rightarrow_G\ &\text{I am always right aren't I.}
\end{aligned}$$

Here, the production

$$\big(\langle \text{I}\rangle, \langle \text{am}\rangle, \langle \text{right}\rangle\big) \rightarrow (\text{I}, \text{am } X, Y \text{ right aren't I})$$

initiates the derivation. When it finds *I am* at the beginning of the sentence, it generates the question tag *aren't I* at its end. In addition, it adds X behind *I am* and Y in front of *right aren't I*. Next, it rewrites all words from $\langle w \rangle \in I$ to $w \in T$. It makes sure that the predicator was chosen properly by productions from

$$\Big\{\big(\langle x \rangle, X\big) \rightarrow (x, X) : x \in T - T_V\Big\}$$

similarly to the previous example. In addition, productions from

$$\Big\{\big(X, \langle y \rangle, Y\big) \rightarrow (X, y, Y) : x \in T - T_V, y \in T\Big\}$$

check whether the question tag was placed at the very end of the sentence. If not, there remains some symbol from the input vocabulary behind Y that cannot be rewritten. Finally, the last production removes X and Y from the sentential form.

When the predicator is a lexical verb in present, the question tag is formed by *does* or *do* depending on person in which the predicator occurs:

$$\begin{aligned} & \langle \text{he} \rangle \langle \text{plays} \rangle \langle \text{the} \rangle \langle \text{violin} \rangle \\ \Rightarrow_G \; & \text{he plays } X \langle \text{the} \rangle Y \text{ violin doesn't he} \\ \Rightarrow_G \; & \text{he plays } X \text{ the violin } Y \text{ doesn't he} \\ \Rightarrow_G \; & \text{he plays the violin doesn't he.} \end{aligned}$$

The rest of the derivation is analogous to the first case.

Based on these derivations, we can see that the set of all input sentences K described in the introduction of this example is transformed by G to $T(G, K)$, which is the set of all sentences constructed from K that are supplemented with question tags. Therefore,

$$\big(\langle \text{I} \rangle \langle \text{am} \rangle \langle \text{always} \rangle \langle \text{right} \rangle, \text{I am always right aren't I}\big) \in T(G, K),$$
$$\big(\langle \text{he} \rangle \langle \text{plays} \rangle \langle \text{the} \rangle \langle \text{violin} \rangle, \text{he plays the violin doesn't he}\big) \in T(G, K).$$

Generation of grammatical sentences

The purpose of the next discussion, which closes this section, is six-fold—(1) through (6), stated below.

1. We want to demonstrate that ordinary scattered context grammars, discussed in the previous chapters of this book, can be seen as a special case of transformational scattered context grammars, whose applications are discussed in the present section.
2. As pointed out in the notes following the general definition of a transformational scattered context grammar (see Definition 8.1), there exists a close relation between ordinary scattered context grammars and transformational scattered context grammars. That is, for every scattered context grammar $G = (V, T, P, S)$, there is a transformational scattered context grammar $H = \big(V, T, P, \{S\}\big)$ satisfying

$$L(G) = \Big\{y : (S, y) \in T\big(H, \{S\}\big)\Big\},$$

and in this way, $L(G)$ is defined by H. Next, we illustrate this relation by a specific example.

3. From a syntactical point of view, we want to show that scattered context grammars can generate an infinite non-context-free grammatical subset of English language in a very succinct way.
4. In terms of *morphology*—that is, the area of linguistics that studies the structure of words and their generation—we demonstrate how to use transformational scattered context grammars to create complicated English words within English sentences so that the resulting words and sentences are grammatically correct.
5. As stated in the beginning of the present section, so far we have assumed that the set of common English words is finite. Next, we want to demonstrate that from a strictly theoretical point of view, the set of all possible well-formed English words, including extremely rare words in everyday English, is infinite. Indeed, L, given next, includes infinitely many words of the form *(great-)*^{i}*grandparents*, *(great-)*^{i}*grandfathers*, and *(great-)*^{i}*grandmothers*, for all $i \geq 0$, and purely theoretically speaking, they all represent well-formed English words. Of course, most of them, such as

   great-great-great-great-great-great-great-great-great-grandfathers

   cannot be considered as common English words because most people never use them during their lifetime.
6. We illustrate that the language generation based upon scattered context grammars may have significant advantages over the generation based upon classical grammars, such as context-sensitive grammars.

Without further ado, consider the language L consisting of these grammatical English sentences:

Your grandparents are all your grandfathers and all your grandmothers.

Your great-grandparents are all your great-grandfathers and all your great-grandmothers.

Your great-great-grandparents are all your great-great-grandfathers and all your great-great-grandmothers.

⋮

In brief,

$$L = \big\{\text{your } \{\text{great-}\}^i \text{grandparents are all your } \{\text{great-}\}^i \text{grandfathers and all your } \{\text{great-}\}^i \text{grandmothers } : i \geq 0\big\}.$$

Introduce the scattered context grammar $G = (V, T, P, S)$, where

$$T = \{\text{all, and, are, grandfathers, grandmothers, grandparents, great-, your}\},$$

$V = T \cup \{S, \#\}$, and P consists of these three productions:

$$\begin{aligned}(S) &\rightarrow (\text{your \#grandparents are all your \#grandfathers}\\ &\qquad \text{and all your \#grandmothers}),\\ (\#, \#, \#) &\rightarrow (\text{\#great-}, \text{\#great-}, \text{\#great-}),\\ (\#, \#, \#) &\rightarrow (\varepsilon, \varepsilon, \varepsilon).\end{aligned}$$

Obviously, this scattered context grammar generates L; formally, $L = L(G)$. Consider the transformational scattered context grammar $H = \big(V, T, P, \{S\}\big)$. Notice that

$$L(G) = \Big\{y : (S, y) \in T\big(H, \{S\}\big)\Big\}.$$

Clearly, L is not context-free, so its generation is beyond the power of context-free grammars. It would be possible to construct a context-sensitive grammar that generates L. However, a context-sensitive grammar like this would have to keep traversing across its sentential forms to guarantee the same number of occurrences of *great-* in the generated sentences. Compared to this awkward way of generating L, the scattered context grammar G generates L in a more elegant, economical, and effective way.

In this chapter, we have illustrated how to transform and generate grammatical sentences in English by using transformational scattered context grammars, which represent a very natural linguistic apparatus straightforwardly based on scattered context grammars. However, from a more general perspective, we can apply these grammars basically in any area of science that formalizes its results by strings containing some scattered context dependencies. This general perspective brings us to the concluding chapter of this book, in which we make remarks about some selected scientific areas that involve a formalization of scattered context, and we also suggest how to make use of scattered context grammars in them.

CHAPTER 9

Concluding remarks

In this concluding chapter, we first make some bibliographical remarks. First, we point out the studies that underlie the present monograph, which represents the very first book that systematically summarizes the concepts and results concerning scattered context grammars. We also recommend some books that cover formal language theory in general and which represent a theoretical background of the present book. Then, we suggest further theoretically oriented investigation areas concerning scattered context grammars. Finally, we bring the reader's attention to some attractive application fields of these grammars, including linguistics, compilers, and biology.

Bibliographical remarks

Scattered context grammars were introduced in [2]. Their original version disallowed erasing productions; that is, in terms of the present monograph, only propagating scattered context grammars were originally considered by Greibach and Hopcroft. Several years later, Virkkunen [15] generalized them to scattered context grammars by allowing erasing productions. References [2, 15–17, 20–22, 25–29, 31–55] represent the most important studies that have discussed these grammars, and in many respects, we have based this monograph upon them. Specifically, the material presented in Sections 3.1 and 3.2 is taken from [2], and Section 3.3 is based on [21, 22, 40]. The results concerning the discussion of Chapter 4 are taken from [44, 52]. Chapter 5 is based on [21, 25, 28, 50, 53, 54]. Studies [29, 38, 39, 42, 43] underlie Chapter 6. The generators discussed in Chapter 7 were introduced and studied in [48, 49, 51]. Finally, the applications of scattered context grammars in linguistics are published in the present book for the first time in Chapter 8.

Although the present treatment of scattered context grammars is self-contained, some background in formal language theory is definitely helpful to grasp the material of this book easily. As an introduction to formal language theory, we recommend [24, 56–64]. The three-volume *Handbook of Formal Languages* (see [1]) gives an overview of the recent important trends in formal language theory. Regarding computational linguistics discussed in Chapter 8, consult [65–78].

Theoretical investigation

Next, we suggest new theoretical directions in the investigation of scattered context grammars.

Grammatical Regulation by Scattered Context. The concept of scattered context can be viewed as a mechanism that restricts or, in other words, regulates grammatical derivations. From this viewpoint, scattered context grammars are closely related to many regulated grammars, which are based upon various derivation restrictions that regulate the generation of their languages. Investigate how to replace some of these mechanisms by suitable scattered-context-based restrictions and vice versa. The theory of regulated grammars is discussed in numerous studies, many of which are summarized in Chapter 3 of the second volume of [1]. The monograph [19] represents a systematic introduction to regulated grammars; however, published in 1989, it is somewhat out of date. The study [27] shows one possibility how to enrich scattered context grammars by the concept of regulation.

Scattered Context Automata. Consider various automata with their tapes restricted in a scattered context way. To give a more specific suggestion, consider classical pushdown automata and place scattered context restrictions on their pushdown lists. Study the properties of automata restricted in this way. For a detailed discussion of automata theory, consult [23, 56, 58–60, 65, 79–85].

Scattered Context Translation. Transformational scattered context grammars, defined in Chapter 8 and applied to linguistics therein, can be seen as a formalism that translates languages instead of generating them. Study their properties from a theoretical point of view by analogy with other well-known studies of formal translation, including [79, 86–92].

Applications

Chapter 8 has demonstrated how to express and describe English syntax by scattered context grammars. Next, we add some more suggestions regarding the linguistically oriented applications of scattered context grammars. Then, in order to demonstrate that scattered context grammars may play an important role in other computer science fields in the future, their potential application is sketched in another field of computer science—compilers. We suggest some scattered context modifications of the traditional construction of compilers. From a broader point of view, we explain how scattered context grammars can formally underlie the design of modern compilers based upon computational concurrency and parallelism, which definitely belong to the fundamental features of the current way of computation. Finally, we propose how to make use of scattered context grammars in a scientific field out of computer science; specifically, we sketch some applications of these grammars in genetics.

Linguistics. As we have seen in Chapter 8 in terms of English syntax, there exist a number of scattered context relations between individual syntactical elements of sentences in natural languages. The examples given in Chapter 8 were chosen because the resulting scattered context grammars were relatively simple. Naturally, significantly more complicated grammars are needed when some complex syntax structures are considered as input. For instance, relative clauses are introduced by *who* or *which* depending on the subject of the main clause. If the subject in the main clause is a person, the relative clause is introduced by *who*; otherwise it starts by *which*. We encourage the reader to design a scattered context grammar that describes this dependency and all other coordination-related dependencies (see [33] for more examples).

Of course, by broadening the discussion of language syntax in terms of other languages than English, we obtain many more examples of scattered context dependencies. To illustrate, in Spanish, all adjectives inflect according to gender of the noun they characterize. Both the noun and the adjective may appear at different parts of a sentence, which makes their syntactical dependency difficult to capture by classical context grammars; obviously, scattered context grammars can describe this dependency in a more elegant and simple way.

Apart from description, specification, and transformation of language syntax, scattered context grammars can be applied to other linguistically oriented fields, such as morphology or lexical derivations, as illustrated by the concluding paragraphs of Chapter 8 and Example 8.3.

Compilers. Parsing, discussed in Chapter 7 from a rather theoretical point of view, represents a crucial phase of the compilation process, and it is traditionally underlain by context-free grammars. Scattered context grammars are stronger than context-free grammars, and in addition, lots of the languages they describe can be generated in a deterministic way. From these favorable properties, we draw inspiration of parsing languages by using scattered context grammars instead of ordinary context-free grammars. Making use of the scattered context grammatical mechanism, the resulting parsers could simultaneously place restrictions on derivation domains, use of productions, and neighborhood of the rewritten symbols. As a result, by a suitable combination of all these restrictions, scattered context parsers could consult their parsing and symbol tables only during some selected steps, after which they would make several consecutive steps under the guidance of the parsing mechanism without any table consultation. Scattered context parsers constructed in this way would be obviously stronger and faster than standard parsers, which consult their tables during every single step of the parsing process. In addition, they could control their derivation process in a deterministic way. In fact, these parsers might be based upon scattered context grammars in which the number of their components, including nonterminals and productions, is significantly reduced as follows from the reduction-related results achieved in Chapter 6.

From a more general point of view, in compilers, some of their fundamental parts, such as scanners and parsers, run concurrently within the compilation process as a whole. Furthermore, through the symbol table, compilers concurrently distribute various pieces of information throughout their components. As concurrency and parallelism represent central computational modes underlying modern information technologies, we can expect that the future's general design of compilers will be even more significantly based upon models that reflect this computational parallelism in order to perform the compilation process in an optimal way. More specifically, some parts of modern compilers may be further divided into various subparts, which are run in parallel, and within these subparts, a similar parallelism can be applied again, and so on. As a matter of fact, even in the present design of compilers, the syntax-directed translation is frequently divided into two parts, which work concurrently. One part is guided by a precedence parser that works with expressions and conditions while the other part is guided by a predictive parser that processes the general program flow. In addition, both parts are sometimes further divided into several subprocesses or threads; for instance, several expressions may be parsed in parallel, not sequentially. Of course, this two-parser design of syntax-directed translation requires an appropriate performance of compilation as a whole. Prior to this syntax-directed translation, a pre-parsing decomposition of the tokenized source program separates the syntax constructs for both parsers. On the other hand, after the syntax-directed translation based upon the two parsers is successfully completed, all the produced fragments of the intermediate code are carefully composed together so the resulting intermediate code is functionally equivalent to the source program.

To give another example of modern compiler design, various optimization methods are frequently applied to generate the resulting target code that itself is run in a parallel way. This way of code generation usually results from an explicit requirement in the source program. Sometimes, however, compilers themselves recognize that a generation like this is appropriate within the given computer framework, so they generate the parallel target code to speed up its subsequent execution. Whatever they do, however, they always have to guarantee that the generated target code is functionally equivalent to the source program. Clearly, this massively parallel design of compilers necessitates an extremely careful control over all the subprocesses running in parallel, and this complicated control has to be based upon a well-developed theory of computational parallelism and concurrency. Within formal language theory, which has always provided compilation techniques with their formal models, this control can be accomplished by scattered context grammars, whose productions naturally and elegantly formalize computational concurrency and parallelism. References [93–101] are good sources regarding compilers and their design.

Genetics. As formal language theory plays an important role in today's science, several scientific areas out of computer science apply the systematically developed knowledge concerning formal languages as well. In some of these scientific areas, scattered context information processing fulfills an important role. Consider, for instance, molecular genetics. Scattered information processing is central to this scientific field although it approaches this processing in a specific way. As opposed to the linguistically oriented transformations described in Chapter 8, genetically oriented studies usually investigate how to simultaneously modify several substrings scattered throughout strings that represent a molecular organism. To illustrate a modification like this, consider a typical molecular organism consisting of several groups of molecules; for instance, take any organism consisting of several parts that slightly differ in behavior of DNA molecules made by specific sets of enzymes. During their development, these scattered groups of molecules communicate with each other, and this communication usually influences the future behavior of the whole organism. A simulation of such an organism might be formally based upon scattered context grammars, which can simultaneously change strings at several different places. Consequently, genetic dependencies of this kind represent another challenging application area of scattered context grammars in the future.

Bibliography

[1] Rozenberg, G. & Salomaa, A., *Handbook of Formal Languages*. Springer, 1997.

[2] Greibach, S. & Hopcroft, J., Scattered context grammars. *Journal of Computer and System Sciences*, **3**, pp. 233–247, 1969.

[3] Greibach, S. & Hopcroft, J., Independence of AFL operations. Technical report, Defense Technical Information Center OAI-PMH Repository, 1967.

[4] Ginsburg, S. & Greibach, S., Abstract families of languages. *Symposium on Switching and Automata Theory*, Austin, pp. 128–139, 1967.

[5] Chomsky, N., On certain formal properties of grammars. *Information and Control*, **2**, pp. 137–167, 1959.

[6] Ginsburg, S., Greibach, S. & Harrison, M., One-way stack automata. *Journal of the ACM*, **14(2)**, pp. 389–418, 1967.

[7] Kuroda, S.Y., Classes of languages and linear-bounded automata. *Information and Control*, **7(2)**, pp. 207–223, 1964.

[8] Geffert, V., Context-free-like forms for the phrase-structure grammars. *Proceedings of the Mathematical Foundations of Computer Science 1988*, New York, pp. 309–317, 1988.

[9] Ibarra, O., Simple matrix languages. *Information and Control*, **17(4)**, pp. 359–394, 1970.

[10] Păun, G., Linear simple matrix languages. *Elektronische Informationsverarbeitung und Kybernetik*, **14(7/8)**, pp. 377–384, 1978.

[11] Rosenkrantz, D.J., Programmed grammars and classes of formal languages. *Journal of the ACM*, **16(1)**, pp. 107–131, 1969.

[12] Hauschildt, D. & Jantzen, M., Petri net algorithms in the theory of matrix grammars. *Acta Informatica*, **31(8)**, pp. 719–728, 1994.

[13] Kasai, T., An hierarchy between context-free and context-sensitive languages. *Journal of Computer and System Sciences*, **4(5)**, pp. 492–508, 1970.

[14] Kleijn, H.C.M. & Rozenberg, G., On the generative power of regular pattern grammars. *Acta Informatica*, **20**, pp. 391–411, 1983.

[15] Virkkunen, V., On scattered context grammars. *Acta Universitatis Ouluensis*, **20(6)**, pp. 75–82, 1973.

[16] Cremers, A.B., Normal forms for context-sensitive grammars. *Acta Informatica*, **3**, pp. 59–73, 1973.

[17] Masopust, T., Scattered context grammars can generate the powers of 2. *EEICT 2007 Proceedings*, Brno, pp. 401–404, 2007.

[18] Masopust, T., *Formal Models: Regulation and Reduction*. Ph.D. thesis, Brno University of Technology, Faculty of Information Technology, 2007.

[19] Dassow, J. & Păun, G., *Regulated Rewriting in Formal Language Theory*. Akademie-Verlag, 1989.

[20] Meduna, A., Syntactic complexity of scattered context grammars. *Acta Informatica*, **32**, pp. 285–298, 1995.

[21] Milgram, D. & Rosenfeld, A., A note on scattered context grammars. *Information Processing Letters*, **1**, pp. 47–50, 1971.

[22] Păun, G., On simple matrix languages versus scattered context languages. *Informatique Théorique et Applications*, **16(3)**, pp. 245–253, 1982.

[23] Wood, D., *Theory of Computation*. Harper and Row, 1987.

[24] Meduna, A., *Automata and Languages: Theory and Applications*. Springer, 2000.

[25] Masopust, T. & Techet, J., Leftmost derivations of propagating scattered context grammars: A new proof. *Discrete Mathematics and Theoretical Computer Science*, **10(2)**, pp. 39–46, 2008.

[26] Mayer, O., Some restrictive devices for context-free grammars. *Information and Control*, **20**, pp. 69–92, 1972.

[27] Fernau, H., Scattered context grammars with regulation. *Annals of Bucharest University, Mathematics-Informatics Series*, **45(1)**, pp. 41–49, 1996.

[28] Gonczarowski, J. & Warmuth, M.K., Scattered versus context-sensitive rewriting. *Acta Informatica*, **27**, pp. 81–95, 1989.

[29] Vaszil, G., On the descriptional complexity of some rewriting mechanisms regulated by context conditions. *Theoretical Computer Science*, **330**, pp. 361–373, 2005.

[30] Wood, D., *Grammars and L Forms: An Introduction*. Springer, 1980.

[31] Ehrenfeucht, A. & Rozenberg, G., An observation on scattered grammars. *Information Processing Letters*, **9(2)**, pp. 84–85, 1979.

[32] Meduna, A., Canonical scattered rewriting. *International Journal of Computer Mathematics*, **51**, pp. 122–129, 1993.

[33] Huddleston, R. & Pullum, G., *The Cambridge Grammar of the English Language*. Cambridge University Press, 2002.

[34] Huddleston, R. & Pullum, G., *A Student's Introduction to English Grammar*. Cambridge University Press, 2005.

[35] Fernau, H. & Meduna, A., On the degree of scattered context-sensitivity. *Theoretical Computer Science*, **290**, pp. 2121–2124, 2003.

[36] Fernau, H. & Meduna, A., A simultaneous reduction of several measures of descriptional complexity in scattered context grammars. *Information Processing Letters*, **86**, pp. 235–240, 2003.

[37] Král, J., On multiple grammars. *Kybernetika*, **1**, pp. 60–85, 1969.

[38] Masopust, T., On the descriptional complexity of scattered context grammars. *Theoretical Computer Science*, **410(1)**, pp. 108–112, 2009.

[39] Masopust, T. & Meduna, A., On descriptional complexity of partially parallel grammars. *Fundamenta Informaticae*, **87(3)**, pp. 407–415, 2008.

[40] Meduna, A., A trivial method of characterizing the family of recursively enumerable languages by scattered context grammars. *EATCS Bulletin*, **56**, pp. 104–106, 1995.

[41] Meduna, A., Four-nonterminal scattered context grammars characterize the family of recursively enumerable languages. *International Journal of Computer Mathematics*, **63**, pp. 67–83, 1997.

[42] Meduna, A., Economical transformations of phrase-structure grammars to scattered context grammars. *Acta Cybernetica*, **13**, pp. 225–242, 1998.

[43] Meduna, A., Generative power of three-nonterminal scattered context grammars. *Theoretical Computer Science*, **246**, pp. 276–284, 2000.

[44] Meduna, A., Terminating left-hand sides of scattered context productions. *Theoretical Computer Science*, **237**, pp. 423–427, 2000.

[45] Meduna, A., Uniform generation of languages by scattered context grammars. *Fundamenta Informaticae*, **44**, pp. 231–235, 2001.

[46] Meduna, A., Coincidental extension of scattered context languages. *Acta Informatica*, **39**, pp. 307–314, 2003.

[47] Meduna, A. & Švec, M., *Grammars with Context Conditions and Their Applications*. Wiley, 2005.

[48] Meduna, A. & Techet, J., Generation of sentences with their parses: the case of propagating scattered context grammars. *Acta Cybernetica*, **17**, pp. 11–20, 2005.

[49] Meduna, A. & Techet, J., Canonical scattered context generators of sentences with their parses. *Theoretical Computer Science*, **389**, pp. 73–81, 2007.

[50] Meduna, A. & Techet, J., Maximal and minimal scattered context rewriting. *FCT 2007 Proceedings*, Budapest, pp. 412–423, 2007.

[51] Meduna, A. & Techet, J., Reduction of scattered context generators of sentences preceded by their leftmost parses. *DCFS 2007 Proceedings*, High Tatras, pp. 178–185, 2007.

[52] Meduna, A. & Techet, J., Scattered context grammars that erase nonterminals in a generalized k-limited way. *Acta Informatica*, **45(7)**, pp. 593–608, 2008.

[53] Meduna, A. & Techet, J., An infinite hierarchy of language families generated by scattered context grammars with n-limited derivations. *Theoretical Computer Science*, 2009. In press.

[54] Techet, J., A note on scattered context grammars with non-context-free components. *MEMICS 2007 Proceedings*, Znojmo, pp. 225–232, 2007.

[55] Techet, J., *Scattered Context in Formal Languages*. Ph.D. thesis, Brno University of Technology, Faculty of Information Technology, 2008.

[56] Floyd, R.W. & Beigel, R., *The Language of Machines: An Introduction to Computability and Formal Languages*. Computer Science Press, Inc., 1994.

[57] Ginsburg, S., *Algebraic and Automata-Theoretic Properties of Formal Languages*. North-Holland, 1975.

[58] Harrison, M., *Introduction to Formal Language Theory*. Addison-Wesley, Reading, 1978.

[59] Hopcroft, J.E. & Ullman, J.D., *Introduction to Automata Theory, Languages, and Computation*. Addison-Wesley, Reading, 1979.

[60] Kelley, D., *Automata and Formal Languages*. Prentice-Hall, 1995.

[61] Lewis, H.R. & Papadimitriou, C.H., *Elements of the Theory of Computation*. Prentice-Hall, 1981.

[62] Martin, J.C., *Introduction to Languages and the Theory of Computation*. McGraw-Hill Higher Education, 1997.

[63] Moll, R.N., Arbib, M.A. & Kfoury, A.J., *An Introduction to Formal Language Theory*. Springer, 1988.

[64] Salomaa, A., *Formal Languages*. Academic Press, 1973.

[65] Arbib, M.A., Moll, R.N. & Kfoury, A.J., *Basis for Theoretical Computer Science*. Springer, 1984.

[66] Beardon, C., Lumsden, D. & Holmes, G., *Natural Language and Computational Linguistics*. Ellis Horwood, 1991.

[67] Beesley, K.R. & Karttunen, L., *Finite State Morphology*. CSLI Publications, 2003.

[68] Bennett, P., *A Course in Generalized Phrase Structure Grammar*. UCL Press, 1995.

[69] Gazdar, G., Klein, E., Pullum, G.K. & Sag, I.A., *Generalized Phrase Structure Grammar*. Harvard University Press, 1985.

[70] Hausser, R., *Foundations of Computational Linguistics: Human-Computer Communication in Natural Language*. Springer, 2001.

[71] Jones, D., *Analogical Natural Language Processing*. UCL Press, 1996.

[72] Jones, D.B. & Somers, H., *New Methods in Language Processing*. Taylor & Francis, 1997.

[73] Jurafsky, D. & Martin, J.H., *Speech and Language Processing: An Introduction to Natural Language Processing, Computational Linguistics and Speech Recognition*. Prentice-Hall, 2000.

[74] Mitkov, R., *The Oxford Handbook of Computational Linguistics*. Oxford University Press, 2003.

[75] Roark, B. & Sproat, R., *Computational Approaches to Morphology and Syntax*. Oxford University Press, 2007.

[76] Rosner, M. & Johnson, R., *Computational Linguistics and Formal Semantics*. Cambridge University Press, 1992.

[77] van Riemsdijk, H. & Williams, E., *Introduction to the Theory of Grammar*. MIT Press, 1986.

[78] Whitelock, P. & Kilby, K., *Linguistic and Computational Techniques in Machine Translation System Design*. UCL Press, 1995.

[79] Aho, A.V. & Ullman, J.D., *The Theory of Parsing, Translation, and Compiling*. Prentice-Hall, 1972.

[80] Carroll, J. & Long, D., *Theory of Finite Automata with an Introduction to Formal Languages*. Prentice-Hall, 1989.

[81] Eilenberg, S., *Automata, Languages, and Machines*. Academic Press, 1974.

[82] Kuich, W. & Salomaa, A., *Semirings, Automata, Languages*. Springer-Verlag, 1985.

[83] Revesz, G.E., *Introduction to Formal Language Theory*. McGraw-Hill, 1983.

[84] Salomaa, A., *Computation and Automata*. Cambridge University Press, 1985.

[85] Sudkamp, T.A., *Languages and Machines: An Introduction to the Theory of Computer Science*. Addison-Wesley, Reading, 2006.

[86] Aho, A.V. & Ullman, J.D., *Principles of Compiler Design*. Addison-Wesley, 1977.

[87] Brookshear, J.G., *Theory of Computation*. Benjamin Cummings Publishing, 1989.

[88] Chomsky, N., *Syntactic Structures*. The Hague, 1957.

[89] Gries, D., *Compiler Construction for Digital Computers*. Wiley, 1971.

[90] Lewis, P.M., Rosenkrantz, D.J. & Stearns, R.E., *Compiler Design Theory*. Addison-Wesley, Reading, 1976.

[91] Pagen, F.G., *Formal Specifications of Programming Language: A Panoramic Primer*. Prentice Hall, 1981.

[92] Sippu, S. & Soisalon-Soininen, E., *Parsing Theory*. Springer-Verlag, 1987.

[93] Aho, A.V., Sethi, R. & Ullman, J.D., *Compilers: Principles, Techniques and Tools*. Addison-Wesley, 1988.

[94] Almasi, G.S. & Gottlieb, A., *Highly Parallel Computing*. Benjamin-Cummings Publishing, 1989.

[95] Cooper, K.D. & Torczon, L., *Engineering a Compiler*. Morgan Kaufmann, 2004.

[96] Grune, D., Bal, H.E., Jacobs, C.J.H. & Langendoen, K., *Modern Compiler Design*. Wiley, 2002.

[97] Kennedy, K. & Allen, J.R., *Optimizing Compilers for Modern Architectures: A Dependence-Based Approach*. Morgan Kaufmann Publishers, 2002.

[98] Meduna, A., *Elements of Compiler Design*. Taylor and Francis, 2008.

[99] Srikant, Y.N. & Shankar, P., *The Compiler Design Handbook*. CRC Press, 2002.

[100] Wolfe, M.J., *High Performance Compilers for Parallel Computing*. Addison-Wesley, 1996.

[101] Zima, H. & Chapman, B., *Supercompilers for Parallel and Vector Computers*. ACM, 1991.

Language family index

Family	Page	Grammatical model
$\mathscr{L}(RE)$	13	phrase-structure grammar
$\mathscr{L}(CS)$	14	context-sensitive grammar
$\mathscr{L}(CF)$	14	context-free grammar
$\mathscr{L}(LIN)$	14	linear grammar
$\mathscr{L}(REG)$	14	regular grammar
$\mathscr{L}(RLIN)$	15	right-linear grammar
$\mathscr{L}(SM)$	16	simple matrix grammar
$\mathscr{L}(SM, n)$	16	simple matrix grammar of degree n
$\mathscr{L}(SM, LIN)$	17	linear simple matrix grammar
$\mathscr{L}(SM, LIN, n)$	17	linear simple matrix grammar of degree n
$\mathscr{L}(SM, RLIN)$	17	right-linear simple matrix grammar
$\mathscr{L}(SM, RLIN, n)$	17	right-linear simple matrix grammar of degree n
$\mathscr{L}(P)$	18	programmed grammar without appearance checking and without erasing productions
$\mathscr{L}(P, \varepsilon)$	18	programmed grammar without appearance checking
$\mathscr{L}(ST)$	19	state grammar
$\mathscr{L}(ST, n)$	19	state grammar of degree n
$\mathscr{L}(SC)$	23	scattered context grammar
$\mathscr{L}(PSC)$	23	propagating scattered context grammar
$\mathscr{L}(P, ac)$	48	programmed grammar with appearance checking and without erasing productions

Hierarchy of language families

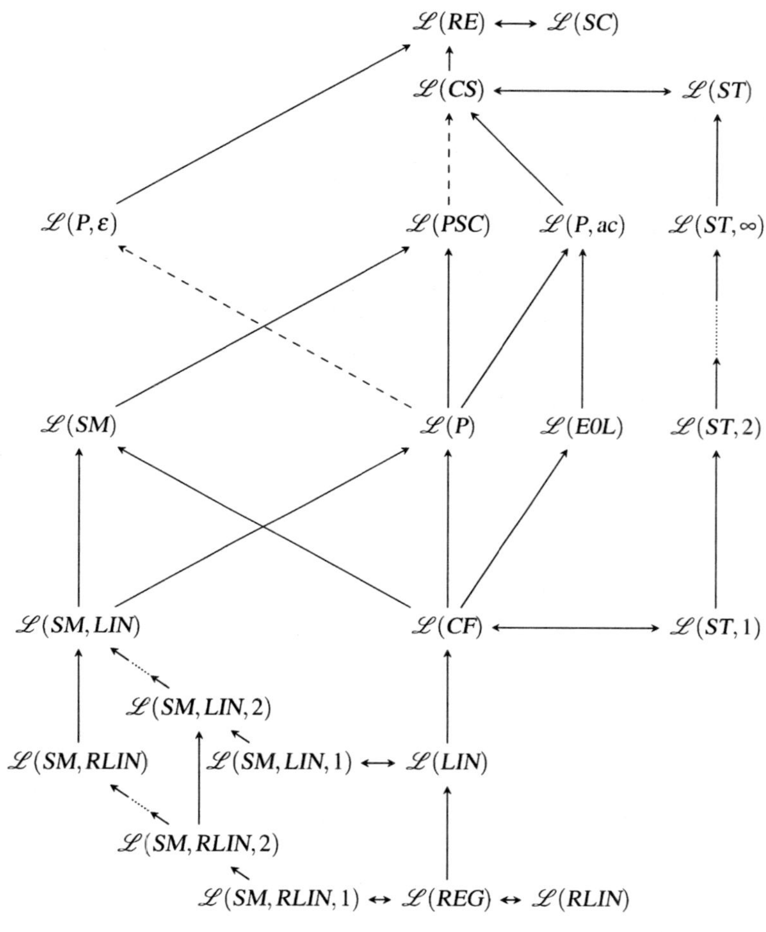

Figure 1: Hierarchy of elementary language families used throughout the book. One-sided arrows with solid lines represent strict inclusion with the more powerful language family located at the arrow tip. Dashed lines indicate an inclusion where the strictness is unknown. Double-sided arrows represent an equivalence of the language families. Dotted lines indicate an infinite hierarchy of language families.

Symbol index

Symbol	Page	Description
$a \in A$	7	a is a member of A
$a \notin A$	7	a is not a member of A
$\|A\|$	7	cardinality of A
$\emptyset$	7	empty set
$\{a_1, \ldots, a_n\}$	7	a set containing $a_1, \ldots, a_n$
$\{a : \pi(a)\}$	7	a set containing elements that satisfy π
$A \subseteq B$	7	A is a subset of B
$A \subset B$	7	A is a proper subset of B
2^A	7	power set of A
$A \cup B$	7	union of A and B
$A \cap B$	8	intersection of A and B
$A - B$	8	difference of A and B
$\bigcup_\pi A$	8	union of elements from A that satisfy π
$\|x\|$	8	length of x
ε	8	empty sequence (string)
$\|x\|_V$	8	number of occurrences of elements from V in x
(a, b)	8	ordered pair
$(a_1, \ldots, a_n)$	8	ordered n-tuple
$A \times B$	8	Cartesian product
ρ^{-1}	8	inverse relation
$a \in \rho(b)$	8	synonym for $(a, b) \in \rho$
$a \rho b$	8	synonym for $(a, b) \in \rho$
$a = \rho(b)$	9	synonym for $(a, b) \in \rho$ if ρ is a function

Symbol	Page	Description
ρ^k	9	k-fold product of ρ
ρ^+	9	transitive closure of ρ
ρ^*	9	reflexive and transitive closure of ρ
T^*	9	set of all strings over T
T^+	9	set of all non-empty strings over T
$x \cdot y$	10	concatenation of strings x and y
x^i	10	ith power of a string x
$L_1 \cdot L_2$	10	concatenation of languages L_1 and L_2
L_1/L_2	10	right quotient of L_1 with respect to L_2
$L_2\backslash L_1$	10	left quotient of L_1 with respect to L_2
L_1 fi L_2	10	exhaustive right quotient of L_1 with respect to L_2
L_2 fl L_1	10	exhaustive left quotient of L_1 with respect to L_2
L^i	10	ith power of a language L
L^*	10	Kleene star
L^+	10	Kleene plus
$\mathscr{L}$	11	family of languages
$x \rightarrow y$	13	production with left-hand side x and right-hand side y
$x \Rightarrow_G y\ [p]$	13	x is rewritten to y by using p in G
$x \Rightarrow_G^k y$	13	k-fold product of $\Rightarrow_G$
$x \Rightarrow_G^+ y$	13	transitive closure of $\Rightarrow_G$
$x \Rightarrow_G^* y$	13	reflexive and transitive closure of $\Rightarrow_G$
$F(G)$	13	set of all sentential forms of G
$L(G)$	13	language of G
$x\ {}_{lm}\Rightarrow_G y$	23	leftmost derivation step
$x\ {}_{rm}\Rightarrow_G y$	23	rightmost derivation step
$\grave{x}$	56	—
$\acute{x}$	56	—
$\check{x}$	61	—
$x \Rrightarrow y$	66	—
$x\ {}_{lim}^{\ n}\Rightarrow_G y$	71	n-limited derivation step
$L(G, lim, n)$	72	—
$L(G, lm)$	86	—
$L(G, rm)$	86	—
$x\ {}_{max}\Rightarrow_G y$	92	maximal derivation step
$x\ {}_{min}\Rightarrow_G y$	92	minimal derivation step
$L(G, max)$	92	—
$L(G, min)$	92	—
$l : p$	138	production p labeled by l
$T(G, K)$	169	transformation of strings from K defined by G
$a \prec b$	170	lexical order of elements a and b

Subject index